deeper experiences of
FAMOUS CHRISTIANS

deeper experiences of
FAMOUS CHRISTIANS

JAMES G. LAWSON

WHITAKER
HOUSE

Publisher's note:
This new edition from Whitaker House is a revision of the complete
original text. The resulting version has been edited for content and also
updated for the modern reader. Words, expressions, and sentence structure
have been revised for clarity and readability. Although the more modern
Bible translation quoted in this edition was not available to the author, the
Bible version used was carefully and prayerfully selected in order to make
the language of the entire text readily understandable while maintaining
the author's original premises and message.

Unless otherwise indicated, all Scripture quotations are taken from the
New King James Version (NKJV), © 1979, 1980, 1982, 1984 by Thomas
Nelson, Inc. Used by permission. All rights reserved. Scripture quotations
marked (KJV) are taken from the King James Version of the Holy Bible.

Deeper Experiences of Famous Christians

ISBN-13: 978-0-88368-517-4 • ISBN-10: 0-88368-517-5
Printed in the United States of America
© 1998 by Whitaker House

Whitaker House
1030 Hunt Valley Circle
New Kensington, PA 15068
www.whitakerhouse.com

Library of Congress Cataloging-in-Publication Data

Lawson, J. Gilchrist (James Gilchrist), 1874–1946.
    Deeper experiences of famous Christians / by James Gilchrist
Lawson
        p.   cm.
    ISBN 0-88368-517-5
    1. Christian biography.   I. Title.
    BR1700.2.L38   1998
    270'.092'2—dc21
                                        98-19190

Contents

Introduction

❦

*T*he purpose of this book is to describe, in their own words as far as possible, the deepest spiritual experiences of the most famous Christians of all ages. I have spent many years searching the whole range of Christian literature in order to glean from it the most spiritual and helpful Christian experiences. I believe that this book contains the very best of the Christian literature of all ages, and I trust that it will be the means of leading many into *"the fullness of the blessing of the gospel of Christ"* (Rom. 15:29).

Although these pages contain an account of the most important facts in the lives of famous Spirit-filled children of God, it would be impossible, in a book of this kind, to describe the deeper experiences of all the famous Spirit-filled Christians. In the early Christian church, and in almost every denomination of Christianity, there have been many whose consecrated lives and spiritual experiences have made them a blessing to multitudes. The deeper experiences of famous living Christians would fill still another volume of this kind.

The deeper spiritual experiences of Christians of many different ages and denominations are given in this book, but there is a wonderful harmony in the experiences related here. The characters may relate their deeper experiences in very different words, yet the deeper Christian experience described is always the same. It is the baptism, filling, or gift of the Holy Spirit, and the experience resulting from being filled with the Spirit.

A person looking at the Niagara Falls from the Canadian side would describe them in very different terms from a person looking at them from the American side, although the Falls would remain the same. Likewise, the Calvinist may describe his deeper Christian experience in terms that agree with his theological views, while the Arminian uses terms that agree with his theological views. Theories differ according to the different standpoints or ways of looking at things. As long as men have different degrees of light, they are bound to differ in theory. *"Now we see in a mirror, dimly,"* said the apostle, *"but then I shall know just as I also am known"* (1 Cor. 13:12).

We can hardly expect all men to agree in theory with regard to the deeper things of God's Word, when they differ so much in theory with regard to politics and every other question imaginable. However, as there is a practical agreement among evangelical Christians with regard to the way of salvation, so there is a practical agreement among those who believe in a Christian experience deeper than conversion. All agree that Christians may be *"filled with the Spirit"* (Eph. 5:18); that we may *"have life, and...have it more abundantly"* (John 10:10); that we may be *"rooted and grounded in love"* (Eph. 3:17); that we can be *"more than conquerors through Him who loved us"* (Rom. 8:37); that if we bring all the tithes into His storehouse, the Lord will open to us the windows of heaven, and pour out a blessing upon us, so that *"there will not be room enough to receive it"* (Mal. 3:10); that we may have *"peace...like a river"* and *"righteousness like the waves of the sea"* (Isa. 48:18); that we may have *"joy unspeakable and full of glory"* (1 Pet. 1:8 KJV); and so on.

In a court of law, the testimony of witnesses would be rejected if they all gave the same evidence and gave it in the same words and manner. It would prove that there had been secret cooperation among the witnesses. But if each witness gave his evidence in his own words and manner, and yet the testimony of the witnesses agreed as to the essential facts, the evidence would be regarded as most convincing. So, when Christians of so many different centuries and countries relate their deeper Christian experiences in their own manners and languages, and yet all agree as to the essential facts, it is overwhelming evidence that such a deep Christian experience may really be attained.

I pray that this account of God's work may be the means of leading you to *"hunger and thirst for righteousness"* (Matt. 5:6), so that you

> *may be able to comprehend with all the saints what is the width and length and depth and height; to know the love of Christ which passes* [human] *knowledge; that you may be filled with all the fullness of God.* (Eph. 3:18–19)

Chapter 1

Old Testament Characters

ᥫᩢ

A careful study of the Old Testament will reveal the fact that in Old Testament times, as in New Testament times, those who accomplished great things for God were first anointed by the Holy Spirit and filled with power from on high. No great work has ever been accomplished except through the power of the Holy Spirit, who is the great Executive of God, carrying out the will of God in all things. From the first chapter of Genesis, we learn that *"the Spirit of God was hovering over the face of the waters"* (Gen. 1:2), and that He created all things in obedience to God's commands.

The Holy Spirit is the source of all life, both spiritual and temporal. *"It is the Spirit who gives life"* (John 6:63), so that in God *"we live and move and have our being"* (Acts 17:28). Scientists have sought in vain to discover the secret of life, not knowing that the Holy Spirit is the great source of all life. But the patriarch Job knew that it was through the power of the Spirit that God created all things, when he said, *"By His Spirit He adorned the heavens"* (Job 26:13). Elihu also understood it when he said, *"The Spirit of God has made me, and the breath of the Almighty gives me life"* (Job 33:4).

Not only did the Holy Spirit bring all things into being at God's command, but He also gave the tabernacle builders the wisdom to perform their work (see Exodus 28:3; 31:2–3; 35:30–31); and He qualified all the great patriarchs, prophets, judges, and kings for the work He had for them to do.

The Patriarchs

It is very evident that the power of the Holy Spirit made the Old Testament patriarchs such princes with God and men. Enoch must have been filled with the Spirit of God, because he *"walked with God"* (Gen. 5:22, 24) and prophesied (Jude 14) and was translated into heaven (Heb. 11:5). It is the work of the Holy Spirit to give grace, to reveal things, and to translate people to heaven. Noah must also have been filled with the Holy Spirit's power, because he also *"walked with God"* (Gen. 6:9) and talked with Him. It seems that the Spirit of God spoke through Noah to those who lived before the time of the Flood, and that they are now imprisoned in hell because they refused to hear him (1 Pet. 3:18–20).

Abraham also must have been filled with the Holy Spirit, for he had many visions and special revelations from the Lord (Gen. 15:1; Acts 7:2; Heb. 11:8). Other Old Testament patriarchs were undoubtedly filled with the Holy Spirit's power in a similar manner, but the deeper experiences of Jacob and Joseph are more fully described in the Word of God than those of the other patriarchs.

Jacob

In the biblical account of Jacob's life, as perhaps in that of no other Old Testament saint, the power of God to change and transform character is revealed. Before God met Jacob at Bethel, there was little to love and admire in his weak, vacillating character. His name, Jacob, means "supplanter," or "deceiver," and such was his character. By deception he obtained his brother Esau's birthright, and he then went away to a strange land to escape his brother's wrath. But God, who foreknows all things, knew that Jacob rather than Esau was prepared to abandon the life of selfishness and sin and to become a chosen vessel in His service. (See Romans 9:10–13.)

One night, as Jacob lay asleep on the lonely mountains north of Jerusalem, with a stone for his pillow, the Lord began to reveal Himself to him. In a dream, the Holy Spirit revealed to him a little of the glories of heaven. He saw a ladder reaching toward heaven and the angels of God ascending and descending on it, and the Lord promised him great blessings (Gen. 28:11–15). Jacob called the name of the place *Bethel,* which means "house of God," and said, *"This is none other than the house of God, and this is the gate of heaven!"* (v. 17).

But this was only the gate, or the beginning, of Jacob's spiritual experience. It was not at Bethel, but at Peniel, that his life was completely transformed. After he had served Laban for many years, and Laban had become envious of him, Jacob started for his old home. Laban pursued him with an army. After making peace with Laban, Jacob heard that his brother Esau was coming with another army to meet him. Jacob seemed to be completely at the mercy of Esau and his army and was at the end of his own resources. But man's extremity is God's opportunity, as the saying goes, and the darkest hour is often before day. *"Weeping may endure for a night, but joy comes in the morning"* (Ps. 30:5).

Those who wait on the LORD shall renew their strength; they shall mount up with wings like

*eagles, they shall run and not be weary, they
shall walk and not faint.*   (Isa. 40:31)

Such was the case with Jacob. He knew that only
God could deliver him from the extremity in which he
had placed himself by his evil deeds. So he spent the
night alone with God, crying for deliverance. Undoubtedly it was a night of bitter repentance and tears. He
wrestled with the angel of the Lord until the break of
day and said to him, *"I will not let You go unless You
bless me"* (Gen. 32:26). Having touched Jacob's thigh
and made him a cripple to punish him for his sins and
to keep him humble before God, the angel pronounced
upon him one of the greatest blessings that man has
ever experienced. He said, *"Your name shall no longer
be called Jacob, but Israel; for you have struggled with
God and with men, and have prevailed"* (v. 28).

Israel means "prince of God," and from that night
at Peniel until his dying day, Jacob was truly a spiritual prince and had power with God and with men. In
one night, God transformed him from a weak, vacillating deceiver into a prince with God and men; from
Jacob (deceiver) to Israel (prince of God); and from a
refugee to a ruler. This wonderful change was brought
about in answer to prayer, and because Jacob said, *"I
will not let You go unless You bless me"* (v. 26).

Joseph

Another Old Testament saint whose deeper religious experiences have been a help to many was the patriarch Joseph. As a youth, Joseph was told by God in
dreams and visions that He would greatly bless him.
(See Genesis 37:5–9.) But the blessings of God did not
come to Joseph until he was prepared by suffering to
receive them. Human nature is such that we cannot
bear great blessings or prosperity without some *"thorn
in the flesh"* (2 Cor. 12:7) or humiliating experiences to

keep us from being *"exalted above measure"* (v. 7), as it
was with Paul.

*"The refining pot is for silver and the furnace for
gold"* (Prov. 17:3). Silver can be melted and refined in
a pot, but the gold must be put right into the fire before it can be melted and refined. Those who are only
to be silver vessels in the house of God may only have
to go through the melting pot of affliction to be refined,
but those who are to be golden vessels in the house of
God often have to go through the fire of affliction, as
did Job, Madame Guyon, and many others.

Joseph was to be a golden vessel for the Master's
use, and he had to be greatly humbled before he could
bear the great honors and blessings that God was
about to shower upon him. He was betrayed by his
brothers, sold as a slave, carried away into the strange
land of Egypt, falsely accused of a horrible crime, and
finally thrown into an Egyptian dungeon. He lost
friends, property, reputation, liberty, and everything
that is held dearest in this life. This did not look like
the prosperity and blessing that God had promised
him, but his faith in God never wavered. Like the patriarch Job, in the midst of his trials, he could say,
"Though He slay me, yet will I trust Him" (Job 13:15).
Although Joseph lost everything except his faith in
God, he did not doubt God or forsake Him, as most
men would have done under similar circumstances.

After the Lord had sufficiently humbled Joseph,
blessings and honor began to pour in upon him. He was
delivered from prison, placed on the throne of Egypt as
the virtual ruler, and had his friends and relatives restored to him. And above all this, God gave him such
wisdom and understanding that even Pharaoh marvelled at it.

> *And Pharaoh said to his servants, "Can we find
> such a one as this, a man in whom is the Spirit
> of God?" Then Pharaoh said to Joseph,*

"Inasmuch as God has shown you all this, there is no one as discerning and wise as you."
(Gen. 41:38–39)

Moses, Joshua, and the Elders

In the life of Moses, the first and greatest of Israel's judges, the Holy Spirit's power was manifested in a preeminent degree. Over five hundred times in the Word of God, we are told about God speaking to Moses or Moses speaking to God. When the Lord first called Moses to lead the children of Israel from Egypt to Canaan, he went in his own strength to deliver Israel, and he killed an Egyptian. Then he became frightened and fled into the wilderness, and he spent forty years feeding sheep for his father-in-law. By that time, all his pride and self-reliance had left him. When God again called him to go and deliver Israel from Egypt, he felt his own weakness as he had not felt it when the Lord first called him to that mission.

"Now the man Moses was very humble, more than all men who were on the face of the earth" (Num. 12:3). Moses pleaded that he was *"slow of speech"* (Exod. 4:10) and was not qualified to lead Israel. But God, who chooses and uses humble instruments, said, *"I will be with your mouth and teach you what you shall say"* (v. 12). Moses still pleaded that the Lord would send someone else, and then the Lord gave him Aaron, his brother, as his spokesman.

After this, the Spirit of God worked through Moses and Aaron in a marvelous manner. At the sway of Moses' rod, the plagues of blood, frogs, lice, flies, pestilence, boils and other sores, locusts, and darkness were sent over the land of Egypt; the Red Sea was divided; water was brought from the smitten rock; and so on. Under the inspiration of the Spirit of God, Moses also wrote more of the Bible than any other person, the five books of Moses being larger than the fourteen letters of

Paul. When Moses came down from the mount, after communing with God, his countenance was so resplendent with the glory of God that he had to veil his face while talking with the people (Exod. 34:33).

When Israel increased to a great nation, and the burden of judging the people was too great for Moses, seventy elders were selected to assist him in judging the people. The Spirit of God fell upon these seventy elders, and they began to prophesy. Joshua was afraid that they would take the leadership away from Moses, so he asked Moses to rebuke Eldad and Medad, two of the seventy, who were prophesying in the camp. Moses said to him, *"Are you zealous for my sake? Oh, that all the Lord's people were prophets and that the LORD would put His Spirit upon them!"* (Num. 11:29).

When Moses was about to be called away by God, he prayed that the Lord would raise up someone to take his place. *"And the LORD said to Moses: 'Take Joshua the son of Nun with you, a man in whom is the Spirit, and lay your hand on him'"* (Num. 27:18). After Moses had prayed for him, Joshua was given great power and wisdom by the Spirit of God. He conquered seven nations and thirty-one kings in the land of Canaan, and took possession of the land.

Other Judges of Israel

Besides Moses and Joshua, all the other great judges of Israel were also qualified by the Holy Spirit's power for the work to which God had called them. Some were farmers who were raised up and anointed by the Holy Spirit to become judges over Israel. Again and again Israel was delivered into the hands of her enemies because of her sins; and when the people of Israel repented, God always raised up a great judge to deliver them from their enemies and to rule over them. We are specifically told concerning many of these judges that the Spirit of the Lord came upon them and prepared them for the work that God had for them to do.

Thus, in Judges 3:9–10, we read concerning Othniel:

> *When the children of Israel cried out to the LORD, the LORD raised up a deliverer for the children of Israel, who delivered them: Othniel the son of Kenaz, Caleb's younger brother. The Spirit of the LORD came upon him, and he judged Israel.*

Likewise, we read, *"The Spirit of the LORD came upon Gideon"* (Judg. 6:34), so that with a little band of 300 men he put to flight the great army of the Midianites who were *"as numerous as locusts"* (Judg. 7:12). Further, we read how *"the Spirit of the LORD came upon Jephthah"* (Judg. 11:29), a man of humble birth, and how mightily God used him to deliver Israel from the Ammonites.

From the book of Judges, we also learn that the strength of Samson was the strength of the Lord, and that when he grieved away the Spirit of God he was weak like other men. *"And the Spirit of the LORD began to move upon him at Mahaneh Dan between Zorah and Eshtaol"* (Judg. 13:25), and he began to perform deeds of valor. One day he met a lion,

> *and the Spirit of the LORD came mightily upon him, and he tore the lion apart as one would have torn apart a young goat, though he had nothing in his hand.* (Judg. 14:6)

The Holy Spirit also came upon Samson when he went to Ashkelon and slew thirty of the wicked Philistines (v. 19). Then we read about another occasion:

> *When he came to Lehi, the Philistines came shouting against him. Then the Spirit of the*

> LORD *came mightily upon him; and the ropes*
> *that were on his arms became like flax that is*
> *burned with fire, and his bonds broke loose from*
> *his hands. He found a fresh jawbone of a donkey,*
> *reached out his hand and took it, and killed a*
> *thousand men with it.* (Judg. 15:14–15)

When the Spirit of the Lord left him, Samson's power
was gone, but when he prayed, the power returned to
him again.

The last and one of the greatest of the judges of
Israel was Samuel. As a child he grew *"in favor both
with the LORD and men"* (1 Sam. 2:26). The Lord spoke
to him and revealed many things to him by the Holy
Spirit. *"And all Israel from Dan to Beersheba knew that
Samuel had been established as a prophet of the LORD"*
(1 Sam. 3:20).

The Kings of Israel and Judah

Just as the great patriarchs and judges were filled
with the Spirit, so were the greatest and best kings of
Israel and Judah. All the good kings of Israel were
anointed for their position by the Spirit of God and
were thus qualified to rule over the people. The
anointing oil poured upon them at their coronations
symbolized the Holy Spirit's anointing, just like the
anointing oil that was poured upon the high priest at
his consecration. Throughout the Scriptures, oil is used
as a symbol of the Holy Spirit and His anointing. The
prophet Samuel told Saul, who was the first king of
Israel, that the Spirit of the Lord would come upon him
and that he would be turned into another man (1 Sam.
10:6).

When the Spirit of God came upon Saul and he
began to prophesy, the people were astonished and
said, *"Is Saul also among the prophets?"* (v. 11). But
someone who knew that the same God who had made

the others prophets had also made Saul a prophet, said, *"But who is their father?"* (v. 12). *"The Spirit of God came upon Saul"* (1 Sam. 11:6), and he prospered until he sinned by sparing Agag. Then *"the Spirit of the LORD departed from Saul, and a distressing spirit from the LORD troubled him"* (1 Sam. 16:14).

When the prophet Samuel poured the anointing oil on David, the next great king of Israel, *"the Spirit of the LORD came upon David from that day forward"* (v. 13). Through the inspiration of the Holy Spirit, David wrote the noblest songs that ever were sung, and he foretold that Christ would come in both humiliation and glory. The shepherd boy on Judea's hills was made one of the world's greatest poets, prophets, and kings. *"The Spirit of the LORD spoke by me, and His word was on my tongue"* (2 Sam. 23:2), said David, and the apostle Peter agreed that the Holy Spirit spoke through David (Acts 1:16). After David sinned, he feared that he had sinned against the Holy Spirit, and he prayed,

> *Do not cast me away from Your presence, and do not take Your Holy Spirit from me. Restore to me the joy of Your salvation, and uphold me by Your generous Spirit. Then I will teach transgressors Your ways, and sinners shall be converted to You.* (Ps. 51:11–13)

When Solomon, the third king over Israel, was a youth, he chose wisdom from God rather than long life, riches, or honor. Because he made this choice, God gave him a wise and understanding heart, so that no one else was as wise as Solomon. (See 1 Kings 3.) His fame went out over all the earth; and when the queen of Sheba came to see him and hear him for herself, *"there was no more spirit in her"* (1 Kings 10:5). She said, *"The half was not told me"* (v. 7), meaning that no one had fully told her of Solomon's wisdom. The wisdom of this world paled into nothingness when compared with the marvelous wisdom that the Spirit of God imparted to King Solomon.

Truly, wisdom and knowledge are still the gifts of God's Spirit (1 Cor. 12:8; James 3:17), and God can give us *"wise and understanding heart*[s]*"* (1 Kings 3:12). The wisdom of Solomon, the wisest man, like the strength of Samson, the strongest man, was a direct gift of the Holy Spirit.

The Old Testament Prophets

Just as the Holy Spirit anointed and qualified the great judges and kings of Israel, He also anointed and qualified the Old Testament prophets. Without the anointing of the Holy Spirit, they would have been only ordinary men. Isaiah was only *"a man of unclean lips"* (Isa. 6:5), unable to speak with divine power, until God touched his lips with the fire of His Holy Spirit. Then he became the world's greatest and most sublime prophet.

Jeremiah felt that he could not be a prophet because he was just a child (Jer. 1:6), but God so anointed him with the Holy Spirit's power that he became *"a fortified city and an iron pillar, and bronze walls"* (v. 18) against sin. God caused him *"to root out and to pull down, to destroy and to throw down"* the evil, and *"to build and to plant"* the good (v. 10). He became the greatest prophet of woe and denunciation against sin that the world has ever had. The Lord said to him, *"I will make My words in your mouth fire"* (Jer. 5:14), and they were like a fire and *"like a hammer that breaks the rock in pieces"* (Jer. 23:29).

Over and over again, we read about the Spirit of the Lord being upon Ezekiel and inspiring him with heavenly visions and revelations. (See Ezekiel 1:1 and 2:2, for examples.) The great prophet Elijah was so anointed with the Spirit of God that Elisha longed for a double portion of his spirit (2 Kings 2:9), and *"the*

spirit and power of Elijah" (Luke 1:17) became prover-
bial. When the mantle of Elijah fell upon Elisha, the
Spirit of God anointed Elisha to become a great
prophet (2 Kings 2), and the sons of the prophets said,
"The spirit of Elijah rests on Elisha" (v. 15).

Daniel was only a Hebrew captive in a heathen
land, but the Spirit of God gave him greater wisdom
than all the wise men of the great Babylonian empire.
(See Daniel 1:17; 5:11–14; 6:3.) Like Joseph, he was
made the real ruler of a world empire. The Holy Spirit
revealed to him the rise and fall of all the empires of
the world. (See Daniel 2 and 7.)

As the Holy Spirit anointed and qualified the ma-
jor prophets, so He also anointed the minor prophets.
Balaam was enlightened by Him (Num. 24:2); so were
Saul's messengers (1 Sam. 19:20–23), Micaiah (1 Kings
22:24; 2 Chron. 18:23), Amasai (1 Chron. 12:18),
Azariah (2 Chron. 15:1), Jahaziel (2 Chron. 20:14),
Zechariah the son of Jehoiada (2 Chron. 24:20), Elihu
(Job 32:8, 18–19), Micah (Mic. 3:8), and all the others.
The Spirit of the Lord was in all the true prophets
(Neh. 9:30; 1 Pet. 1:10–11). *"For prophecy never came
by the will of man, but holy men of God spoke as they
were moved by the Holy Spirit"* (2 Pet. 1:21).

Chapter 2

New Testament
Characters

᳭

ot only was the Holy Spirit the source of all
spiritual power in Old Testament times, but
He also imparted power to John the Baptist,
to the Son of God Himself, to the Galilean fishermen,
and to all the great saints of New Testament times. By
His death on the cross, Christ opened the way for God to
pour His Spirit upon all men, which He did on the Day
of Pentecost, ushering in the more glorious dispensation
foretold by Joel and other Old Testament prophets.
Since the Day of Pentecost, the Holy Spirit has been
convicting the whole world of sin and convincing them of
righteousness and of judgment (John 16:8) in a way that
He did not do in Old Testament times, except with a few
individuals. Thus, in this dispensation of the Holy Spirit,
the world has become more responsible to God because
of its increased light and privileges.

John the Baptist

John the Baptist, the great forerunner, or herald,
of the coming of Jesus, was specially anointed for His

mission by the Holy Spirit. The angel, in announcing
His birth, said,

> For he will be great in the sight of the Lord, and
> shall drink neither wine nor strong drink. He
> will also be filled with the Holy Spirit, even from
> his mother's womb. And he will turn many of the
> children of Israel to the Lord their God. He will
> also go before Him in the spirit and power of Eli-
> jah, "to turn the hearts of the fathers to the chil-
> dren," and the disobedient to the wisdom of the
> just, to make ready a people prepared for the
> Lord.   (Luke 1:15–17)

When he had grown to manhood, John the Baptist
preached in the wilderness, proclaiming the coming of
the Christ and commanding the people to repent. The
multitudes were strangely affected by the preaching of
this great prophet.

> Then Jerusalem, all Judea, and all the region
> around the Jordan went out to him and were
> baptized by him in the Jordan, confessing their
> sins.   (Matt. 3:5–6)

Even the proud Pharisees, the materialistic Sad-
ducees, the despised publicans, and the hardened soldiers went to him for counsel and advice. And what
was the secret of the wonderful power of this lonely
preacher in the wilderness, which enabled him to thus
sway the multitudes? Jesus said to the people,

> What did you go out into the wilderness to see? A
> reed shaken by the wind? But what did you go
> out to see? A man clothed in soft garments? In-
> deed, those who wear soft clothing are in kings'
> houses. But what did you go out to see? A
> prophet? Yes, I say to you, and more than a
> prophet.   (Matt. 11:7–9)

John the Baptist was no *"reed shaken by the wind,"* swayed by every breeze of public opinion, pandering to the people in order to please them. That was not what drew the multitudes to hear him. He denounced their sins, and he rebuked them to their faces (Luke 3:7–9). Nor did they flock out into the wilderness to see his fine clothing, for he wore only a garment of camel's hair, secured with a leather belt. Nor did they flock to him to get something good to eat, for he lived on locusts and wild honey. But John the Baptist was the voice of God speaking to the people, through the inspiration of the Holy Spirit, and that was the secret of his wonderful power.

John the Baptist summed up the whole Gospel in two brief sentences: *"Behold! The Lamb of God who takes away the sin of the world!"* (John 1:29), and, *"He will baptize you with the Holy Spirit and fire"* (Luke 3:16). One is the gospel of pardon for the sinner, and the other is the gospel of power for the believer. The gospel of pardon is also summed up in John 3:16: *"God so loved the world,"* and so on. Too many people lay great stress on the gospel of pardon while neglecting the gospel of power. Let us remember Luke 3:16 and 1 Corinthians 3:16, as well as John 3:16.

Jesus, the Christ

The Son of God Himself was especially anointed for service by the Holy Spirit, who descended upon Him in the form of a dove after His baptism. The name *Christ* itself is from the Greek word for oil, *chrism,* and means "the Anointed One." All through the Scriptures, oil is used as a symbol of the Holy Spirit, and the psalmist referred to this fact when he said concerning Christ, *"You love righteousness and hate wickedness; therefore God, Your God, has anointed You with the oil of gladness more than Your companions"* (Ps. 45:7).

The Holy Spirit was the *"oil of gladness"* with which Jesus was anointed.

In the synagogue at Nazareth, Christ applied to Himself the prophecy in Isaiah 61:1–2:

> *The Spirit of the LORD is upon Me, because He has anointed Me to preach the gospel to the poor; He has sent Me to heal the brokenhearted, to proclaim liberty to the captives and recovery of sight to the blind, to set at liberty those who are oppressed; to proclaim the acceptable year of the LORD.* (Luke 4:18–19)

The apostle Peter also referred to this Scripture when he spoke of

> *how God anointed Jesus of Nazareth with the Holy Spirit and with power, who went about doing good and healing all who were oppressed by the devil, for God was with Him.* (Acts 10:38)

Jesus was undoubtedly a better medium for the Spirit than any human being, for the Holy Spirit brought about greater miracles through Him and was more manifest in His life than in the life of any human being. He spoke as no other man had ever spoken (John 7:46); all the sick who touched even the hem of His garment were made perfectly whole; with a few loaves and fishes He fed the hungry multitudes; and even the unbelievers of Nazareth *"marveled at the gracious words which proceeded out of His mouth"* (Luke 4:22). Christ Himself said that all these miracles were brought about by the *"finger of God"* (Luke 11:20) or by His Spirit (Matt. 12:28).

Christ is our great example and pattern, and His life on earth was truly a Spirit-filled one. If the Son of God Himself was anointed for His ministry by the Holy Spirit, how necessary it is that we should be also!

Pentecostal Experience of the Apostles

On the Day of Pentecost, the world was given the greatest example of God's power to transform the lives and character of men, so as to make the weak strong and powerful. Pentecost was the pouring out of the *"former rain"* (Hos. 6:3) of God's Spirit, just as in these last days there will be an outpouring of the *"latter rain"* (James 5:7). By His death on the cross, Jesus made such a great atonement for sin that God could safely pour out His Spirit on all mankind without the universe thinking that He was regarding sin lightly. It was the atonement of Christ, therefore, that purchased the great Pentecostal gift for the world.

"When He ascended on high, He led captivity captive, and gave gifts to men" (Eph. 4:8). Before the ascension of Christ, the Holy Spirit was not yet poured upon all flesh, *"because Jesus was not yet glorified"* (John 7:39). Jesus told His disciples that it was expedient, or profitable, that He should go away, because if He did not go away, the Comforter would not come (John 16:7). He had to complete His great work of atonement for the world before the Comforter could come. And it was better for the followers of Jesus that the Holy Spirit should be poured upon them and upon the world than that Jesus Himself should remain with them.

While in the body, Jesus could be in only one place at a time, but the Comforter can be present everywhere to convict men *"of sin, and of righteousness, and of judgment"* (v. 8). His first objective is to convince men of coming judgment. He does this by influencing men's hearts and minds from without, or by coming to dwell within them. Upon those in whom He dwells, He bestows one or more of His seven different spiritual gifts.

The seven different gifts of the Holy Spirit seem to be spoken of in Revelation as *"the seven Spirits of God"*

(Rev. 4:5). They were probably symbolized by the golden candlestick, with its seven branches and seven lamps in the tabernacle and temples of the Old Testament. The apostle Paul enumerated nine gifts of the Holy Spirit in 1 Corinthians 12:7–10, but healing and miracles are probably the same gift, and tongues and the interpretation of tongues probably belong to one gift, so that there are only seven distinct gifts mentioned.

Before Pentecost, Jesus said to His disciples,

> *I still have many things to say to you, but you cannot bear them now. However, when He, the Spirit of truth, has come, He will guide you into all truth.* (John 16:12–13)

He knew that His disciples were only weak spiritual babes, even after everything He had taught them, and He commanded them to wait in Jerusalem until they were filled with power from on high (Luke 24:49). He also said to them,

> *But you shall receive power when the Holy Spirit has come upon you; and you shall be witnesses to Me in Jerusalem, and in all Judea and Samaria, and to the end of the earth.* (Acts 1:8)

If the disciples had not believed that promise, there might have been no Pentecost. If they had said that they were already converted and that they were not looking for any deeper experiences, the world might still be groping in heathen darkness. But their faith laid hold of the promise, and great were the results.

The disciples seem to have prayed together for ten days before the promised Comforter came. One, two, three days went by, and then a whole week, and still no Comforter came, but their faith did not waver. They waited in the Upper Room until the morning of the tenth day before the Comforter came. We do not know why they had to wait so long for the Holy Spirit, for there is no other Bible example of men praying so long a time before they received the Pentecostal gift. Perhaps they did not fully meet God's conditions before the tenth day, or He may have planned that they would be fully prepared and humbled by long and earnest prayer so that they would not be puffed up and exalted by the great blessing He was about to pour upon them.

It is more probable, however, that the great reason why God did not send the Holy Spirit sooner was that He intended to send Him on the Day of Pentecost, or the fiftieth day after the Passover (Pentecost means "fiftieth"), when multitudes of Jews from all over the world were present in Jerusalem. Pentecost was one of the three great annual feasts, or religious gatherings, of the Jews. It was a time of rejoicing over the firstfruits, and it was appropriate that on that day the *"firstfruits of the Spirit"* (Rom. 8:23) would be poured upon the world.

It is estimated that, in the time of Christ, between one and two million Jews were in Jerusalem to attend the feast of Pentecost. The Bible tells us about Jews of every nation being present to hear the disciples bear witness to the outpouring of the Spirit. The Jews were God's husbandmen, or chosen people, through whom He was revealing Himself to the world. By waiting until Pentecost to pour His Spirit upon them, He secured witnesses from every nation to testify to the outpouring of the Spirit.

Early on the morning of Pentecost, the Holy Spirit came with such demonstration and power that no one present could ever doubt the reality of His coming.

When the Day of Pentecost had fully come, they were all with one accord in one place. And suddenly there came a sound from heaven, as of a rushing mighty wind, and it filled the whole

> *house where they were sitting. Then there ap-*
> *peared to them divided tongues, as of fire, and*
> *one sat upon each of them. And they were all*
> *filled with the Holy Spirit and began to speak*
> *with other tongues, as the Spirit gave them utter-*
> *ance.*   (Acts 2:1–4)

William Arthur, in his book, *The Tongue of Fire,*
suggests that the *"divided tongues"* symbolized the
new power that the disciples would receive to preach
the Gospel, and this is the generally accepted opinion.
The *"divided tongues"* may have symbolized the fact
that their power of speech would be doubled, and also
that they would not speak of themselves but that another would speak through them. When the Holy Spirit
fell on them, He gave them power to witness for Christ.
When Jesus called the ignorant fishermen from the Sea
of Galilee to come and follow Him, He promised to
make them *"fishers of men"* (Matt. 4:19).

On the Day of Pentecost, this promise was fulfilled, and they indeed became *"fishers of men."* On
that day, the Lord enabled them to catch more men
than they caught fish when the miracle occurred on the
Sea of Galilee. Peter and John, two of the Galilean
fishermen, afterward spoke with such boldness that
the people, who knew that they were uneducated and
ignorant men, *"marveled. And they realized that they*
had been with Jesus" (Acts 4:13).

Before leaving His disciples, Jesus had promised
that they would do even greater works than He had
done (John 14:12), and this promise was also fulfilled
at Pentecost. During Christ's earthly ministry, very
few people seem to have been converted to God
through Him. The greatest number of converts mentioned is *"five hundred brethren"* (1 Cor. 15:6). But after He ascended to the Father and sent the promised
Comforter, the disciples led 3,000 converts to the foot
of the cross in one day (Acts 2:41), and several days

later 5,000 more were converted (Acts 4:4). Surely these were greater works than Jesus accomplished during His earthly ministry!

In a moment of time, God changed the ignorant fishermen of Galilee into the world's greatest preachers. In a moment of time, they learned more about Christ than they had learned in three years walking and talking with Him before they were filled with the Spirit, although He was the greatest teacher who ever appeared in human form. Although the apostles had been with the Son of God Himself for a long time, had seen all His miracles, and had listened to all His teachings, they were only spiritual babes and did not understand the first principles of the Gospel until the Day of Pentecost.

The disciples quarreled among themselves as to who should be greatest. They looked for Christ to immediately set up an earthly kingdom and subdue His enemies. Some of them resorted to the use of carnal weapons. All deserted Christ in His trial and condemnation; Peter denied Him with swearing and cursing; and in many other ways the apostles showed their lack of spiritual power and understanding. But on the Day of Pentecost, this was all changed, and they received power from on high.

Poor, weak, vacillating Peter, who had promised to be true to Christ though all others should forsake Him—and yet he soon afterward denied Him—was now transformed into another man. In the power of the Spirit, he arose and preached such a sermon that 3,000 people were greatly affected and cried out, *"Men and brethren, what shall we do?"* (Acts 2:37). All the apostles suddenly became spiritual giants, faced the enemy with courage, preached the Gospel with boldness, and afterward carried it throughout the world. And all except John seem to have suffered as martyrs for Christ.

The multitudes who gathered together to hear the disciples on the Day of Pentecost did not believe that

Jesus was divine. They thought that they had crucified a mere man and not the Son of God. But the Holy Spirit, witnessing through the disciples, convinced them that Jesus was divine and that they had crucified the Son of God. Then they were greatly convicted and cried aloud for mercy. It is the work of the Holy Spirit to glorify Jesus and to show men that He is the divine Son of God. *"No one can say that Jesus is Lord except by the Holy Spirit"* (1 Cor. 12:3), but when the Holy Spirit lays hold of a man's heart, that man is soon convinced of Christ's divinity. It is His work to draw all men to Christ.

The great Spirit-filled evangelist Charles Finney said that wherever he went, all forms of unbelief vanished when the Holy Spirit was poured upon the people. The Holy Spirit can teach men more about Christ in one hour than the greatest preacher can teach them in fifty or even in a hundred years without the Spirit enlightening them.

Deeper Experiences of the Apostle Paul

As Moses was the greatest leader and writer among Old Testament saints, so Paul was the greatest leader and writer among the New Testament saints. Though he was a persecutor, murderer, blasphemer, and the "chief of sinners" (see 1 Timothy 1:15) before his conversion, God completely transformed his life and made him one of the greatest examples of what divine grace and power can do in and through a human being. On his way to Damascus to arrest the saints and deliver them to death, he was suddenly struck down in the road by a light from heaven far more powerful than the noonday sun.

Some of the so-called higher critics, who know little about the grace and power or God, have suggested that Paul had a sunstroke on his way to Damascus. Someone has replied that if a sunstroke can so transform the life and character of a man, it is a pity these higher critics could not all have sunstrokes, too. Paul seemed to have been blinded by the glory and power of the light that shone from heaven, and after his conversion to Christ, he had to be led into Damascus. Then God appeared in a vision to an earnest Christian named Ananias and sent him to instruct and pray for Paul. Laying his hands on Paul, as was then the usual custom in praying for a person, he said,

> *Brother Saul, the Lord Jesus, who appeared to you on the road as you came, has sent me that you may receive your sight and be filled with the Holy Spirit.* (Acts 9:17)

Paul's eyesight was immediately restored, and he was baptized.

At this time, he was undoubtedly filled with the Spirit, whether before or after his baptism we cannot say. Soon after this, he went into Arabia, and in the interval between Acts 9 and 13, little mention is made concerning him. Conybeare and Howson, in their book about the life and labors of Paul, and other authorities on the subject, believe that Paul was in the desert of Arabia during this interval of about three years, learning of God. (See Galatians 1:17–18.) They believe that it was then that he was caught up into heaven and heard things unlawful to be uttered (2 Cor. 12:4).

No matter what happened, it is certain that Paul had an abundance of visions and revelations from God such as no human being could have unless he also had something to keep him humble. D. L. Moody, the great evangelist, used to say that if God had revealed anything more concerning heaven, we would be so homesick to go there that we could not attend to our everyday duties on earth. Also, if God had revealed anything more concerning future punishment in hell, men would be so terrified that they would not be able to attend to their ordinary occupations.

Perhaps that is what Paul meant when he said that it was not lawful for a man to utter what he had heard in paradise. Paul himself could not have borne the glory of these revelations if a *"thorn in the flesh...a messenger of Satan"* had not been allowed to buffet him, *"lest* [he] *should be exalted above measure by the abundance of the revelations"* (2 Cor. 12:7) that had been given to him. Three times he asked God to remove this thorn, before he realized that the Lord allowed it for the purpose of keeping him humble. When at last he realized how God's strength was made perfect through his weakness, he said,

> *Therefore most gladly I will rather boast in my infirmities, that the power of Christ may rest upon me. Therefore I take pleasure in infirmities, in reproaches, in needs, in persecutions, in distresses, for Christ's sake. For when I am weak, then I am strong.* (vv. 9–10)

In other words, he could say, "Lord, if I need afflictions and troubles to keep me humble when I have such great revelations of Your glory, I will be glad to have such afflictions, so that Your power may rest upon me."

There are many different opinions about the nature of Paul's thorn in the flesh. Some people think that it was a sin of some kind that he could not overcome, and they use this as an excuse for living in sin. But Paul represented himself as *"free from sin"* (Rom. 6:18), as *"dead to sin"* (v. 2 KJV), and as more than a conqueror (Rom. 8:37). Whatever Paul's thorn was, it certainly was not sin, for the apostle would not glory in sin as he gloried in his infirmities. He said that charity, or love, *"does not rejoice in iniquity"* (1 Cor. 13:6).

Some people have thought that Paul's thorn was epilepsy, others that it was dyspepsia, and so on; but the most reasonable supposition seems to be that it was weak eyes. That would make his bodily presence seem weak (2 Cor. 10:10) and would account for him saying that the Galatian believers would have plucked out their own eyes and given them to him if it had been possible for them to do so (Gal. 4:15). It would also explain the fact that nearly all of his letters were written by secretaries, and that sometimes two or three secretaries were employed in writing one letter. (See notes at the close of his epistles.)

One of the longest epistles written by Paul himself was the book of Galatians; and at the close of it he wrote, *"See with what large letters I have written to you with my own hand!"* (Gal. 6:11). And yet the epistle is not a remarkably long one for such a great scholar to write if he had had good eyesight and nerves, for Paul was one of the greatest scholars of his time. Finally, at his trial before the high priest, Paul did not seem to recognize him (Acts 23:4–5), although anyone with good eyesight ought to have been able to recognize the high priest by his robes. All these facts seem to point to the conclusion that Paul had weak eyes, and some people think that his eyes never fully recovered from the dazzling effect of the great supernatural light he saw on his way to Damascus.

Whatever Paul's thorn in the flesh may have been, it was necessary to keep him humble when God was showing him such great revelations. None of us, perhaps, have had such great revelations as Paul, yet it may be that afflictions have been necessary to keep us humble also.

The power of the Holy Spirit was so manifest in the preaching of Paul that even the great Roman ruler Felix trembled when the little apostle stood before him and reasoned about righteousness, temperance, and judgment to come. King Agrippa was almost persuaded by Paul to be a Christian. Like a firebrand, Paul went through Asia Minor and Greece, and finally to Rome, kindling a mighty fire that soon enveloped the whole world. When Paul and Silas came to Thessalonica, all the city was in an uproar, saying, *"These who have turned the world upside down have come here too"* (Acts 17:6). Someone has said that when they turned the world upside down, they turned it right side up for God. Truly, the apostle Paul could say, *"And my speech and my preaching were not with persuasive words of human wisdom, but in demonstration of the Spirit and of power"* (1 Cor. 2:4). He also said, *"Our gospel did not come to you in word only, but also in power, and in the Holy Spirit and in much assurance"* (1 Thess. 1:5). And in another place he said, *"The weapons of our warfare are not carnal but mighty in God for pulling down strongholds"* (2 Cor. 10:4).

The apostle Paul had drunk so deeply from *"the wells of salvation"* (Isa. 12:3) that he longed for others to enjoy the same experience. He exhorted the Roman believers to be *"dead indeed to sin"* (Rom. 6:11), to bring forth *"fruit unto holiness"* (v. 22 KJV), to pray in the Spirit (Rom. 8:26), to present their bodies as *"a living sacrifice"* (Rom. 12:1) to God, and to be led by the Spirit in everything (vv. 6–8). He wrote to them, *"But I know that when I come to you, I shall come in the fullness of the blessing of the gospel of Christ"* (Rom. 15:29). How I wish that every one of God's children could say the same!

Paul urged the Corinthian believers not to remain weak and carnal, like babes in Christ, but to become strong and spiritual (1 Cor. 3:1–3). He wrote to them, *"Now concerning spiritual gifts, brethren, I do not want you to be ignorant"* (1 Cor. 12:1), after which he devoted a great part of his letter to explaining spiritual gifts, without which the church would be like a body without eyes, hands, feet, and so on. In his second epistle to them, he explained how the Spirit of the Lord changed people into the image of the Lord, *"from glory to glory"* (2 Cor. 3:18). He also urged them to be separate from the world (2 Cor. 6:17), to perfect their holiness (2 Cor. 7:1), and to be perfect and complete (2 Cor. 13:11).

Paul told the Galatian believers how he was so eager for them to be like Christ that he was in great agony of prayer for them until this would be accomplished (Gal. 4:19), or until they would be transformed into the Lord's image. He told them to walk in the Spirit, and they would *"not fulfill the lust of the flesh"* (Gal. 5:16).

In his epistle to the Ephesians, Paul again and again urged them to *"be filled with the Spirit"* (Eph. 5:18). He said,

> [I] *do not cease to give thanks for you, making mention of you in my prayers: that the God of our Lord Jesus Christ, the Father of glory, may give to you the spirit of wisdom and revelation in the knowledge of Him, the eyes of your understanding being enlightened; that you may know what is the hope of His calling, what are the riches of the glory of His inheritance in the saints, and what is the exceeding greatness of His power toward us who believe, according to the working of His mighty power.* (Eph. 1:16–19)

He also said to them,

> *I bow my knees to the Father of our Lord Jesus Christ, from whom the whole family in heaven and earth is named, that He would grant you, according to the riches of His glory, to be strengthened with might through His Spirit in the inner man, that Christ may dwell in your hearts through faith; that you, being rooted and grounded in love, may be able to comprehend with all the saints what is the width and length*

and depth and height; to know the love of Christ
which passes knowledge; that you may be filled
with all the fullness of God. Now to Him who is
able to do exceedingly abundantly above all that
we ask or think, according to the power that
works in us, to Him be glory in the church by
Christ Jesus to all generations, forever and ever.
Amen.   (Eph. 3:14–21)

Paul explained to the Ephesians that spiritual gifts
were for the perfecting of the saints, so that they might
become mature men:

Till we all come to the unity of the faith and of
the knowledge of the Son of God, to a perfect
man, to the measure of the stature of the fullness
of Christ.   (Eph. 4:13)

Without these spiritual gifts in the church, Christians
would never become strong and mature. Paul urged
the Ephesian believers to put on the whole spiritual
armor of God, so that they might be able to stand
against every temptation (Eph. 6:11). With this armor,
they would *"be able to quench all the fiery darts of the*
wicked one" (v. 16).

In a similar manner, Paul prayed for the Colossian
believers to be *"filled with the knowledge of* [God's]
will in all wisdom and spiritual understanding" (Col.
1:9). He also prayed for the Thessalonian believers,
that God would sanctify them wholly and that their
"whole spirit, soul, and body [would] *be preserved*
blameless at the coming of our Lord" (1 Thess. 5:23).
He urged both the Thessalonian and Hebrew believers
to pursue holiness, without which no man would see
the Lord (Heb. 12:14). These are only a few of the
many examples of Paul's longings and prayers that
others might partake of the same deep, rich, full spiritual experience that he enjoyed.

Deeper Experiences of the Samaritan Disciples

Philip, the evangelist, was among the men *"full of the Holy Spirit and wisdom"* (Acts 6:3) who were selected as deacons of the first Christian church at Jerusalem. In Acts 8, we read the story of how he went to Samaria and preached the Gospel. There was a great revival in that city under his preaching. Many believed the things he preached, for Christ had prepared the way when He preached to the woman at the well of that city and then to all the people (John 4). Great miracles occurred, and there was much joy in the city. The people who were converted under Philip's preaching were baptized, both men and women.

> *Now when the apostles who were at Jerusalem heard that Samaria had received the word of God, they sent Peter and John to them, who, when they had come down, prayed for them that they might receive the Holy Spirit. For as yet He had fallen upon none of them. They had only been baptized in the name of the Lord Jesus. Then they laid hands on them, and they received the Holy Spirit.* (Acts 8:14–17)

The Ephesian Disciples Filled with the Spirit

In Acts 19, we read about Paul going to the city of Ephesus. *"And finding some disciples he said to them, 'Did you receive the Holy Spirit when you believed?'"* (vv. 1–2). If every believer had received the Holy Spirit, then Paul's question would have been a very foolish one. But these believers had *"not so much as heard whether there is a Holy Spirit"* (v. 2). This surprised Paul, for he thought that they should have heard about the Holy Spirit when they were baptized. He said, *"Into what then were you baptized?"* (v. 3). They then told him, *"Into John's baptism"* (v. 3).

This explained why they had not heard about the Holy Spirit when they were baptized, for John only baptized unto repentance and not in the name of the Father, Son, and Holy Spirit. *"When they heard this, they were baptized in the name of the Lord Jesus"* (v. 5), and in the name of the Father and the Holy Spirit. *"And when Paul had laid hands on them, the Holy Spirit came upon them, and they spoke with tongues and prophesied"* (v. 6).

Paul may have referred to this experience of the Ephesian disciples, and to other similar experiences, when he later wrote, in his epistle to the Ephesians,

> *In Him you also trusted, after you heard the word of truth, the gospel of your salvation; in whom also, having believed, you were sealed with the Holy Spirit of promise.* (Eph. 1:13)

The early Christian writers all referred to the filling of the Spirit as the sealing of the Spirit.

The Early Christian Church

Most of the great Bible scholars and commentators, and most of the great church historians, agree that it was the custom of the early church to pray for all believers to be filled with the Spirit. The usual custom was to baptize the converts, and then the elders would lay hands on them and pray for them to receive the gift of the Holy Spirit. The laying on of hands (in prayer for the Holy Spirit) is mentioned in Hebrews 6:2 as one of the first principles, or foundation principles, of the Gospel. In the case of Paul, the Samaritan disciples, and the Ephesian disciples, we have examples of this early custom.

The Holy Spirit came without the laying on of hands on the Day of Pentecost, but some people think that this was because there were then no Spirit-filled believers to lay hands on the disciples and pray for them to be filled with the Spirit. The Holy Spirit also fell upon Cornelius and his household and friends without the laying on of hands in prayer, while Peter was preaching to them (Acts 10:44), but some suppose that this was because no Jew would lay hands on Gentiles to pray for them to be filled with the Spirit until after God poured His Spirit on Cornelius. Cornelius also received the Holy Spirit before he was baptized, but this was because no Jew would have baptized Gentiles. The Scriptures say that the Jews were astonished when they saw that God had poured His Spirit upon the Gentiles also (v. 45).

Dr. Lightfoot, a scholar and Bible commentator, has written that it was a maxim among the Jews "that the Holy Spirit is never imparted to any Gentile." Undoubtedly, Peter would have refused to preach to Gentiles if God had not shown him three times in a vision to do so (Acts 10:9–16). Nevertheless, it seems certain that the usual order in the early Christian church was first conversion, then baptism, then the laying on of hands in prayer for the Holy Spirit.

Peter undoubtedly referred to this order of things on the Day of Pentecost, when the people were greatly convicted of sin and cried aloud, *"Men and brethren, what shall we do?"* (Acts 2:37). Peter said,

> *Repent, and let every one of you be baptized in the name of Jesus Christ for the remission of sins; and you shall receive the gift of the Holy Spirit. For the promise is to you and to your children, and to all who are afar off, as many as the Lord our God will call.*　　　　　(vv. 38–39)

The laying on of hands in prayer was a very ancient custom, and the early Christians probably adopted it from the Jews. Jacob laid his hands upon the sons of Joseph when blessing them (Gen. 48:14). Moses

laid hands on Joshua, as the Lord commanded him to
do, when praying for Joshua to be filled with the Spirit
(Num. 27:18, 23). The early Christians usually laid
hands on the sick when praying for their recovery
(Mark 16:18). Paul spoke of the gift given to Timothy
by the laying on of the hands of the elders (1 Tim. 4:14;
2 Tim. 1:6). And there are many more examples of this
throughout the Scriptures.

The custom of laying hands on ministers when
ordaining them is practiced in the churches today, but
the ancient custom of laying hands on all believers and
praying for them to be filled with the Spirit is no longer
observed by many of the Protestant churches. While
God can, and undoubtedly often does, give the Holy
Spirit without the laying on of hands, it might be best
to restore this ancient custom. It is a means of
strengthening the faith and concentrating the thoughts
of the person prayed for.

The Greek Church and other Eastern churches,
the Roman Catholic Church, the Lutheran Church, the
Church of England, and a few smaller churches still
retain a relic of the old apostolic custom of laying on
hands in prayer for the Holy Spirit in what they call
confirmation services. In the confirmation services of
all these churches, the bishops, or priests, lay hands on
the individuals and pray for them to be filled with the
Holy Spirit. The mere form of this, however, amounts
to little unless the Holy Spirit actually comes to dwell
within. If He does this either with or without laying on
of hands, there will be new life and power in the experience of the Christian.

The early Christian church believed in and prayed
for the filling of the Holy Spirit, and this was the secret
of its power. It lived in the Spirit, walked in the Spirit,
prayed in the Spirit, and sang in the Spirit. Its meetings were conducted in the Pentecostal manner, with
everyone praying, singing, or testifying as they were
moved by the Spirit. The Holy Spirit prayed through

them, spoke through them, sang through them, comforted them, anointed them, strengthened them, and enlightened them. Of the first church at Jerusalem, we read, *"And great grace was upon them all"* (Acts 4:33).

Soon after Pentecost, the apostles were gathered together in prayer, and the Holy Spirit again came with such power that He shook the place in which they were assembled, and all who were not previously filled with the Spirit were then filled, so that *"they were all filled with the Holy Spirit, and they spoke the word of God with boldness"* (v. 31). Concerning other churches in the Holy Land, we read:

> *Then the churches throughout all Judea, Galilee, and Samaria had peace and were edified. And walking in the fear of the Lord and in the comfort of the Holy Spirit, they were multiplied.*
> (Acts 9:31)

The Gentiles had their Pentecost when the Holy Spirit fell upon Cornelius and his household and friends (Acts 10), and after that, Jews and Gentiles were all one in Christ (Gal. 3:28). Some people believe that Cornelius and his friends were justified, or saved, before the Holy Spirit fell upon them, and the words of Peter seem to indicate this (Acts 10:34–35). But if they were not justified before Peter spoke to them, they were both justified and filled with the Spirit while he was speaking to them (v. 44).

The apostle Paul could say to the church at Corinth, *"Do you not know that you are the temple of God and that the Spirit of God dwells in you?"* (1 Cor. 3:16). And to Christians in general, the apostle John could write, *"But you have an anointing from the Holy One, and you know all things"* (1 John 2:20). These, and many other Scriptures, show that the New Testament church was truly a Spirit-filled one. The men chosen as deacons of the first Christian church were *"full of the*

Holy Spirit and wisdom" (Acts 6:3). One of these, Stephen, was so filled with the Spirit that his face shone like *"the face of an angel"* (v. 15). With such anointed believers, it is little wonder that the early church went forth conquering and soon won the world to Christ—a few Judean peasants overturning the entire fabric of paganism.

> Oh, for the Spirit's quickening power;
> Oh, for a soul-refreshing shower;
> Oh, for the Pentecostal power;
> Lord, send it now.

Chapter 3

Other Early
Writers

⚜

*T*he early Christian writers, both the Greek and
Roman fathers of the church, testify to the fact
that in the second century and later, it was
customary to pray for Christians to be filled with the
Spirit, just as they were prayed for in Bible times. In
the days of Tertullian, a church father who wrote in
the second century, it was also customary to anoint
baptized believers with oil before praying for them to
be filled with the Spirit. The oil was used as a symbol
of the Holy Spirit, as it is used all through the Scriptures, although there is no biblical example of anointing before prayer for the Holy Spirit.

In Old Testament times, oil was used in anointing
the priests and kings, as a symbol of the Holy Spirit's
anointing. In New Testament times, it was used to
anoint the sick before prayer was offered for their recovery (James 5:14), thus symbolizing that the Holy
Spirit would do the healing. The custom of anointing
people before praying for them to be filled with the
Spirit, however, seems to have become common soon
after the time of the apostles, as it was very widespread in the second century. As the baptism in water

symbolized the cleansing from sin, so the anointing with oil was used to symbolize the anointing of the Holy Spirit.

Tertullian, in his book called *Baptism,* wrote, "The baptized, when they come up out of the bath, are anointed with the holy oil, and then the hand is laid upon them with the invocation of the Holy Spirit." This is clear testimony from one of the earliest Christian writers to show that in his day it was customary to pray for the newly baptized converts to be filled with the Spirit.

Near the close of the second century, no one could become a member of the church at Rome (one of the largest and most influential churches) unless he believed in praying for those who were newly converted and baptized in water to then be clothed with the Holy Spirit. In his book entitled *The Resurrection of the Body,* Tertullian wrote the following to explain the need to be filled with the Spirit:

> The flesh is consigned or sealed, so that the soul may be guarded or defended; and the body is overshadowed by the imposition of hands, so that the soul may be enlightened by the Holy Spirit.

Prayer for the Holy Spirit was no mere form in the second century. This is evident from the testimony of Irenaeus. Writing about A.D. 150, he indicated that in his time, "When God saw it necessary, and the church prayed and fasted much, miraculous things occurred, even of bringing back the spirit to a dead man."

Theophilus of Antioch, writing about A.D. 170, or not long after the time of the apostles, said that the name *Christian* is derived from the Greek word for oil, *chrism,* and means "anointed one," referring to the fact that the followers of Christ were anointed with the Spirit. Living at such an early time, and in the city where they were first called Christians (Acts 11:26), his explanation seems to be a reasonable one. Perhaps Christians came to be called "anointed ones" because Christ was commonly called "the Anointed" (that is what the word *Christ* means). Theophilus said, "We are called Christians because we are anointed with the blessing of God."

Jeremy Taylor, a bishop of the Church of England, explained how the imposition of hands in prayer for the Holy Spirit came to be known as "the sacrament of chrism." He said,

> It was very early in the church that they used oil and balsam to represent the grace that was ministered in confirmation, the anointing from above. They so constantly used this in their confirmation that from the ceremony it had the name, *sacramentum chrismatis* (the sacrament of anointing).

The filling of the Spirit was commonly called "the Lord's seal" or "the Lord's signature" by the early Christian writers. After the church began to anoint people with oil before praying for them to be filled with the Spirit, the ceremony of anointing with oil was called *signaculum,* or sealing. The term *sealing* was probably derived from Ephesians 1:13, where Paul spoke about the Ephesians being sealed with the Holy Spirit after they had believed. He probably referred to the time when they were filled with the Spirit in answer to his prayer, as recorded in Acts 19:6, and to other similar experiences. Nevertheless, it is certain that the early Christian writers referred to the filling of the Spirit as "the sealing of the Spirit."

One bishop compared the gift of the Holy Spirit through the laying on of hands after baptism, to the ring that the father put on the finger of the Prodigal Son after his return. It was said that the spiritual anointing is like a royal signature.

In Bible times, any Spirit-filled Christian could pray for another to be filled with the Spirit, just as Ananias, who was not an apostle, prayed for Paul. But, gradually, the Western church, which afterward became the Roman Catholic Church, came to believe that only bishops had the power or authority to pray for others to be filled with the Spirit. Bishops no longer held the humble offices that they held in the early church, when there were several bishops, or elders, in each church. (See Philippians 1:1, for example.) The Eastern church, which afterward became the Greek Church, has always held that any ordinary priest has the right to lay on hands in prayer for the Holy Spirit.

Around A.D. 250, Saint Cyprian wrote about how the officials of the church in his day prayed for the newly converted and baptized to be filled with the Spirit. Peter and John had prayed for the Samaritan disciples to be filled with the Spirit, and Cyprian said that this same thing could be done among people in his own time, as long as "those who are already baptized are brought to the rulers of the church to obtain the Holy Spirit by our prayer and imposition of hands."

These words show that at that time the Western church had already become formal enough to imagine that the Holy Spirit could only be obtained through the prayers and laying on of hands of a bishop. They also show that it was the rule of the church in the third century that only baptized converts could be prayed for so that they might receive the Holy Spirit. I have already shown that this was the custom of the church in the first and second century.

Firmillian, also writing in the third century, compared Paul's confirming of the disciples at Ephesus (Acts 19:1–7) to the confirming of people in his own time. Firmillian and Saint Ambrose seem to have been among the first to use the word *confirmation* to describe the laying on of hands in prayer for the Holy

Spirit. The term is undoubtedly derived from 2 Corinthians 1:21–22:

> *Now He who establishes* [or, confirms] *us with you in Christ and has anointed us is God, who also has sealed us and given us the Spirit in our hearts as a guarantee.*

The ancient writers of the church believed that the establishing, anointing, and sealing referred to in these verses meant the filling of the Holy Spirit. In the time of Saint Ambrose, the Latin word *confirmatio,* which means "confirmation" or "establishing," began to be the common word for describing imposition of hands in prayer for the Holy Spirit.

The Holy Spirit does confirm, or establish, people; and the word *confirmation* is a good word to describe the filling of the Holy Spirit. However, the word has been used so much to describe what is often a mere form or ceremony that it has lost much of the simplicity and power of its meaning.

In his epistle to the Bishop of Spain around A.D. 320, Melchiades described the need of being filled with the Spirit, which he called "confirmation":

> What does the mystery of confirmation profit me after the mystery of baptism? Certainly we did not receive everything in our baptism, if after the washing we need something of another kind. The military requires that when the general enlists a soldier, he not only marks him, but also furnishes him with arms for the battle. Likewise, in one who is baptized, this blessing is his ammunition. A soldier requires weapons. What good is it if a father gives a great estate to his son if he does not care to provide guidance for him? Therefore, the Holy Spirit is the Guardian of our regeneration in Christ; He is the Comforter, and He is the Defender.

The above comparison of the regenerated person who is not filled with the Spirit to a soldier without armor or weapons is not only a striking one, but it is also scriptural. Recall how Paul exhorted Christians to *"put on the whole armor of God"* (Eph. 6:11). Regeneration makes us soldiers, but the filling of the Spirit clothes us with armor and weapons.

Concerning the imposition of hands in prayer for the Holy Spirit, Gregory of Nazianzen, around A.D. 370, said, "We therefore call it a seal or signature, as being a guard and custody to us, and a sign of the Lord's dominion over us." He also said, "How will the angel know what sheep belong to his charge; how will he snatch them from the enemy, if he does not see their mark and signature?" The mark and signature he referred to is the seal of the Holy Spirit.

Many of the early Christian writers referred to the filling of the Spirit as the Lord's seal. They believed that in regeneration they became the Lord's, but that the filling of the Spirit was the Lord setting His seal on them just as a man might brand the sheep that were already his.

Saint Ambrose, in his book *Concerning the Mystery,* commented on the words of Paul, *"He who establishes us with you in Christ...is God"* (2 Cor. 1:21). Ambrose said,

> Remember that you who have been confirmed have received the spiritual signature, the spirit of wisdom and understanding, the spirit of counsel and strength, the spirit of knowledge and godliness, the spirit of holy fear. Keep what you have received; the Father has sealed you, and Christ your Lord has confirmed you.

In the time of Saint Jerome, which was near the end of the fourth century, the whole Christian world seemed to believe in the laying on of the bishops' or elders' hands in prayer for the Holy Spirit. This had become so much of a form or ceremony that many imagined that God would not give the Holy Spirit in any other way. The simple New Testament form of church government had already grown into a great ecclesiastical hierarchy seeking to usurp power over both the souls and bodies of men.

The church was losing sight of the grand simplicity of God's promises to pour His Spirit upon every hungering, thirsting believer. In New Testament times, the elders and church officers usually prayed for individuals to be filled with the Spirit, because the most spiritual men were selected as church officers. However, God never meant to confine this authority or privilege to any individuals or class of individuals. This is proved by His promise:

> *Ask, and it will be given to you; seek, and you will find; knock, and it will be opened to you. For everyone who asks receives, and he who seeks finds, and to him who knocks it will be opened. If a son asks for bread from any father among you, will he give him a stone? Or if he asks for a fish, will he give him a serpent instead of a fish? Or if he asks for an egg, will he offer him a scorpion? If you then, being evil, know how to give good gifts to your children, how much more will your heavenly Father give the Holy Spirit to those who ask Him!* (Luke 11:9–13)

Saint Augustine, the most celebrated of all the early Christian writers, writing around the year A.D. 380, explained Acts 2:38 as follows:

> *"Then Peter said to them, 'Repent, and let every one of you be baptized in the name of Jesus Christ for the remission of sins; and you shall receive the gift of the Holy Spirit.'"* In the church in which the Holy Spirit truly resided, both were

brought to pass, that is, both the remission of sins and the receiving of the gift.

This is indisputable evidence that the church of the fourth century believed in both the remission of sins and the gift of the Holy Spirit. It is also evident from his *Confessions* that Augustine himself seemed to have felt that the Holy Spirit was leading and directing him.

Lucherius Lugdenenses, writing in the fifth century, said,

> The same thing that is done now in the imposition of hands on individual persons, is no different from what was done upon all believers in the descent of the Holy Spirit; it is the same ministry, and all derived from the same authority.

John of Damascus, about A.D. 700, mentioned the incoming of the Holy Spirit. He said, "He (the Lord) makes us His anointed ones, and by His Spirit He declares His eternal mercy toward us."

Amalarius, in the ninth century, affirmed that Pope Sylvester, "foreseeing how dangerous a journey he takes who abides without confirmation, brought remedy as far as he could and commanded that in the absence of bishops they should be anointed by the priest." He then went on to explain how the custom of laying on of hands in prayer for the Holy Spirit was derived from the apostles themselves.

Reformed Churches and the Filling of the Spirit

Both the Eastern and Western churches, from apostolic times to the present, have prayed for converts to receive the gift of the Holy Spirit—even though the prayer has often been ritualistic, formalistic, and purely ceremonial. The ceremony of laying on of hands in prayer for the Holy Spirit has been maintained through all the centuries of the Christian era by the Eastern churches and sects, and by the Roman Catholic Church and the early sects in the West. A quarrel concerning the anointing oil used in this ceremony led to the division of the Catholic Church into the Eastern and Western churches, which are now known as the Greek Church and the Roman Catholic Church.

For a long time, the Greeks obtained anointing oil blessed by the bishop of Rome, who, on account of Rome being the leading city of the world, was rapidly coming to be recognized as the pope, or father, of all the churches. But when the Romans demanded eighty pounds of gold and some other gifts in exchange for the anointing oil, the Greeks rejected the authority of the bishop of Rome and began to consecrate their own oil. Since that time, the two great churches have remained separate.

When infant baptism became common in the church, infant confirmation and infant communion also became common. In the time of Augustine, infants received both confirmation and communion after baptism. But they often vomited the wine and bread of the communion, which were forced into their mouths, and this led the Roman Catholic Church to stop the practice of infant communion, although it is still the rule and practice of the Greek Church. Both the Greek and Roman Catholic churches decided that it would be better not to continue the practice of confirming little infants, and both those great churches now wait until children have reached the age of accountability before confirming them.

The Protestant Churches, formed during and since the great Protestant Reformation, are divided with regard to the practice of confirmation. The Lutheran Church and the Church of England retained the practice, while most of the other Protestant churches rejected it as an empty form and adopted nothing in its place. John Calvin, the great reformer, acknowledged that the custom of praying for converts to be filled with the Spirit was derived from the apostles, and that the Protestant churches ought to have something in the place of it, and yet he seems to have made little effort to impress the need of it upon the churches with which he had so much influence. Calvin said, with regard to the laying on of hands in prayer for the Holy Spirit,

> This rite had its beginning with the apostles, but afterward, however, was turned into superstition, as the world almost always degenerates into corruptions....Therefore the pure institution at this day ought to be retained, but the superstition ought to be removed.

There were at least two great and sincere efforts to make the Roman Catholic and Protestant churches feel the need for being filled with the Spirit and led by the Spirit. These were the Quietist movement and the Quaker movement. Both of these great spiritual movements have had a tremendous influence for good in deepening the spiritual life of the churches. Although I am a firm believer in the outward ordinances of baptism and the Lord's Supper, I cannot help believing that the Lord raised up the Quakers to call the churches away from dependence on outward forms and ceremonies, and to emphasize the thought that *"the kingdom of God is not eating and drinking, but righteousness and peace and joy in the Holy Spirit"* (Rom. 14:17).

Chapter 4

Girolamo
Savonarola

~~~⟡~~~

G irolamo Savonarola, from Italy, was one of the greatest reformers, preachers, prophets, politicians, and philosophers the world has ever known. His public career as a preacher began the same year that Martin Luther was born, which was 1483. If Italy had been as open as Germany was to a Protestant Reformation, he, instead of Luther, might have been the instrument in bringing about that reformation.

As it was, however, Savonarola was the precursor of the Protestant Reformation. By his terrific denunciation of the corruptions of the Roman Catholic Church, he prepared all of Europe for the Reformation. His life and teachings had a great influence upon Luther, who acknowledged his indebtedness to him and spoke of him as "a Protestant martyr." Not only was Savonarola the herald of the coming reformation, but he also did more than any other man to rescue mankind from the abyss of skepticism and corruption into which the world had been plunged by the example of the most degraded and dissolute church that ever bore the Christian name.

Before the days of the Spanish Inquisition, the Roman Catholic Church was never as corrupt as in the fifteenth century, when those monstrous criminals, the Borgias, reigned as popes and cardinals. By his powerful preaching, by his profound philosophy, and by the divine anointing resting upon him, Savonarola convinced the masses that religion was not all sham and formalism, and a new day dawned for Christianity and for the world.

Born in Ferrara, Italy, on September 14, 1452, Savonarola was the third in a family of seven children. His parents were cultured but worldly people, moderately wealthy but having great influence at the court of the duke of Ferrara. Girolamo's paternal grandfather, who tutored him during his earlier years, was an eminent physician at the court of the duke, and Girolamo's parents intended him to follow the same profession and to become his grandfather's successor. But God had chosen another calling for the youth.

From his infancy, Girolamo had been rather quiet. As a child, he was never playful, but always serious and subdued. At an early age, he became a very diligent student, and he afterward attained great proficiency in the liberal arts and in philosophy. He was an earnest student of Aristotle, but the writings of the great Greek philosopher left the deepest longings of his soul unsatisfied. The philosophy of Plato gave him a little more satisfaction, but it was not until he began to study the writings of the Christian philosopher Thomas Aquinas that he found real food for his soul. The writings of that celebrated saint led Savonarola, at a very early age, to yield his whole heart and life to God, and these writings probably continued to influence his life more than any other writings except the Scriptures.

Concerning his visions, Savonarola said,

> They came to me when I was very young, but it was only at Brescia, a community in northern Italy, that I began to proclaim them.

> Then I was sent by the Lord to Florence, which
> is in the heart of Italy, so that the reformation of
> Italy might begin.

As a boy, his devotion and fervor increased as he grew
older, and he spent many hours in prayer and fasting.
He would kneel in church for hours at a time engaged
in prayer. He was very contemplative, and his soul was
deeply stirred by the vice and worldliness he saw wherever he went. The luxury, splendor, and wealth displayed by the rich, and the awful poverty of the poor,
weighed heavily on his heart.

Italy was the prey of petty tyrants and wicked
priests, and dukes and popes vied with each other in
lewdness, lavishness, and cruelty. These things
brought great sorrow to Savonarola's young soul,
which was burning for virtue and truth. Some of the
rough, impassioned verses of his youth show how
deeply his soul was stirred by the evils he saw all
around him. Thus, in one of his earliest poems, he
spoke of

> Seeing the whole world overset;
> All virtue and goodness disappeared;
> Nowhere a shining light;
> No one taking shame for his sins.

This profound awareness of the evils around him
made Savonarola a sad and sorrowful youth. He talked
little, and he kept to himself. He loved to be in lonely
places, in the open fields or along the green banks of
the river Po. There he would wander, sometimes singing, sometimes weeping, and he would give utterance
to the strong emotions that boiled in his breast. His
great, soulful eyes were resplendent and were the color
of the heavens, but they were often filled with tears.
Prayer was his one great solace, and his tears would often fall upon the altar steps, where, stretched prostrate

for hours at a time, he sought aid from heaven against the vile, corrupt, and dissolute age.

At one time, in the midst of Savonarola's deep musings, there came a brief time when he fell in love with a young Florentine maiden and began to have a more cheerful view of things in general. But the affair ended when the maiden scornfully rejected him because she belonged to the proud Strozzi family and did not consider Savonarola's family to be exalted enough to mate with hers. He resented her arrogance and sought her hand no more.

After this little episode of happy delusion, when the magical mist and the glamour of love almost blinded him for a time to the evils around him, the mists were dispelled, and Savonarola again saw clearly the corruption abounding everywhere he looked. Religious desires again took complete possession of his soul, and his prayers were uttered with daily increasing fervor. Disgusted with the world, disappointed in his personal hopes, finding no one to sympathize with his feelings, and weary with the sight of constant wrongs and evils that he could not remedy, he decided to enter the monastic life.

It was on April 24, 1475, while his relatives were all away celebrating the festival of Saint George, that Girolamo ran away to Bologna and applied for admittance to the Dominican convent. The fact that his favorite writer, Thomas Aquinas, was a Dominican probably influenced him to enter that order. He did not ask to become a monk, but only to be a drudge and to do the most menial services in the kitchen, garden, and monastery. He was accepted, and as soon as he reached his cell he wrote an affectionate letter to his family, explaining why he entered the monastery and begging his parents to forgive him and give him their blessing. He had left behind him at home a paper entitled "Contempt of the World," in which he described the condition of things as similar to that of Sodom and

Gomorrah. Even at this time, he seems to have had a presentiment that someday God would use him mightily in calling men to repentance.

In the Dominican monastery, Savonarola fasted and prayed and led a silent life, and he became increasingly absorbed in spiritual contemplation. His modesty, humility, and obedience surpassed that of all the others. Soon after he entered the monastery, he was made lecturer on philosophy to the convent, a position he held during the remainder of the years that he spent there. During this time, his fury and indignation against the sins of the church increased so much that he longed to denounce them and did so in a poem entitled, "The Ruin of the Church."

In 1481, after spending seven years in the monastery at Bologna, Fra (Brother) Girolamo went to the convent of Saint Mark's in Florence, the most beautiful and cultured city in Italy and the city where he was to become famous. The modern world was then just coming into being and found its best expression in the great Italian Renaissance, of which the de Medici family, who ruled Florence, were the principal patrons. The Renaissance, or revival of learning, had affected Florence more than any other city. The de Medici had done much to make it a learned and cultured city, and most of the people knew Greek and Latin and could read the classics.

Savonarola had high ideas concerning the culture and refinement of Florence, and he expected to find the Florentines leading purer and nobler lives than those of other cities. But his hopes were doomed to disappointment. He had yet to learn that only faith in God will save people from sin. Florence was indeed outwardly beautiful, as it was situated in the midst of a rich and green valley that blossomed with flowers. But Savonarola soon found that beneath their facade of learning, the people were utterly corrupt and were entirely given over to worldliness. They were dissolute, selfish, pleasure-loving, and had little thought about God or spiritual things.

In the year after he entered the convent of Saint Mark's, Savonarola was made instructor of the novices, and he was finally raised to the rank of preacher in the monastery. Although the monastery had a vast library, Savonarola came more and more to use the Bible as his textbook. He was filled with a sense of approaching judgment, terror, and the vengeance of God. When he was sent to preach in the neighboring towns, he sometimes expressed these feelings of impending judgment. In the towns of Brescia, San Geminiano, and Florence, he thundered from the pulpit a thousand woes against the wicked, but his sermons made scarcely any impression. The cultured people of Florence hardly paid any attention to this monk whose accents were harsh and whose sentences were not daintily formed.

In the Church of San Lorenzo, where Savonarola first preached in Florence, there were not even 25 people in the audience. He made a somewhat deeper impression in the remote villages and towns. However, his preaching had so little effect that he decided to give up preaching and to confine himself to teaching the novices. But, as God called Moses from the desert where he had retired to feed sheep, so He called Savonarola from the monastery to preach.

In 1482 Savonarola was sent to Reggio d'Emilia to represent his convent at a Dominican general assembly. During the first day, while the monks were discussing dogma, he remained silent. But on the second day, when a question of discipline was brought up, he arose and in a powerful voice railed against the sins and corruption of the church and the clergy. His soul was on fire, and he spoke with an eloquence that made a deep impression upon those who heard him.

Returning to Florence, Savonarola found it impossible to refrain from preaching, and he began to deliver sermons at the little church of the Murate convent. His sermons, however, still made little impression on the pleasure-loving Florentines. Fra Mariano, an Augustinian monk, was preaching to immense crowds in the Great Church of Santo Spirito, and the people preferred him to Savonarola. He never rebuked them for their sins, but he entertained them with classical quotations, philosophy, astronomy, and poetry, and the whole city was flocking to hear him. This only strengthened the resolve of Savonarola to denounce the sins and vices of the age. "These verbal elegancies and ornaments will have to give way to sound doctrine simply preached," he said.

In prayer and meditation, Savonarola waited upon God and yearned for a direct revelation from Him, which was eventually granted to him. One day, while engaged in conversation with a nun, he suddenly saw in a vision the heavens opened, and all the future calamities of the church passed before his eyes. He seemed to hear a voice calling him to announce these future events to the people. From that moment, he was convinced of his divine mission and was filled with a new anointing and power. His preaching was now with a voice of thunder, and his denunciation of sin so terrific that the people who heard him sometimes went about the streets half-dazed, bewildered, and speechless. His congregations were often in tears, so that the whole church resounded with their sobs and weeping. Men and women of every age and condition—workmen, poets, philosophers—would burst into passionate tears.

Savonarola's ardor for prayer, his faith, and his devotion increased day by day. His friend, Fra Sebastiano, from Brescia, said that when Savonarola was engaged in prayer, he frequently fell into a trance and was sometimes so transported by holy zeal that he was obliged to retire to some solitary place. Some of his biographers relate that on Christmas Eve, 1486, while seated in the pulpit, Savonarola remained in a trance for five hours, that his face seemed illuminated to all in the church, and that this occurred several times afterward. Savonarola told his friend and biographer, the younger Pico della Mirandola, that on one occasion while meditating on the text, *"Blessed are You, O LORD! Teach me Your statutes"* (Ps. 119:12), he felt his mind illuminated, all doubts left him, and he felt entirely certain of the things that were shown to him.

In 1484 Savonarola was sent as a preacher to the little republic of San Gimignano. Here he preached with such power that he returned to Florence with greater confidence in his mission. He retained his post of lecturer to the novices of Saint Mark's until Lent of 1486, when he was sent to preach in various cities of Lombardy, especially in Brescia. Everywhere he went, his denunciations of sin awakened much alarm, and his fame continued to spread across Italy. He remained in Lombardy until January 1489.

In a letter to his mother, describing his meetings in Lombardy, he wrote, "When I have to depart, men and women shed tears and hold my words in much esteem." In 1489 he returned to Florence, the Lord revealing to him that great things awaited him there. He began to explain the book of Revelation to the friars, in the garden of Saint Mark's convent. But his fame had spread through Florence, and laymen begged for admittance to his lectures. His congregations increased daily until he had to preach from the pulpit of the church. The church was crowded, and many clung to the iron gratings or stood in order to see and hear the preacher. The voice of Savonarola seemed to have an almost superhuman effect, and the audience experienced great spiritual delight.

After that service, all of Florence spoke of Savonarola, and even the most educated individuals flocked to hear him. By Lent of 1491, San Marco Church had become too small to hold the people, and Savonarola had to preach in the famous Duomo, or cathedral church of Florence, where he remained during the rest of the eight years that he preached in Florence. The people were so eager to hear him that they rose in the middle of the night and waited for hours for the cathedral doors to open. They came along the streets singing and rejoicing and listened to the sermons with such interest that when they were finished, the people thought that they had scarcely begun.

Savonarola seemed to be swept onward by a power not his own, and he carried his audiences with him. Soon all of Florence was at the feet of the great preacher, and Lorenzo de Medici, the corrupt ruler of the city, was greatly alarmed. He tried by flattery and bribery, by threats and persuasion, to induce Savonarola to cease denouncing the sins of the people, and especially his own sins. But Savonarola continued his fearless preaching. Then Lorenzo hired Fra Mariano, the once popular preacher, to denounce Savonarola; but his eloquence and rhetoric had no effect on the people, and after preaching one sermon against Savonarola, he ceased his opposition.

When Lorenzo was opposing Savonarola, the fearless preacher predicted that Lorenzo, the Pope, and the King of Naples would all die within a year, and that is exactly what happened. As Lorenzo de Medici lay dying, he thought of the wrongs he had done, and he was in an agony to obtain pardon. He did not call for his own priests or for Fra Mariano for consolation, but he sent for Savonarola, the only preacher who had dared to oppose him. Savonarola said to the messenger, "I am not the person he wants; it is not good for me to go to him." Lorenzo sent the messenger back, promising to do everything that Savonarola required of him.

Savonarola then went to the beautiful villa of Carregi, amid the olive gardens, where Lorenzo lay dying. He was led into the sick chamber. "Father," said Lorenzo, "there are three things that drag me back and throw me into despair, and I know not if God will ever pardon me for them." These were the sack of Volterra, the robbery of the Monte della Fanciulle, and the massacre of the Pazzi. Savonarola replied, "Lorenzo, do not despair, for God is merciful and will be merciful to you, if you will do three things I will tell you."

"What are these three things?" asked Lorenzo.

"The first is that you should have a great and living faith that God can and will pardon you," replied Savonarola.

"This is a great thing, and I do believe it," said Lorenzo.

"It is also necessary that everything wrongfully acquired should be given back by you, insofar as you can do this and still leave to your children as much as will allow them to remain private citizens," continued Savonarola.

These words nearly drove Lorenzo into despair again, but he finally said, "This also will I do."

Savonarola then said, "Lastly, it is necessary that freedom, and popular government according to her republican usage, should be restored to Florence." At this Lorenzo turned his back to him and was silent, and Savonarola went away without absolving him.

A year and a half after Lorenzo's death, Charles VIII, king of France, invaded Italy, sacked Naples, and then advanced on Florence. Savonarola had long predicted that God would send "a new Cyrus from across the Alps" to punish the people for their sins, and in their dire circumstances the people flocked to the Duomo to hear what Savonarola would say. He urged them to repent of their sins, and he went himself to meet the French king and to entreat him to spare Florence. Charles did so very reluctantly, after remaining in the city for some time, and after Savonarola warned him to leave Florence if he did not wish to incur the vengeance of God.

For some time, the people of Florence debated as to what kind of government they should adopt in the place of that of the de Medici, which was overturned during the French invasion. They could come to no agreement, and then Savonarola deemed it necessary to advise them in his sermons. Through his advice, they adopted one of the most advanced and enlightened forms of democratic government. A just form of taxation, abolition of torture, laws against usury and gambling, a court of appeal, and abundant provision for the poor were some of the principal features. The laws and government of the Florentine republic have served as a model to all nations and have had a mighty influence in shaping the modern world.

The influence of Savonarola in Florence and all of Italy was now greater than ever. The people of Florence abandoned their vile and worldly books and read Savonarola's sermons. Everyone prayed and went to church, and the rich gave freely to the poor. Merchants restored all the merchandise they had dishonestly acquired, and this constituted a great monetary loss for them. Even the hoodlums and street urchins stopped singing their crude songs and sang hymns instead. All the people forsook the carnivals and vanities in which they had indulged, and they made huge bonfires of their masks, wigs, worldly books, obscene pictures, and other things of the kind. The children marched from house to house in procession, singing hymns and collecting everything they called vanities. With these a great pyramid was built in the public square and was sent up in flames amid the singing of hymns and pealing of bells. This was in 1497.

But the triumph of Savonarola was short. During his first sermon in Florence, he predicted that he would only preach there eight years. He also foretold his own martyrdom. Although people from all over Italy flocked to Florence to hear him, until the great Duomo itself would not hold the crowds, his fearless sermons aroused the anger of many, and especially of the corrupt pope, cardinals, and priests. He was threatened, excommunicated, and persecuted; and finally, in

1498, by order of Alexander VI, one of the vilest of popes, he was burned to death in the public square of Florence, the city he loved so well.

Savonarola's last words were, "The Lord has suffered so much for me." Thus perished one of the world's greatest saints and martyrs. His sermons and books on humility, prayer, love, and other devotional subjects have continued to exert a very wide influence in the world. Although he held many of the superstitious beliefs of the Roman Catholic Church, he was far in advance of the people of his day, and he may almost be regarded as the first great Protestant reformer. He taught that all believers were in the true church, and he continually fed upon the Word of God. The margin of his Bible was covered with notes of ideas that occurred to him while poring over its pages. His sermons were often expositions of the Scriptures, and it was claimed that there was not a passage to which he could not turn at a moment's notice. He knew a great portion of the Bible by heart. He spent whole nights in prayer, and real visions and revelations seem to have been granted to him. He foretold many important events, and all his biographers have marvelled at the accuracy of his prophecies.

In appearance, Savonarola was of medium height and of dark complexion, and he had a high forehead, a curved nose, thick lips, and a large mouth. When he was preaching, a divine light seemed to beam from his eyes and illuminate his face. His words flowed like a torrent, and he had a voice like thunder.

Chapter 5

Madame Guyon

◢◣◥◤

*M*adame Jeanne Guyon, a Frenchwoman, was one of the greatest Christian leaders of all time. What Savonarola was to Italy, Madame Guyon was to France. Her influence was felt not only throughout her native land of France, but also all over Europe and the world. Fénelon, John Wesley, and other great spiritual leaders have acknowledged that they were greatly indebted to Madame Guyon for the deep spiritual lessons learned from her life and writings. Although she was a Roman Catholic, Jeanne Guyon very much resembled the Quakers, or Friends, in her teachings. She has been termed "a Quaker born out of due time." Dr. J. Rendel Harris, one of the most eminent Friends, said, "No society has been so influenced by Madame Guyon as the Quakers have been."

Jeanne was the center of the spiritual movement known as Quietism, which was perhaps the greatest spiritual movement ever originated within the Roman Catholic Church. In its emphasis on the work of the Holy Spirit, the Quietist movement very much resembled the Quaker movement, and the original Friends were often considered Quietists on this account. The name *Quietist* refers to the quiet submission to the will of God and to the promptings of the Holy Spirit.

As a girl, Jeanne was religiously inclined, but as a young woman she became a vain, proud society butterfly, with few thoughts about God or the world to come. Living in fashionable Paris, in the corrupt and profligate times of Louis XIV, it was very easy for her to be carried away by the worldliness surrounding her. The rule of Louis XIV was perhaps the most pleasure-loving, corrupt, and dissolute that ever cursed the sunny land of France; and the great talents and beauty of Jeanne Guyon, or Mademoiselle de La Mothe, as her maiden name was, made her particularly susceptible to the influences of fashionable society.

But her proud heart was gradually subdued by the destruction of her beauty through an attack of smallpox and by the loss of everything that was dearest to her in this world. Her vanity and pride were completely crushed out, and then she became *"a vessel for honor, sanctified and useful for the Master"* (2 Tim. 2:21). Perhaps no other person except Job was so made *"perfect through sufferings"* (Heb. 2:10), the sufferings of our divine Savior not being considered as the sufferings of a human being.

Jeanne Marie Bouvieres de La Mothe was born at Montargis, France, about 50 miles north of Paris, on April 13, 1648, about a century after the beginning of the Protestant Reformation. Her parents belonged to the aristocracy of France, were highly respected, and were religiously inclined, as were their ancestors for many generations. Her father bore the title of Seigneur, or Lord, de La Mothe Vergonville. In infancy, Jeanne was afflicted with an illness that caused her parents to fear she would die. She rallied, however, and at the age of two and a half years was placed in the Ursuline Seminary in her own town to be educated by the nuns. After a short time, she was taken home, where she remained for some time, but her mother left her chiefly under the care of the servants. During this period, her education was neglected.

In the year 1651, the duchess of Montbason came to Montargis to reside with the Benedictine nuns established there, and she asked Jeanne's father to allow his little daughter, then four years of age, to keep her company. While in the house of the Benedictines, though earlier in life she had some religious impressions, Jeanne was brought to realize her need of a Savior by a dream she had. Her dream showed her the future misery of impenitent sinners, and so she yielded her heart and life to God, and she even vowed her willingness to become a martyr for God.

When the nuns heard this, they pretended that they thought God really wanted her to become a martyr, and they made her believe that they were going to put her to death. She said her prayers, and then they led her to a room prepared for the purpose and caused her to kneel on a cloth they had spread. One of the older girls then appeared as executioner and raised a machete over her head. But at this critical moment Jeanne cried out that she was not at liberty to die without her father's permission. The nuns told her afterward that she was not willing to die for Christ and that she had made an excuse on that account. They made the little girl believe that she had denied the Lord, and it brought great darkness over her mind.

While she was with the Benedictines, Jeanne was generally treated kindly, but her health was very poor. She was again taken to her home and again left most of the time under the care of the servants. Her two half sisters had entered the Ursuline convent, and after she was at home for a short period, Jeanne returned to the Ursuline convent in order to be with them. She was then seven years of age. Her fraternal half sister took her under her special care, and under her instruction Jeanne made rapid progress in learning and piety.

When Jeanne was eight years of age, Henrietta Maria, queen of England, fled to her native land of France to take refuge from the civil war in England.

She visited the La Mothe family and was so charmed by the learning and beauty of little Jeanne that she entreated Lord de La Mothe to allow her to take the child with her, promising to make her maid of honor to the princess. But the father would not consent.

At ten years of age, Jeanne was again taken home, but in a short time she was placed in the Dominican convent at the request of the prioress, who seemed to have a great affection for her. Here she remained eight months, and made much improvement, though her health was very poor. Here she found a Bible, which in some unknown way had been left in her chamber. Young as she was, she became deeply absorbed in reading it. "I spent whole days," she said,

> in reading it, giving no attention to other books or other subjects from morning to night. And having great powers of recollection, I committed to memory the historical parts entirely.

This study of the Scriptures undoubtedly laid the foundations of her wonderful life of devotion and piety. After eight months in the Dominican convent, she returned to her home. She intended to take the sacrament at twelve years of age, but for some time she had been very remiss in her religious duties. A feeling of melancholy entered her mind, and she gave up what religious profession and practices she had. Later in life, she made it known that her religion at that time was chiefly in appearance, and that the love of God was not at the bottom of it. Her father again placed her in the Ursuline Seminary, and through the influence of her pious and prayerful half sister, she was led to think of "giving herself to God in good earnest." She partook of the sacrament, but still her heart was not reached.

She grew tall, and her features began to develop into the beauty that later distinguished her. Her mother, pleased with her appearance, indulged her in dress. Then the world gained full sway over her, and Christ was almost forgotten. Such changes frequently occurred in her early experience. One day she would have serious thoughts and good resolutions, and the next day they were shattered; then gaiety and worldliness filled her life.

A devout young man, a cousin of hers, named de Tossi, was going as a missionary to Cochin China (the southern region of Vietnam), and while passing through Montargis called to see the family. His visit was short, but it made a deep impression on Jeanne, although she was out walking at the time and did not see him. When she was told of his sanctity and consecration, her heart was so touched that she cried the rest of the day and night. She was greatly affected by the thought of the contrast between her own worldly life and the pious life of her cousin. Her whole soul was now aroused to a sense of her true spiritual condition.

She tried to give up her worldliness, to bring herself into a religious frame of mind, and to obtain the forgiveness of all those whom she had wronged in any way. She visited the poor, gave them food and clothing, taught them the catechism, and spent much time in private reading and prayer. She read devotional books, such as the *Life of Madame de Chantal* and the works of Thomas à Kempis and Francis de Sales. She even thought of becoming a nun. But she had not yet learned the lesson of finding peace and rest of soul through faith in Christ. Perhaps God allowed her to go through many struggles and trials to find salvation, so that she might be better suited to teach others the way of salvation through faith after she herself discovered it.

After about a year spent in earnestly seeking after God, she fell deeply in love with a young man, a relative of hers, though she was only fourteen years of age. Her mind was so occupied with thoughts of him that she neglected prayer, and she began to seek in him the pleasure she had formerly sought in God. She still kept up religious appearances, but religion became a matter of indifference in her heart. She read romances, spent much time before the mirror, and became very vain. The world thought highly of her, but her heart was not right with God.

In the year 1663, the La Mothe family moved to Paris, a step not calculated to benefit them spiritually. Paris was a worldly, pleasure-loving city, especially under the reign of Louis XIV, and Mademoiselle de La Mothe's vanity swelled and increased. Jeanne and her parents were led into worldliness by the society in which they now found themselves. The world now seemed to her the one object worth conquering and possessing. Her beauty, intellect, and brilliant powers of conversation made her a favorite of Parisian society. Her future husband, Monsieur Jaques Guyon, who was a man of great wealth, and numerous others, sought her hand in marriage.

Although she had no great affection for Monsieur Guyon, her father arranged the marriage, and she yielded to his wish. The wedding took place in 1664. Jeanne had nearly completed her sixteenth year, while her husband was thirty-eight. She soon discovered that the home to which he took her would be a house of mourning to her. Her mother-in-law, a woman without education or refinement, governed it with a rod of iron.

Jeanne's husband had good qualities and had considerable affection for her, but many factors made life a burden to the young bride: he was often very ill, he was much older than she, and her mother-in-law had a fierce temper. Jeanne's great intellect and sensitivity made her sufferings all the more keen. Her earthly hopes were ruined. She did not know that God had permitted her to be placed under such circumstances for a purpose, nor did she realize His power to alter those circumstances whenever it suited His purposes to do so. But she afterward believed that everything had been ordered in mercy to call her from her life of pride and worldliness.

God seems to have allowed her to go through the furnace of affliction, so that the dross might be purged out and that she might come forth a vessel of pure gold. "My natural pride was so strong" said Madame Guyon, "that nothing but deep sorrow would have broken down my spirit and turned me to God." Later, she said, "You have ordered these things, my God, for my salvation! In goodness You have afflicted me. Enlightened by the result, I have since clearly seen that these dealings of Your providence were necessary, in order to make me die to my vain and haughty nature." Although she ate the bread of sorrow and mingled her drink with her tears (see Psalm 80:5), all these things inclined her mind toward God, and she began to look to Him for comfort in her sorrow. About a year after her marriage, a little son was born to her, and then she felt the need of looking to God for his sake as well as for her own.

However, one calamity after another now befell Madame Guyon. Soon after the birth of her son, her husband lost a great part of his wealth, and this greatly embittered her greedy mother-in-law. In the second year of her marriage, Jeanne fell sick, and it seemed that she would die, but her sickness was a means of causing her to think more of spiritual things. Her beloved half sister died, and then her mother also. As great as these trials were, they worked for her *"a far more exceeding and eternal weight of glory"* (2 Cor. 4:17). Bitterly, she learned that she could find rest nowhere except in God, and she now sought Him in earnest and found Him. Never again did she forsake Him.

From the works of Thomas à Kempis, Francis de Sales, and Madame Chantal, and from her conversations with a pious English lady, Madame Guyon learned much about spiritual things. After an absence of four years, her cousin returned from Cochin China, and his visit was a great help to her spiritually. A humble Franciscan monk felt led by God to visit her home, and he also helped her much in spiritual things. It was this Franciscan who first led her to see clearly the need of seeking Christ through faith, and not through outward works alone, as she had been doing.

Through his instruction, she was led to see that true religion was a matter of the heart and soul, rather than a mere routine of ceremonial duties and observances, as she had supposed. With regard to certain words spoken by this Franciscan, concerning salvation through faith, she said,

> They were to me like the stroke of a dart, which pierced my heart asunder. I felt at this instant deeply wounded with the love of God—a wound so delightful that I desired it never might be healed. These words brought into my heart what I had been seeking so many years; or, rather, they made me discover what was there, and what I did not enjoy because I did not know of it.

Later, she said,

> I told this good man that I did not know what he had done to me, that my heart was quite changed, that God was there. From that moment, God had given me an experience of His presence in my soul—not merely as an object intellectually perceived by the application of the mind, but as a thing really possessed in the sweetest manner. I experienced those words in the Canticles: *"Your name is ointment poured forth; therefore the virgins love you"* (Song 1:3). For I felt in my soul an anointing that healed all my wounds in a moment. I did not sleep at all that night, because Your love, O God, flowed in

me like delicious oil, and burned as a fire that was going to destroy all that was left of self in an instant. I was suddenly so altered that I and others could hardly recognize myself.

Madame Guyon was twenty years of age when she received this definite assurance of salvation through faith in Christ. It was on July 22, 1668. After this experience, she said,

> Nothing was easier to me now than to practice prayer. Hours passed away like moments, while I could hardly do anything else but pray. The fervency of my love allowed me no intermission. It was a prayer of rejoicing and of possession, in which the taste of God was so great, so pure, so unblended and uninterrupted, that it drew and absorbed the powers of the soul into a profound recollection, a state of confiding and affectionate rest in God, existing without intellectual effort.

Some time later she said to the Franciscan,

> I love God far more than the most affectionate lover among men loves the object of his earthly attachment. This love of God occupied my heart so constantly and strongly, that it was very difficult for me to think of anything else. Nothing else seemed worth attention.

Madame Guyon then said,

> I bade farewell forever to assemblies that I had visited, to plays and diversions, to dancing, and to parties of pleasure. The amusements and pleasures that are so much prized and esteemed by the world now appeared to me dull and insipid—so much so, that I wondered how I ever could have enjoyed them.

A second son was born to Jeanne and her husband in 1667, or a year before she was led into the above remarkable experience. Her time was now occupied in caring for her children, and in visiting and ministering to the poor and needy. She caused many beautiful but poor young girls to be taught a trade, so that they would have less temptation to lead a life of sin. She also did much to rescue those who had already fallen into sin. With her means she often assisted poor tradesmen and craftsmen to get a start in business. But she did not neglect prayer. She said, "So strong, almost insatiable, was my desire for communion with God that I arose at four o'clock to pray."

Prayer was the greatest pleasure of her life. Worldly people were astonished to see one so young, so beautiful, and so intellectual, wholly given up to God. Pleasure-loving society felt condemned by her life, and so they sought to persecute and ridicule her. Even her own relatives did not refrain from mocking her feelings, and her mother-in-law sought to make her life more miserable than ever and succeeded to some extent in alienating the affections of her husband and of her eldest son. But trials did not trouble her now as they had before, as she now regarded them as permitted by the Lord to keep her humble. A third child, a daughter, was born to her in 1669. This little girl was a great comfort to her but was destined to leave her soon.

For about two years Madame Guyon's religious experience continued to be a mountaintop one, and then she was drawn away to some extent into worldly conformity. On a visit to Paris, she neglected prayer too much and conformed too much to the worldly society with whom she formerly associated. Realizing this, she rushed back to her home, and her anguish for her shortcomings was like a consuming fire. During a journey through many parts of France with her husband, in 1670, she also felt many temptations to the old life of worldly pleasure. Her sorrow was so great that she even felt that she would be glad if the Lord, by some sudden stroke of His providence, should take her out of this world of temptation and sin.

Jeanne's chief temptations were in the areas of worldly dress and behavior. But the reproaches of her conscience were like a fire burning within her, and the sense of her shortcomings filled her with bitterness and tears. For three months, she did not enjoy her former communion with God. As a result, her mind was turned to the question of holy living. She yearned for someone to instruct her how to live a more spiritual life, how to have a closer walk with God, and how to be more than a conqueror (Rom. 8:37) over the world, the flesh, and the Devil.

Christians of deep spiritual insight were scarce in France. But in Genevieve Grainger, a Benedictine prioress, Madame Guyon found a friend who helped her much in spiritual things. As already mentioned, she also obtained much spiritual help from reading the works of Thomas à Kempis, Francis de Sales, and the biography of Madame Chantal. One day, as she was walking across one of the bridges of the Seine, in Paris, on her way to Notre Dame Church, a poor man in religious garb suddenly joined her and entered into religious conversation. "This man," said Jeanne, "spoke to me in a wonderful manner about God and divine things." He seemed to know all about her history, her virtues, and her faults. Jeanne described the results:

> He led me to understand that God required not merely a heart that is forgiven, but also a heart that could properly, and in some real sense, be designated as holy. This man also showed me that it was not sufficient merely to escape hell, but that God also demanded the subjection of the evils of our nature, and the utmost purity and height of Christian attainment.

The Spirit of God bore witness to what this man said to me. The words of this remarkable man, whom I never saw before and whom I have never seen since, penetrated my very soul. Deeply affected and overcome by what he had said, I had no sooner reached the church than I fainted.

Having already felt her weakness and her need for a deeper spiritual experience, and having received such a direct message through the providence of God, Madame Guyon resolved that day, before leaving the church, to give herself to the Lord anew. Taught by sad experience the impossibility of serving both God and the world, she resolved, "From this day, this hour, if it is possible, I will be wholly the Lord's. The world will have no portion of me." Two years later, she drew up and signed her historic covenant of consecration, but the real consecration seems to have been completed that day when she visited Notre Dame Church. She yielded herself without reservations to the will of God.

Almost immediately, her consecration was tested by a series of overwhelming afflictions that served to purge the dross that was in her nature. Her idols were destroyed one after the other, until all her hopes and joys and ambitions were centered in the Lord, and then He began to use her mightily in the building up of His kingdom. Her beauty had been the greatest cause of her pride and worldly conformity, and that was the first of her idols to be smitten. On October 4, 1670, when she was little more than twenty-two years of age, the blow came upon her like lightning from heaven. She was stricken with smallpox in a most virulent form, and to a very great extent her beauty was destroyed.

"But the external devastation was counterbalanced by internal peace," said Jeanne.

My soul was kept in a state of contentment, greater than can be expressed. Reminded continually of one of the causes of my religious trials and falls, I indulged the hope of regaining my inward liberty by the loss of the outward beauty that had been my grief. This view of my condition caused my soul to be so satisfied and so united to God, that it would not have exchanged its condition for that of the happiest king in the world.

Everyone thought that she would be inconsolable. But she said,

As I lay in my bed, suffering the total deprivation of what had been a snare to my pride, I experienced unspeakable joy. I praised God with profound silence....When I was again well enough to be able to sit up in my bed, I asked for a mirror; out of curiosity I viewed myself in it. I was no longer what I once was. It was then I saw that my heavenly Father had not been unfaithful in His work, but He had ordered the sacrifice in all reality.

The next of her most loved idols to be removed was her youngest son, to whom she was most fondly attached. "This blow," said Jeanne,

struck me to the heart. I was overwhelmed, but God gave me strength in my weakness. I loved my young boy tenderly; but though I was greatly afflicted at his death, I saw the hand of the Lord so clearly that I shed no tears. I offered him up to God, and I said in the language of Job, *"The LORD gave, and the LORD has taken away; blessed be the name of the LORD"* (Job 1:21).

In 1672, Madame Guyon's father died, and her beautiful little three-year-old daughter died as well.

The death of her friend and counselor, Genevieve Grainger, followed soon after, so that she no longer had anyone to lean upon in her spiritual trials and difficulties. In 1676 her husband, who had become reconciled to her, was taken away in death. Like Job, she lost everything that was dearest in this world, but she believed that the Lord allowed all these things for the humbling of her proud heart and will. She saw the hand of God so clearly in them that she exclaimed,

> Oh, adorable conduct of my God! There must be no guide, no prop for the person whom You are leading into the regions of darkness and death. There must be no conductor, no support, to the man whom You are determined to destroy to all the carnality and selfishness of the natural life.

As great as these trials were, Madame Guyon had yet to pass through one of her greatest and most prolonged trials. In 1674 she entered upon what she afterward called her "state of privation, or desolation," which lasted for seven years. During that entire period, she was without religious joy, peace, or emotions of any kind, and she had to walk by faith alone. She continued her devotions and her works of charity, but without the pleasure and satisfaction she had previously felt. She seemed to be left without God, and she made the mistake of imagining that God had really forsaken her. She had yet to learn how to walk by faith instead of by feelings.

True joy and peace come from living by faith, without regard to feelings. We are filled *"with all joy and peace in believing"* (Rom. 15:13). But when we look at our feelings and take our eyes off the Lord, then all true joy and peace leave us. Madame Guyon seems to have made this great mistake, and for seven years she kept looking for feelings and emotions before she learned to live by simple faith in God. Then she found that the life of faith is much higher, holier, and happier than the life governed by feelings and emotions. She had been thinking more about her emotions than about the Lord, more about the gift than the Giver, but at last her faith rose triumphantly above circumstances and feelings.

Almost seven years after she lost her joy and emotion, she began to correspond with Father La Combe, an eminent Superior of the Barnabite order, to whom she had shown the light of salvation some years previously. Now he was the instrument of leading her out into the clear light and sunshine of Christian experience. He showed her that God had not forsaken her, as she was so often tempted to believe, but that He was crucifying the self life in her. The light began to dawn upon her, and gradually the darkness was driven away.

Jeanne then appointed July 22, 1680, as a day on which Father La Combe should pray especially for her if her letter should reach him in time. Although he was a long way off, her letter providentially reached him in time, and both he and Madame Guyon spent the day in fasting and prayer. It was a day she would remember for a long time. God heard and answered their prayers. The clouds of darkness lifted from her soul, and floods of glory took their place. The Holy Spirit opened her eyes to see that her afflictions were God's mercies in disguise. They were like the dark tunnels that are shortcuts through mountains of difficulty into the valleys of blessing beyond. The vessel had been purified and prepared for His abode, and the Spirit of God, the heavenly Comforter, now took up His residence in her heart.

Madame Guyon's whole soul was now flooded with His glory, and everything seemed full of joy. She described her experience as follows:

> On July 22, 1680, that happy day, my soul
> was delivered from all its pains. From the time of

the first letter from Father La Combe, I began to recover a new life. I was formerly like a dead person who is in the beginning of his restoration and is raised up to a life of hope rather than of actual possession; but on this day I was restored, as it were, to perfect life, and set wholly at liberty. I was no longer depressed, no longer weighed down under the burden of sorrow. I thought that I had lost God, and lost Him forever; but I found Him again. And He returned to me with unspeakable magnificence and purity.

In a wonderful manner, difficult to explain, all that had been taken from me was not only restored, but it was also restored with increase and new advantages. In You, my God, I found it all, and more than all! The peace I now possessed was all holy, heavenly, inexpressible. What I had possessed some years before, in the period of my spiritual enjoyment, was consolation, peace—the gift of God rather than the Giver Himself. But now, I was brought into such harmony with the will of God that I might now be said to possess not merely consolation, but the God of consolation; not merely peace, but the God of peace. This true peace of mind was worth all that I had undergone, although it was only in its dawning.

When describing the experience she now enjoyed, Jeanne wrote,

I had a deep peace that seemed to pervade my whole soul and resulted from the fact that all my desires were fulfilled in God. I feared nothing; that is, my strong faith placed God at the head of all perplexities and events. I desired nothing besides what I now had, because I had full belief that, in my present state of mind, the results of each moment constituted the fulfillment of the divine purposes. As a sanctified heart is always in harmony with the divine providences, I had no will but the divine will, of which such providences are the true and appropriate expression.

In another place she wrote,

> One characteristic of this higher degree of experience was a sense of inward purity. My mind had such a oneness with God, such a unity with the divine nature, that nothing seemed to have power to soil it and to diminish its purity. It experienced the truth of that declaration of Scripture, *"To the pure all things are pure"* (Titus 1:15)....From this time, I found myself in the enjoyment of liberty. My mind experienced a remarkable ability to do and suffer everything that presented itself in the order of God's providence. God's order became its law.

Madame Guyon's life was now characterized by great simplicity and power. After she had found the way of salvation through faith, she was the means of leading many in France into the experience of conversion, or regeneration. And now, since she had received a deeper, richer, fuller experience, she began to lead many others into the experience of sanctification through faith, or into an experience of "victory over the self life," or "death to the self life," as she was fond of calling it. Her soul was all ablaze with the anointing and power of the Holy Spirit, and everywhere she went she was besieged by multitudes of hungering, thirsting souls who flocked to her for the spiritual meat that they failed to get from their regular pastors.

Revivals of religion began in almost every place she visited, and all over France earnest Christians began to seek the deeper experience that she taught. Father La Combe began to spread the doctrine with great anointing and power. Then the great Archbishop Fénelon was led into a deeper experience through the prayers of Madame Guyon, and he, too, began to spread the teaching all over France. So many people were led to renounce their worldliness and sinfulness, and to consecrate their lives wholly to God, that many who had claimed to have faith felt condemned.

Then some began to persecute Madame Guyon, Father La Combe, Fénelon, and all who held the doctrine of pure love, or entire death to the self life. Finally, the corrupt and dissolute King Louis XIV imprisoned Madame Guyon in the convent of Saint Marie. But Jeanne had learned how to suffer, and she bore her persecutions patiently and grew stronger and stronger spiritually. Her time in prison was spent in prayer, praise, and writing, although she was sick part of the time because of the poor air and other inconveniences in her little cell. After eight months in prison, her friends secured her release.

Her enemies tried to poison her while she was in prison, and she suffered for seven years from the effects of the poison. Her writings were now sold and read all over France and in many other parts of Europe, and in this way multitudes were brought to Christ and into a deeper spiritual experience through her teachings. In 1695 Jeanne was again imprisoned by order of the king, and this time was placed in the Castle of Vincennes. The following year she was transferred to a prison at Vaugiard. In 1698 she was placed in a dungeon in the Bastille, the historic and dreaded prison of Paris. For four years she was in this dungeon, but her faith in God was so great that her prison seemed like a palace to her. In 1702 she was banished to Blois, where she spent the remainder of her life in her Master's service. She died in perfect peace, and without a cloud on the fullness of her hopes and joy, in the year 1717, at sixty-nine years of age.

Madame Guyon left behind her about sixty volumes of her writings. Many of her sweetest poems and some of her most helpful books were written during her imprisonment. Some of her poems were translated into English by the poet William Cowper. Some of her hymns are very popular, and her writings have been a mighty influence for good in this world of sin and sorrow. Perhaps her own Christian experience is best described in the following words from her own pen:

> To me remains nor place nor time;
> My country is in every clime;
> I can be calm and free from care
> On any shore since God is there.

Chapter 6

Fénelon

⌒⌒⌒

*F*or piety, talent, and saintliness of character, few names have ranked so high as that of Fénelon, the celebrated archbishop of Cambray, France. Although the Pope, the king of France, and the greatest literary genius of the period united and conspired to ruin Fénelon, his sweet Christian spirit and commanding genius triumphed over all and made him one of the most loved of men. Not only in France, but also throughout the world, his name is today a synonym for piety.

Francois de Salignac de La Mothe Fénelon was of noble birth. He was a younger son of Count Pons de Salignac, a Gascon nobleman, and was born in the Castle of Fénelon, in Perigord, France, in 1651. He was carefully trained at home until twelve years of age, when he was sent to the University of Cahors, and afterward to the College of Plessis, in Paris. His mind was turned very early to the subject of religion, and at the age of fifteen he preached his first sermon. His theological studies were continued at the Seminary of Saint Sulpice, the principal of which was the celebrated Abbé Tronson, a man known for his piety, talents, and learning.

Francois became a favorite pupil of Tronson, who gave him the most careful intellectual and spiritual training. From Tronson, he undoubtedly acquired many of the views concerning inward Christian experience and real consecration to God that afterward made him such a champion and advocate of the higher Christian life. In 1675, at the age of twenty-four, he was ordained as a priest, and for three years he ministered in the parish of Saint Sulpice.

Before his ordination, he was strongly inclined to go as a missionary either to Canada or to the Levant (countries bordering the eastern Mediterranean), but his uncle kept him from doing so, although he did visit Canada for a brief time.

Early in life, Fénelon's remarkable intellect and talents began to display themselves in devotional, philosophical, and educational writings. Some of his books on educational subjects have been greatly prized. The king of France, Louis XIV, was so attracted by the qualifications of Fénelon that in 1689 he entrusted him with the education of the young duke of Burgundy, grandson of the king and heir apparent to the throne of France. The duke was very headstrong, self-willed, and passionate; but through the instruction and influence of Fénelon he gained the mastery of himself and would undoubtedly have been a great and good king had he ever mounted the throne. After serving five years as tutor of the duke, Fénelon was made archbishop of Cambray. That was in 1694.

At a time when he was honored by the king of France and was rapidly rising to fame, Fénelon became acquainted with Madame Guyon, and through her prayers and conversation he was led into a deeper, richer, fuller Christian experience. This experience made him willing to sacrifice anything in the service of Christ. He had often heard of the piety and talents of Madame Guyon, who was suffering great persecution from members of the Roman Catholic Church on account of her teachings. While passing through the old home of Madame Guyon, on his return from a mission to the Protestants of Poitou, he made many inquiries concerning her and heard so much about her piety that he decided to visit her, although he knew that it might cost him the King's favor and also his reputation and position to do so.

I have no doubt that the Lord put it into his heart to visit her under such trying circumstances. He met her first at the village of Beine, at the home of the duchess of Charost. They conversed for some time on the subject of inward experience—the subject that interested them most. The experiences of Madame Guyon made a deep impression upon the mind of Fénelon. On the next day, he visited her again at the home of the Duchess of Bethune, in Paris. They spent some time in prayer together. Fénelon was not yet filled with the Spirit, although his eyes were opened to see more clearly what the Lord had in store for him.

During the next eight days, a great burden of prayer for Fénelon rested upon the heart of Madame Guyon; then the agony of soul passed away, and she found inward rest. Near the end of this period of travail of soul, she wrote Fénelon a letter, dated November 1688, telling of her burden of prayer for him and urging him to make a complete surrender of his will to God. In this letter she wrote,

> For the past seven days I have been in a state of continual prayer for you. I call it prayer, although the state of mind has been somewhat odd. I have desired nothing in particular. But my soul has continually presented its purpose before God, that God's will might be accomplished and God's glory might be manifested in it. It has been like a lamp that burns without ceasing.

Later, in the same letter, she said,

> It seems to me that the merciful plans that God has for you are not yet accomplished. Your

soul is not yet brought into full harmony with God, and therefore I suffer. My suffering is great. My prayer is not yet heard. The prayer that I offer for you is not my own handiwork. It is the voice of the Holy Spirit in my soul, an inward voice that man cannot prevent or control. The Holy Spirit always prays effectively. When the inward voice ceases, it is a sign that the grace that has been prayed for has been sent down. I have been in this state of mind before for other souls, but never with such struggle of spirit, and never for such a long time. God's plans will be accomplished within you. I speak with confidence, but I think it cannot be otherwise.

The next day she wrote him again:

The application of my soul to God on your account has been so deep that I have slept very little during the past night. At this moment, I can tell you how I feel only by saying that my spirit, out of concern for your entire renovation, burns and consumes itself within me. I have an inward conviction that the obstacle that has separated you from God before now, is diminishing and passing away.

Fénelon was humble in spirit, and he hungered for a deeper spiritual experience. Although he was an intellectual giant, he was willing to be taught by a little child. His first great struggle was to be absolutely willing to utterly abandon himself to the will of God, for as Madame Guyon said, "A will surrendered is not always a will abandoned." Many who have surrendered their wills to God are still anxious to carry out their own plans and ambitions and are greatly annoyed when their plans are thwarted. Fénelon finally abandoned himself completely to the will of God, but he struggled long before realizing the experience for which his soul was hungering and thirsting.

Sometimes Fénelon met with Madame Guyon, and he frequently corresponded with her concerning the experience that he so much desired. Finally, Madame Guyon wrote him a letter concerning the steps necessary for the entire crucifixion of the life of self. Fénelon seemed to have clearly grasped them with his intellect, for he summarized them in a subsequent letter to Madame Guyon. In this letter he wrote,

I think, Madame, that I understand, in general, the statements in the letter that you had the kindness to send me, in which you describe the various experiences that characterize a person's return to God by means of simple or pure faith. I will endeavor, however, to recapitulate some of your views as I see them, so that I may learn whether I correctly understand them.

The first step that is taken by the person who has formally and permanently given himself to God, would be to bring what may be called his external powers—that is, his natural appetites and propensities—under subjection. The religious state of the soul at such times is characterized by a simplicity that shows its sincerity and is sustained by faith. The individual does not act alone, but he follows and cooperates with the grace that is given to him. He gains the victory through faith.

The second step is to cease to rest on the pleasures of inward sensibility. The struggle here is, in general, more severe and prolonged. It is hard to die to those inward tastes and pleasures that make us feel so happy, and that God usually permits us to enjoy and to rest upon in our first experience. When we lose our inward happiness, we are very apt to think that we lose God, not considering that one's moral life does not consist in pleasure, but in union with God's will, whatever that may be. The victory here is also by faith, though its operation is a little different.

Another step is that of entire crucifixion to any reliance upon our human virtues, either outward or inward. The habits of the self life have become so strong that there is hardly anything in which we do not become complacent to some degree. Having gained the victory over his senses, and having gained the strength to live by faith, independently of inward pleasures, an individual begins to take on a degree of satisfaction. This satisfaction is secretly a selfish one, glorying in and resting in virtues, truth, temperance, faith, and benevolence, as though they were one's own. We are to be dead to them while they come from ourselves, and alive to them only as they are the gifts and the power of God. We are to have no perception or life in them, in the sense of taking secret satisfaction in them; and we are to have satisfaction only in the Giver of them.

A fourth step consists in dying to the repugnance that men naturally feel toward the process of inward crucifixion. The blows that God sends upon us are received without the opposition that once existed and oftentimes existed with great power. A person's perception of God's presence in everything is so clear, his faith is so strong, that those apparently adverse dealings, which were once so exceedingly trying, are now received, not merely with acquiescence, but also with cheerfulness. He kisses the hand that smites him.

When we have gotten this far, we may say with a good deal of truth that the natural man is dead. But then there is a fifth step in this process: the new life. This is not merely the beginning of a new life, but it is a new life in the higher sense of the term: it is the resurrection of the life of love. All the gifts that a person previously sought in his own strength, and perverted and made poisonous and destructive to himself, are now richly and fully returned to him by the great Giver of all things. It is not the plan of God to deprive His creatures of happiness, but only to pour the cup of bitterness into all that happiness, and to destroy all the joy and prosperity that a person has *outside of God*.

There is a moral law of happiness that is as unchangeable as moral principles. God strikes out the false happiness, or the happiness that is founded on false principles and is only the precursor of real permanent misery, so that He may establish the true and everlasting happiness. He does this by bringing people into perfect communion and union with Himself, and by enabling them to drink the living water from the Everlasting Fountain. An individual obtains this new life, and all the goodness and happiness involved in it, by ceasing from his own actions (that is, from all actions that are not in cooperation with God), and letting God live and act in him.

This life, in the sixth place, becomes a truly transformed life, a life in union with God, when a person's will becomes conformed to God in everything that it does and in all of its relationships. At this point, there is such a harmony between the human will and the divine will that they may be properly regarded as having become one. This, I suppose, was the state of Paul, when he said, *"I live; yet not I, but Christ liveth in me"* (Gal. 2:20 KJV). When a person allows his soul to become a temple of the Holy Spirit, as Paul did, God Himself dwells within him and is his light.

This transformed soul does not cease to advance in holiness. It is transformed without remaining where it is; it is new without being stationary. Its life is love, all love, but the capacity of that love continually increases.

Although Fénelon had such a clear intellectual understanding of the steps necessary to reach a life of complete consecration and abandonment to the will of God, it was some time before he obtained the experience for himself. But, finally, he laid hold of the truth with his heart as well as with his intellect, and his whole life and character were completely transformed. He became such a great example of Christian love and piety that his name carries with it a sweet savor of Christ wherever he is known. This is true even though many people have tried to justify the Pope's treatment of Fénelon by degrading Fénelon's character.

It was well for Fénelon that he *"put on the whole armor of God"* (Eph. 6:11), for he had a great battle to fight on behalf of the doctrine of entire death to the self life. He was to become the greatest champion of the doctrine in his time. Arrayed against him were the dissolute King Louis XIV, the greatest literary genius of the day, Bishop Bossuet, and many of the most corrupt priests and people of the Catholic Church. Madame Guyon's teachings concerning the interior life had already aroused their opposition when Fénelon took up the challenge on her behalf.

The doctrine of entire death to the self life, or of pure or impartial love, was spreading over the world so rapidly that worldly professors of religion became alarmed and resolved to crush it out. Father La Combe was thrown into prison and so cruelly tortured that his reason became affected. As already mentioned, Madame Guyon was also thrown into prison, by direct order of the king. Fénelon, who was now foremost in teaching the doctrine of pure or impartial love, was not thrown into prison, because his influence was so great that even the king feared to imprison him.

Bishop Bossuet wrote a book against the teachings of Madame Guyon and sent it to Fénelon for his approval. The influence and standing of Fénelon were so great that Bossuet knew that his approval of the book would mean much to the masses of the people, and he thought that Fénelon would be afraid to displease him and the king by withholding his approval. But the book was such a personal attack against Madame Guyon that Fénelon felt he could not give it his approval, and he wrote Bossuet to this effect.

Fénelon knew that he would have to defend himself for not endorsing Bossuet's book against Madame Guyon. He therefore wrote a great work in reply to Bossuet. It was entitled, *Maxims of the Saints Concerning the Interior Life*. In this work, he showed that the greatest and most spiritual believers throughout the ages had believed and taught the interior life of self-crucifixion and pure love. Many of the most eminent saints were quoted to this effect, including Francis de Sales, Francis of Assisi, John of the Cross, Father Alvarez, Thomas Aquinas, Saint Bernard, Saint Theresa, Dionysius the Areopagite, and Gregory Lopez. Many decisions of ancient church councils concerning the subject were also quoted.

There was nothing personal in Fénelon's book, but it stirred the anger and indignation of Bossuet to see how the people received it. He had been accustomed to swaying the multitudes by his writings, and it was a great trial to him to see that Fénelon's books were becoming more popular than his own. He did not have the sweet Christian spirit of Fénelon and could not tolerate opposition. He determined to crush Fénelon at any cost, and for this purpose wrote book after book against him. As great and masterly as these works were, the replies of Fénelon were still more masterly and decisive and were certainly written in a more Christian spirit. Public opinion was then more favorable toward Fénelon.

Concerning Fénelon's victory over Bossuet, Charles Butler, one of Fénelon's biographers, said, "Never did virtue and genius obtain a more complete triumph. Fénelon's reply, by a kind of enchantment, restored to him every heart." Bossuet, finding that he was no match for Fénelon in argument, decided to take a more direct method. He appealed to the Pope to condemn Fénelon's writings as heretical. The Pope, Innocent XII, had been a great admirer of the genius and writings of Fénelon and had expressed himself favorably toward him. It was a matter of great grief to him that the controversy had been brought to Rome. He did not want to condemn the writings of Fénelon, nor did he wish to offend the king of France or Bishop Bossuet. He delayed his decision for many months, and it was only after the most urgent appeals and almost commands from the king that he finally pronounced a mild condemnation on some of the expressions used by Fénelon.

A commission of cardinals was appointed by the Pope to examine the writings of Fénelon. They were men of great learning, and they maintained that the doctrines taught by Fénelon were held by the great and pious men of the church in all ages. They also claimed that these doctrines were supported both by the Scriptures and by reason. But, for two years, the board of cardinals continued to discuss the question without coming to any decision.

King Louis XIV then became so impatient for the condemnation of Fénelon that he decided to take a step that would intimidate the Pope and cardinals and hurry their decision. He banished Fénelon to his own diocese of Cambray and also began a series of persecutions against Fénelon's friends. Urged on by Bossuet, the king wrote again and again to the Pope, asking him and almost commanding him to condemn the teachings of Fénelon. Finally, in 1699, the Pope issued his mild condemnation of them. But he did not condemn them in the sense in which they were intended by Fénelon.

From the time of his banishment to his own diocese until his death, Fénelon confined his work to the diocese of Cambray, where he was greatly beloved by the people, most of whom were Flemish peasants.

Many stories can be told about his love for these simple country folk. One day, during one of his rural excursions, he met a poor peasant grieving over the loss of a cow. He gave the poor man enough money to buy another cow but noticed that he was still sad. This was because he was so fond of his cow that he thought there was no other cow like her. Fénelon continued his walk and found the cow the peasant had lost. Although the sun had set and it was quite dark, he drove her back to the peasant's cottage.

Although his revenues as archbishop of Cambray were considerable, Fénelon spent everything he had in making others happy. During his absence one time, before his banishment to his own diocese, word was brought to Fénelon that his palace at Cambray had burned to the ground and that his fine library was destroyed. His friend, the Abbé de Langeron, seeing him conversing with some friends, thought he had not heard the sad news and started to break it to him gently. Fénelon, noticing the kindness of the good Abbé and figuring the cause of it, informed him that he was already acquainted with the news of what had happened. His faith in God and resignation to His will and providence were too great for such a thing to deeply affect him.

For six days before his death, Fénelon listened constantly to the reading of the Scriptures, and the greater part of his last two nights on earth were spent in listening to the reading of his favorite texts. He died January 7, 1715, and was buried in the cathedral at Cambray.

In personal appearance, Fénelon was very imposing. His biographer wrote of him, "He was a tall, thin man, well made, pale, with a large nose, and eyes from which life and talent streamed like a torrent." Fénelon's political views were far in advance of his times, and undoubtedly this was one of the main causes of the king's opposition to him. His devotional writings,

especially his *Letters to Men* and *Letters to Women,* rank among the world's best Christian literature. They will certainly continue to exert a mighty influence in the building up and deepening of Christian character and experience until the end of this dispensation.

Chapter 7

George Fox

❧

*P*erhaps no other small denomination of Christians has so influenced the world for good as
have the Quakers, also known as the Friends.
When George Fox, the founder of the Friends' Societies, began his preaching, the churches everywhere
were dead and formal. And when the churches drift
into formalism, the world drifts into unbelief. A formal
church has always resulted in an unbelieving world.
The Quaker movement seems to have been raised up
by God just in the nick of time to save the church from
formalism and the world from unbelief.

George Fox, like the ancient prophets, was sent by
God to call the church from formalism to a real spiritual worship. Like many other great reformers, he was
an extremist in some areas, but sometimes it is necessary for reformers to be extremists in order to thoroughly arouse the people. The Friends should not have
discarded all the outward scriptural laws that were
practiced by the early Christian church and by the
churches throughout the centuries of the Christian
era, but perhaps the Lord allowed the Friends to dis-
card all outward ordinances in order to more clearly
direct the minds of the people toward the spiritual
worship that God requires, and not mere forms and
ceremonies.

On many issues, the Friends were far ahead of the times. They raised their voices clearly against slavery nearly two hundred years before others were brought to see the injustice, cruelty, and sin of it. Another matter in which the Friends were far ahead of others was in their opposition to war. They have probably been more instrumental than any other group of people in bringing about the present opposition to warfare. The peace and arbitration movements of today owe their origins to the Quakers more than to any other group of people.

The Friends have also been foremost in freeing women from the bondage and subjection in which they have been kept throughout the ages, especially in Oriental lands. Believing that Paul's instructions concerning the subordination of women were only a temporary concession to the prejudice of the age in which he lived, the Friends have encouraged the teaching, preaching, and ministry of women more than any other denomination of Christians, with perhaps the exception of the Salvation Army. From the beginning of the movement, the Friends have not only opposed war and slavery of every kind, but they have also done much to secure the abolition of capital punishment for minor offenses, imprisonment for debt, and religious persecution of every kind.

Some people have said that the reason why the Quakers have been leaders in so many great reformations, and the reason why they have been so prosperous in business affairs, is that their form of worship appeals to and attracts only people of great intelligence and does not appeal to the masses. While there is some truth in this assertion, some believe that it is also true that the great reason why the Friends were leaders in spiritual thought and business enterprises was that God enlightened and blessed them because of their consecration to His service.

The remarkable thing about the Quaker movement, so far ahead of its time on so many weighty issues, was that it was founded by a poor and uneducated shoe-maker, whose name was George Fox. But many of the greatest leaders, like John Bunyan, D. L. Moody, and Charles Spurgeon, have been raised up from among the common people. *"God has chosen the weak things of the world to put to shame the things which are mighty"* (1 Cor. 1:27).

George Fox began his preaching without a follower, without belonging to anything, without any special training, without a place to preach in, and without social prestige of any kind. He raised his voice uncompromisingly against all the popular evils of the age, against the formalism of both the established and free churches, and against the religious persecutions for which the king and magistrates were responsible. He was persecuted, beaten, stoned, arrested, and imprisoned perhaps more frequently than any other person who ever lived. There are few pages in his large journals that do not contain some reference to his being mobbed, stoned, arrested, or brought before the magistrates. In a similar manner, his followers were persecuted and imprisoned because they opposed so many popular evils and refused to conform to certain ceremonies and practices.

It is probable that George Fox and the early Quakers suffered more for conscience' sake and the cause of religious freedom, and did more to bring about religious liberty, than did any other group of people since the days of the Reformation. Over and over again, they were thrown into prison for not doing things against their consciences, especially for not conforming to the state church, for refusing to enter the army and navy, and because they would not take judicial oaths. It is estimated that at one time, in the year 1662, no less than 4,500 Quakers were in prison in England and Wales for causes of this kind.

Even so, despite all that they suffered for the cause of religious freedom, George Fox and the early

Quakers increased in favor with God and man. Prejudice against them gradually died away. People found that they could trust them, and Friends in business were better patronized than any other businesspeople. More and more, people recognize the right to religious liberty and freedom of conscience for which the Friends suffered so much. All over the world, there is talk of abolishing war and settling differences in a judicial and reasonable way rather than by murder and brute force. Thus, mighty movements for the advancement of peace on earth were brought about to a great extent by the humble ministry of a poor English cobbler.

George Fox was born in 1624, in Leicestershire, England. His father, he said,

> was a weaver, an honest man; and there was a seed of God in him. The neighbors called him Righteous Christer. My mother was an upright woman; her name was Lago, and she was of the stock of the martyrs.

Like Girolamo Savonarola, Fox was solemn and grave even as a child and was unlike other children around him. At eleven years of age, he yielded his heart to God and sought to live an honest, upright life from then onward. His parents, who were members of the Church of England, desired to train him in their way of worship but did not urge him to conform to the Established Church. As he grew up, some of his relatives wished him to become a priest, but others persuaded him to the contrary. He apprenticed himself to a shoemaker who also dealt in wool and had many sheep. In this position, a great deal of money went through his hands, but he said that the Lord's power was with him so that he "never wronged a man or woman in all that time."

At the age of nineteen, Fox was deeply grieved and shocked at the levity of some professing Christians, one of them being his own cousin, who asked him into a booth at a fair and then began to drink "to their health." Fox was so deeply grieved over this that he could not sleep all night, and he paced back and forth in his room, praying to the Lord. Even as a young man, he was very careful about his conduct and conversation. "For the Lord showed me," he said,

> that the people of the world have mouths full of deceit—their words change—yet I was to keep to yea and nay in all things. (See Matthew 5:37.) I saw that my words should be few (Eccl. 5:2), seasoned with grace (Col. 4:6), and that I should not eat and drink to make myself wanton, but for health. (See Ephesians 5:18.)

In 1643 George Fox became so deeply grieved with the lightness and frivolity of the world that he broke off all companionship with both old and young. He began to travel to many strange places to be away from all friends, relatives, and acquaintances, and to be alone with God. He avoided conversing even with professing Christians, "for I was aware," said he, "that they did not possess what they professed." He was in great distress, and strong temptation and despair seized him.

> I was about twenty years of age when these things came upon me, and I continued in that condition for several years, in great trouble, and gladly would have parted with it. I went to many priests to look for comfort, but found no comfort from them.

The remedies suggested for his state of mind were that he should marry, that he should enlist in the army, that he should find a physician and be bled, and one priest even advised him to use tobacco and sing psalms. "But," said Fox, "tobacco was a thing I did not love, and I was not in a state to sing psalms." He was grieved that he had opened his mind to a man who would give such advice. He found his advisers all miserable comforters. One man who lived at Tamworth was said to be a man of experience, but Fox went to see him and found him to be "like an empty, hollow cask." Dr. Craddock, of Coventry, to whom Fox went for advice, flew into a rage because the despondent youth accidentally stepped on the edge of his flower bed.

Finding that he could get no help from men, Fox began to look to the Lord alone for help, and slowly the light began to dawn upon him. He was led to see "that being bred at Oxford and Cambridge did not qualify or prepare a man to be a minister of Christ." His eyes were also opened to see that "only those who had passed from death unto life were really believers in Christ." (See John 5:24.) With this realization, he stopped going to the Established Church with his relatives. In fact, he stopped going to any church. Instead, he went out into the fields with his Bible to study it for himself.

He also spent much time in fasting and prayer. The Lord showed him many "openings," as he called them. Fox said, "It was opened in me that God, who made the world, did not dwell *'in temples made with hands'* (Acts 17:24)." At first this seemed strange to him, because both priests and people used to refer to their temples or churches as places of reverence, holy ground, and the temples of God. "But," he said,

> the Lord showed me clearly that He did not dwell in those temples that men had set up, but in people's hearts. Both Stephen and the apostle Paul bore testimony that He did not dwell *"in temples made with hands,"* not even in those that He had once commanded to be built; but that His people were His temple, and He dwelt in them.

Fox also claimed that the Lord gave him many openings concerning the meaning of the book of Revelation. After this, when clergymen or others told him that Revelation was "a sealed book," he would tell them that Christ could open the seals.

The Lord continued to lead him on from step to step in his Christian experience, but his troubles were not completely removed, although he often felt some degree of peace and joy. He hungered and thirsted for a deeper experience, and the Lord showed him that it was possible for him to have complete spiritual victory. He was led to see that there are two laws controlling men—the law of the flesh and the law of the Spirit—and that through the indwelling Spirit of God the Christian can have liberty and victory over the flesh and its works. (See Galatians 5:16.)

Fox now began to win many souls for Christ wherever he went. In 1647 he began to declare to professing Christians the deep truths that God had been revealing to him. "But the professing Christians were in a rage," said Fox, "all pleading for the causes of sin and imperfection, and they could not endure to hear talk of perfection, and of a holy and sinless life."

Soon after he began to preach, Fox passed through a remarkable spiritual experience that made him a wonder to many. A certain man named Brown, while on his deathbed, prophesied many great things concerning Fox. "When this man was buried," said Fox,

> a great work of the Lord fell on me, to the admiration of many who thought I had been dead; and many came to see me for about fourteen days. My appearance and demeanor at the time were altered, as if my body had been newly formed. While I was in that condition, I had a sense and discernment given me by the Lord, through which I saw plainly that when people talked about God and Christ, many times the

Serpent spoke in them. But this was hard for others to swallow.

Even so, the work of the Lord occurred in some people, and my sorrows and troubles began to wear off. Tears of joy dropped from me, so that I could have wept night and day with tears of joy to the Lord, in humility and brokenness of spirit. I saw into what was without end, and things that cannot be uttered, and the greatness and infinitude of the love of God, which cannot be expressed by words.

A report went before me that I was a young man who had a discerning spirit. Many people came to me, from far and near—professors, priests, and people—and the Lord's power broke forth. I had great revelations and prophecies, and I spoke to them of the things of God, and they heard with attention and silence. When they went away, they spread the news of what I had said.

After passing through the experience described above, Fox was used mightily by God, and great conviction of sin fell upon the people to whom he preached. "The Lord's power began to shake them," said Fox, "and we began to have great meetings, and there was a mighty power and work of God among people, to the astonishment of both people and priests." Later, Fox went to Mansfield, where a great meeting of leaders and people was being held. There he was moved to pray, and the Lord's power was so great that the house seemed to be shaken.

Fox now went around the country, preaching wherever he could find an opening. He frequently entered the "steeplehouses," as he called the state churches. When the priest finished speaking, he would stand up and exhort the people. He often pointed out to them that their meetinghouses were not churches, but that the people who truly believed in Christ are the real church of God.

The Friends never call their places of worship churches. They call them meetinghouses. Although Fox, or any other person, had a legal right to speak in the state churches when the priest had finished, as long as the rules of decency and order were observed, his speeches often led to controversies with the priests and others, and this often led to his arrest and frequently to his imprisonment. But as soon as he was set free, he would again speak in the state churches or wherever he could find an open door. No amount of persecution or suffering seemed to dampen his zeal or cool his ardor. Many spiritually-minded individuals who were dissatisfied with the formalism of the times began to rally around him, and soon societies of Friends were formed all over the country.

Notwithstanding all he suffered, Fox continued to advance in his own Christian experience, although he sometimes underwent times of great temptation and trial. He seemed to have frequently had real visions and revelations from the Lord, similar to those of Savonarola. While in a sort of trance, he seemed to discern many deep spiritual truths. "The Lord led me into many great things," he said, "and wonderful depths were opened unto me."

Among other things that he claimed the Lord revealed to him were the medical properties of many herbs. Because so many cures were attributed to Quaker remedies, one can assume that Fox really understood the medicinal properties of some herbs. Like Savonarola, Fox seemed to have had a number of future events revealed to him. Thus, in 1664, he saw in a vision the Lord's power checking the westward advance of the Turks. On several occasions, while on the tops of mountains or hills, he had visions of places in the surrounding country where Friends' Societies would be raised up, or where believers would be gathered to him. He had a presentiment of the death of Oliver Cromwell just before the great commoner was called from this life.

A remarkable power seemed to accompany the preaching of Fox wherever he went, whether in Britain or America, Germany, Holland, or the West Indies. He usually went about the country on foot, dressed in his famous leather clothes, said to have been made by himself, and often sleeping outdoors or in some haystack. He was ridiculed and persecuted, beaten and stoned, arrested and imprisoned, and yet the Lord seemed to greatly bless and acknowledge his labors. Describing his meetings at Ticknell, England, he said,

> The priest scoffed at us and called us Quakers. But the Lord's power was so over them, and the Word of Life was declared in such authority and dread to them, that the priest began trembling himself; and one of the people said, "Look how the priest trembles and shakes; he is turned Quaker also."

In describing his meetings, Fox often used words similar to the following:

> And a precious meeting there was, in which the Lord's power was over all; and the people were directed to the Spirit of God, by whom they might come to know God and Christ and understand the Scriptures rightly,

and so on. He also frequently used words such as,

> I had much work in those days, both with priests and people, concerning their old meetinghouses, which they called their churches. The priests had persuaded the people that it was the house of God, whereas the apostle said, *"Whose house we are"* (Heb. 3:6). So the people are God's house, in whom He dwells. And the apostle also said, "Christ purchased the church with His own blood" (see Acts 20:28), and Christ calls His

church His spouse, His bride, and the Lamb's wife. Thus, these titles, church and spouse, were not given to an old house, but to His people, the true believers.

Describing an occasion when he spoke in Carlisle, Fox said, "The power of the Lord was awe-inspiring among them in the steeplehouse, so that the people trembled and shook; and some of them feared that it would fall down on their heads." Later, he said, "Now I went into the country, and had mighty great meetings. The everlasting Gospel and Word of Life flourished, and thousands were turned to the Lord Jesus Christ, and to His teaching." At Sutton he spoke to a multitude of people. "People were greatly convicted," said he, "and many hundreds were turned from darkness to the light." Describing one of his meetings in another place, he said, "I stood a while before I began to speak; after some time I felt the power of the Lord go over the whole assembly, and His everlasting truth and life were shown over all." Thus he went from place to place in Britain and other lands, preaching the Gospel with wonderful anointing and power.

In spiritual matters, Fox seemed to have had a discernment far in advance of any other person of his day. Thus, while others were contending that the "body of sin" was the natural body, or the body of flesh, Fox taught that the natural body was not the "body of sin," or we would not have been commanded to put it off. (See Ephesians 4:22–23.) While others called the days of the week and the months of the year by the names derived from heathen gods (Sunday, Monday; and January, February, and so on), the Quakers rejected these pagan names and called the days, "First Day, Second Day," and the months, "First Month, Second Month," and so on. They waited for the Holy Spirit to move them to speak, sing, or pray; and if no one felt led by the Spirit to take part in the meeting, the meetings were spent in silence and prayer and would break up without a word being spoken.

The early Friends did not use the titles *Mister, Missus,* or *Miss,* but called each other by their given names, as though they were all members of one great family, as God's children truly are. Nor did they apply the title of *Reverend* to their ministers or leaders, for they had no salaried ministers. In their dress, manners, language, and every other way, they displayed a commendable simplicity and avoided extravagance. They seem to have had great power in prayer. Fox told of cases in which sick people were healed and devils cast out in answer to prayer.

The great secret of Fox's own power was his faith in God. William Penn, the famous Quaker, wrote concerning him,

> But above all, he excelled in prayer. The inwardness and weight of his spirit, the reverence and solemnity of his dress and behavior, and the fewness and fullness of his words, have often struck even strangers with admiration, and they used to reach others with consolation. The most wonderful, living, reverent frame I ever felt or beheld, I must say, was his in prayer.

In his journal, Fox wrote,

> The Lord had said unto me, "If only one man or woman were raised up by His power, to stand and live in the same spirit that the apostles and prophets were in, who gave forth the Scriptures, that man or woman would shake the whole country in their profession for miles around."

This proved to be more than true in his case. He started with scarcely any advantages, and soon he influenced the whole world for God. Although he began his preaching with a limited education, without any special training, and without special advantages of any kind, he soon had England, Ireland, Scotland, and Wales ablaze for God, and his influence was powerfully exerted in America and other lands. His followers are now numbered by the hundreds of thousands. Truly, in him we have an example of how God can use the weak things of the world to put to shame the mighty (1 Cor. 1:27).

In personal appearance, Fox was a large man with remarkably piercing eyes. His eyes pierced sinners so that they could hardly endure to have him look at them, and his words were like a flash of lightning. He seemed to be able to read the characters of men just by looking at them. The character of one appeared like that of a fox; another was like that of a wolf, a serpent, a lion, or a wasp, and so on. His judgment was so clear and his logic so convincing that he seemed to have always been able to baffle the judges and magistrates before whom he was so frequently arraigned, although that fact did not save him from frequently going to prison for conscience' sake. Even the Lord Chief Justice of England and the great Protector, Oliver Cromwell, seem to have been impressed by his arguments against the persecution of the Friends, although it was a long time before they secured exemption from the army and from taking judicial oaths.

The one great purpose of all George Fox's preaching and ministry was to turn the eyes of the people away from outward forms and ceremonies and to direct them to the need of real holiness of heart and life. And such was also the real objective of the ministry of Jesus. The entire Sermon on the Mount, all the parables of Jesus, and all the words He uttered were for the purpose of showing people that mere outward forms and ceremonies, or outward works of any kind, would not save them. He taught them that they must be pure in heart, meek in spirit, that they must love God and their neighbor, or they would not enter the kingdom of heaven. Neither Christ nor the apostles esteemed good works lightly when they taught that the outward deeds of the law would not save, but their purpose was to show the people the real need of inward holiness.

So the great mission of George Fox and the Quakers was not to depreciate outward forms and ceremonies so much as to emphasize the need of inward purity and righteousness. In doing this, they may have set too light a value on the outward ordinances prescribed in the Scriptures, but they accomplished their objective so well that the world owes to them a very great debt of gratitude. In the writings of such eminent Friends as George Fox, William Penn, Robert Barclay, and others, may be found some of the most helpful spiritual teachings outside the Word of God.

Chapter 8

John Bunyan

⎯⎯⎯⎯⎯⎯

I t is not to be wondered at that John Bunyan, the author of *The Pilgrim's Progress,* had a very deep inward experience of the grace of God. Without such an experience, an illiterate tinker would hardly have been able to write the book that has reached almost as many people as the Bible has. *The Pilgrim's Progress* is certainly one of the world's most popular books. It has been translated into almost every major language, has been adapted for children's books, and has been adapted for Catholics as well as Protestants.

"Illustrious dreamer" that he was, John Bunyan did not dream up all of his immortal allegory. *The Pilgrim's Progress* is almost as much his own experience as is *Grace Abounding.* The struggles and triumphs of Christian in *The Pilgrim's Progress* represent the real spiritual conflicts and conquests of Bunyan himself, on his way to heaven, and so I want to trace the history of his spiritual experiences as recorded in the novel.

In *The Pilgrim's Progress,* Christian is first seized with conviction. He then leaves the City of Destruction, struggles through the Slough of Despond, endeavors to find help at Mr. Legality's, and then enters the Wicket Gate, after which his burden rolls away at the foot of the cross. After entering the Wicket Gate, he is shown by Interpreter some of the things that he will encounter on his way to the Celestial City. "Then he took him by the hand," says the narrative,

> and led him into a very large parlor that was full of dust, because never swept; the which after he had reviewed it a little while, the Interpreter called for a man to sweep. Now, when he began to sweep, the dust began so abundantly to fly about, that Christian had almost therewith been choked. Then said the Interpreter to a damsel that stood by, "Bring hither water, and sprinkle the room"; the which when she had done, it was swept and cleansed with pleasure.
>
> Then said Christian, "What means this?"
>
> The Interpreter answered, "This parlor is the heart of a man that was never sanctified by the sweet grace of the Gospel. The dust is his original sin, and inward corruptions, that have defiled the whole man. He that began to sweep at first, is the law; but she that brought water, and did sprinkle it, is the Gospel. Now whereas thou sawest, that so soon as the first began to sweep, the dust did so fly about that the room by him could not be cleansed, but that thou wast almost choked therewith; this is to show thee, that the law, instead of cleansing the heart (by its working) from sin, doth revive (Rom. 7:9), put strength into (1 Cor. 15:56), and increase it in the soul (Rom. 5:20), even as it doth discover and forbid it; for it doth not give power to subdue.
>
> "Again, as thou sawest the damsel sprinkle the room with water, upon which it was cleansed with pleasure, this is to show thee, that when the Gospel comes in the sweet and precious influences thereof to the heart, then, I say, even as thou sawest the damsel [settle] the dust by sprinkling the floor with water, so is sin vanquished and subdued, and the soul made clean,

through the faith of it, and consequently fit for the King of glory to inhabit" (John 15:3; Eph. 5:26; Acts 15:9).

Again, Christian is shown by Interpreter that the fire of God's grace will "burn higher and hotter" in the human heart, no matter how much water Satan casts upon it, so long as the oil of grace (the Holy Spirit) is continually feeding the flame. This is shown by a fire that burns higher and hotter although a man (representing Satan) is constantly throwing water on it. The fire is next to a wall, and hidden by the wall is a man (representing the Holy Spirit) who is constantly feeding the fire with oil.

When Christian leaves the house of Interpreter, the latter says, "The Comforter be always with thee, good Christian, to guide thee in the way that leads to the city!"

During his pilgrimage, Christian meets with many enemies and difficulties, and with many friends and blessings. At last he reaches the palace Beautiful, where he is much instructed in the things of God by Piety, Prudence, and Charity. He sleeps all night in the Chamber of Peace, and next morning gets a glimpse of Immanuel's Land.

> When the morning was up, they had him to the top of the house, and bid him look south. So he did, and behold, at a great distance, he saw a most pleasant mountainous country, beautified with woods, vineyards, fruits of all sorts, flowers also, with springs and fountains, very delectable to behold (Isa. 33:16–17). Then he asked the name of the country. They said it was Immanuel's Land. "And it is as common," said they, "as this hill is, to and for all the pilgrims. And when thou comest there, from thence thou mayest see to the gate of the celestial city, as the shepherds that live there will make appear."

Christian is very anxious to reach the beautiful land, and after they clothe him with armor he sets out upon his journey.

Until he reaches the palace Beautiful, Christian has no armor or weapons, just as spiritual babes have not *"put on the whole armor of God"* (Eph. 6:11). But when he has enough courage to pass the great lions and enter the palace, Piety, Prudence, and Charity clothe him with armor from head to toe, just as they will lead other Christians to put on the full armor of God by being *"filled with the Spirit"* (Eph. 5:18).

The narrative says,

> The next day they took him, and had him into the armory, where they showed him all manner of furniture which the Lord had provided for pilgrims, as sword, shield, helmet, breast-plate, all-prayer, and shoes that would not wear out. And there was here enough of this to harness as many men for the service of their Lord as there be stars in the heaven for multitude.

Christian's departure is thus described:

> Now he bethought himself of setting forward, and they were willing he should. "But first," said they, "let us go again into the armory." So they did; and when he came there, they harnessed him from head to foot with what was proof, lest perhaps he should meet with assaults in the way.

It was well that they did so, for Christian had many conflicts awaiting him, and he would have barely reached the Celestial City had he not been clad in spiritual armor at the palace Beautiful. As it was, he was almost slain in his great battle with Apollyon.

After many trials and conflicts, Christian arrives at Vanity Fair, through which all pilgrims must pass

on their way to the Celestial City. Here the worldly
people do not understand Christian and his friend
Faithful.

> And as they wondered at their apparel, so
> they did likewise at their speech; for few could
> understand what they said. They naturally spoke
> the language of Canaan; but they that kept the
> fair were men of this world.

The merchants of Vanity Fair are greatly amused
as well as displeased because "these pilgrims set very
light by all their wares. They cared not so much as to
look upon them." This causes a mighty uproar among
the people of Vanity Fair, and the Great One of the
Fair has the pilgrims arrested. At their trial, Christian
and Faithful state that "they were pilgrims and
strangers in the world, and that they were going to
their own country, which was heavenly Jerusalem." The
men of Vanity Fair conclude that they are insane and
shut them up in an iron cage, but their peaceable and
pious behavior wins friends for them even in Vanity
Fair. These friends try to stop the baser men from per-
secuting the pilgrims and tell them that there are many
wicked men who ought to be punished instead of these
pilgrims. A quarrel ensues, and the two pilgrims are
blamed for the disturbance. A second trial takes place,
before Judge Hate-good. Envy testifies that Faithful

> doeth all he can to possess all men with certain
> of his disloyal notions, which he in the general
> calls principles of faith and holiness. And, in par-
> ticular, I heard him once myself affirm, that
> Christianity and the customs of our town of
> Vanity were diametrically opposite, and could
> not be reconciled.

Superstition also witnesses against him; and finally
Pickthank testifies, among other things, that Faithful

...hath railed on our noble prince Beelzebub, and hath spoken contemptibly of his honorable friends, whose names are the Lord Old Man, the Lord Carnal Delight, the Lord Luxurious, the Lord Desire of Vain Glory, my old Lord Lechery, Sir Having Greedy, with all the rest of our nobility.

Faithful is then condemned to death by the jury, whose names are Mr. Blindman, Mr. No-good, Mr. Malice, Mr. Love-lust, Mr. Live-loose, Mr. Heady, Mr. High-mind, Mr. Enmity, Mr. Liar, Mr. Cruelty, Mr. Hate-light, and Mr. Implacable.

Christian escapes, and continuing on his way is joined by Hopeful. They are led aside by Vain-confidence and leave the King's highway, or "the way of holiness," as Bunyan called it in his description of the encounter between Christian and Apollyon. Giant Despair seizes them and throws them into the dungeon of Doubting Castle, where they almost perish. But Christian finally opens the prison door with the key of Promise, and he and Hopeful find their way back to the King's highway.

They continue their journey and soon reach the Delectable Mountains, where they enjoy the richest blessings of Immanuel's Land. From these mountains, they obtain a glimpse of the Celestial City. They eat and drink freely of the best that "the gardens and orchards, the vineyards and fountains of water" afford. Greatly refreshed, they continue their journey. After traveling for some time on the highway, they are again led aside and snared in the net of Flatterer. A Shining One delivers them and leads them back to the narrow way.

Journeying on their way, they enter the country of Beulah, in which they continue to the end of their pilgrimage. Bunyan described the Beulah experience in the following words:

Now I saw in my dream, that by this time the pilgrims were got over the Enchanted Ground, and entering into the country of Beulah, whose air was very sweet and pleasant (Isa. 62:4); the way lying directly through it, they solaced themselves there for a season. Yea, here they heard continually the singing of birds, and saw every day the flowers appear in the earth, and heard the voice of the turtle in the land (Song 2:10–12). In this country the sun shineth night and day: wherefore this was beyond the Valley of the Shadow of Death, and also out of the reach of Giant Despair; neither could they from this place so much as see Doubting Castle. Here they were within sight of the city they were going to; also here they met some of the inhabitants thereof; for in this land the shining ones commonly walked, because it was upon the borders of heaven.

In this land also the contract between the Bride and the bridegroom was renewed; yea, here, *"as the bridegroom rejoices over the bride, so* [does their] *God rejoice over* [them]" (Isa. 62:5). Here they had no want of corn and wine; for in this place they met with abundance of what they had sought for in all their pilgrimage (vv. 8–9). Here they heard voices from out of the city, loud voices, saying, *"Say to the daughter of Zion, 'Surely your salvation is coming; behold, His reward is with Him'"* (v. 11). Here all the inhabitants of the country called them "the holy People, the redeemed of the Lord, sought out," etc.

Now, as they walked in this land, they had more rejoicing than in parts more remote from the kingdom to which they were bound; and drawing near to the city, they had yet a more perfect view thereof. It was builded of pearls and precious stones, also the streets thereof were paved with gold; so that, by reason of the natural

glory of the city, and the reflection of the sun-
beams upon it, Christian with desire fell sick;
Hopeful also had a fit or two of the same disease:
wherefore here they lay by it a while, crying out
because of their pangs, *"If you find my beloved...tell him I am lovesick"* (Song 5:8).

But being a little strengthened, and better
able to bear their sickness, they walked on their
way, and came yet nearer and nearer, where
were orchards, vineyards, and gardens, and their
gates opened into the highway. Now, as they
came up to these places, behold the gardener
stood in the way; to whom the pilgrims said,
"Whose goodly vineyards and gardens are
these?" He answered, "They are the King's, and
are planted here for His own delight, and also for
the solace of pilgrims." So the gardener had
them into the vineyards, and bid them refresh
themselves with the dainties (see Deuteronomy
23:24); he also showed them there the King's
walks and the arbors where He delighted to be:
and here they tarried and slept.

Now I beheld in my dream, that they talked
more in their sleep at this time, than ever they
did in all their journey; and, being in a muse
thereabout, the gardener said even to me,
"Wherefore musest thou at the matter? It is the
nature of the fruit of the grapes of these vineyards, to go down so sweetly, as to cause the lips
of them that are asleep to speak." (See Song of
Solomon 7:9.)

So I saw that when they awoke, they addressed themselves to go up to the city. But, as I
said, the reflection of the sun upon the city (for
the city was pure gold, Rev. 21:18) was so extremely glorious, that they could not as yet with
open face behold it, but through an instrument
made for that purpose (2 Cor. 3:18). So I saw,
that as they went on, there met them two men in
raiment that shone like gold, also their faces
shone as the light.

These angels accompany the pilgrims (because of their faith) until they reach the river of Death and cross it to the Celestial City.

Having traced the deeper spiritual experiences of Christian in *The Pilgrim's Progress,* I will briefly state in plain words how Bunyan's burden rolled away at the foot of the cross and how he reached a Beulah experience.

John Bunyan was born in the village of Elstow, England, in 1628, "of a low, inconsiderable generation," to use his own words. He was probably referring to the fact that he was born and bred to the profession of a tinker, or mender of pots and kettles, as his father was before him. This profession, in those days, was carried on principally by Gypsies, and for that reason some have supposed that Bunyan was of Gypsy descent. He received some schooling when a boy but claims to have forgotten most of it before his conversion. He served his apprenticeship and learned his trade in Bedford. His parents seemed to have given him religious counsel and advice, but he was a very wicked boy. He said,

> I had but few equals (especially considering my years, which were tender, being few), both for cursing, swearing, lying, and blaspheming the name of God. Indeed, I was so settled and rooted in these things that they became a second nature to me. But these things, as I have with soberness considered since, did so offend the Lord that even in my childhood He did scare and affright me with fearful dreams, and did terrify me with dreadful visions. For often after spending one day and another in sin, I have while asleep in my bed been greatly afflicted with appearances of devils and wicked spirits, who still, as I then thought, labored to draw me away with them; of which I could never be rid.

Thoughts about hell and the Judgment Day also greatly troubled him. "These things," he said,

> when I was but a child, but nine or ten years old, did so distress my soul, that then in the midst of my many sports and childish vanities, amid my vain companions, I was often much cast down and afflicted in my mind because of them, yet could I not let go of those sins.

Later, he said,

> A while after, these terrible dreams did leave me, and I soon forgot them, for my pleasures quickly cut off the remembrance of them, as if they had never been. Therefore, with more greediness, according to the strength of nature, I set loose the reins to my lust, and delighted in all transgression against the law of God, so that, until I came to the state of marriage, I was the very ringleader of all the youth who kept me company, in all manner of vice and ungodliness.

Describing this period of his life, he also said, "In these days, the thoughts of religion were grievous to me. I could neither endure it myself, nor that any other should." But he did not like to see professed Christians sin. "Yet this I well remember," said Bunyan,

> that though I could myself sin with the greatest delight and ease, and also take pleasure in the vileness of my companions; yet, even then, if I have at any time seen wicked things by those who professed godliness, it would make my spirit tremble.

Twice he barely escaped drowning, once he came very near to being bit by a poison adder, and a man who took his place in the army was killed while on sentinel duty; but God mercifully preserved Bunyan's life. "Here," said he,

> were judgments and mercy, but neither of them awakened my soul to righteousness; so I continued to sin, and grew more and more rebellious against God and careless of my own salvation.
>
> Soon after this, when I was about twenty years of age, I changed my condition into a married state; and my mercy was to have a wife whose father was considered godly. This woman and I came together as poor as poor might be— not having so much as a dish or a spoon between us both—yet this she had for her part: *The Plain Man's Pathway to Heaven,* and *The Practice of Piety,* which her father had left her when he died. I would sometimes read these books with her, in which I also found some things that were somewhat pleasing to me; but all the while I experienced no conviction. My wife also told me very often what a godly man her father was.
>
> As a result of these books and the thought of my wife's father, though they did not reach my heart to awaken it about my sinful state, some desires for religion were birthed within me. And because I knew no better, I fell in very eagerly with the religion of the times, which was to go to church twice a day, and to very devoutly say and sing as others did there, yet retaining my wicked life.

At this time Bunyan had great reverence for the clergy, their ceremonial robes, the Liturgy, and all that belonged to the worship of the Church of England. "But all this while," said he,

> I was not aware of the danger and evil of sin. I was kept from considering that sin would damn me, no matter what religion I followed, unless I was found in Christ.

Finally, his pastor preached a sermon against the popular sins and vices with their fearful consequences, which awakened Bunyan's conscience for the first time to the evil nature of sin. But on returning home, he soon forgot the sermon. "I shook the sermon out of my mind," said he, "and to my old custom of sports and gaming I returned with great delight."

The same Sunday, however, while he was playing a game of tipcat,* the conviction returned with such power that he stood still for a while before all the players, none of whom knew what was passing in his mind. After a few minutes spent in silent thought, he concluded that he had gone too far in sin to ever find salvation, and he determined to get what comfort he could out of sin. He said,

> So I went on in sin with great greediness of mind, still grudging that I could not be satisfied with it as I wanted to be. But one day, as I was standing at a neighbor's shop window, cursing and swearing and playing the madman after my usual manner, the woman who was sitting inside the house heard me. Though she was a very loose and ungodly wretch herself, she protested that I swore and cursed at that most fearful rate, that she was made to tremble to hear me. And she told me further that I was the ungodliest fellow for swearing that ever she heard in all her life; and that I, by doing so, was able to spoil all the youth in a whole town if they were to come near me.

This well-merited rebuke had a sobering influence on Bunyan. He gave up swearing, and a conversation with a friend led him to read the Bible. This led to

---

* Tipcat: a game in which a player using a bat lightly strikes a wooden peg and as it flies up strikes it again to drive it as far as possible while fielders try to recover it.

some outward reformation, and then he imagined that he "pleased God as well as any man in England." Even his dancing was given up, and for about a year he continued to live a better outward life, to the great surprise of his neighbors. But he had not yet found peace and rest and joy through faith in Christ.

"But one day the good providence of God did send me off to Bedford, to work my trade," said Bunyan, "and in one of the streets of that town, I came to where there were three poor women sitting at a door in the sun, talking about the things of God." These three women are described in *The Pilgrim's Progress* under the allegory of the three princesses at the palace Beautiful. Bunyan's conversations with them opened his eyes to see that he had been trusting in his own outward works for salvation instead of in the Lord Jesus Christ. He saw that these poor women were basking in the sun on the mountaintop of Christian experience, while he was "shivering and shrinking in the cold, afflicted with frost, snow, and dark clouds."

Bunyan now tried to look to Christ for salvation, but like many others was plunged into fearful despondency and despair by the thought that he might not be one of God's elect. He imagined that God had reprobated him to be lost, and for weeks and months he was in such great agony that he could hardly endure it. The three Christian women he had met introduced him to Mr. Gifford, the Baptist minister in the town. Mr. Gifford took a great interest in him, but probably never dreamed that Bunyan would be his successor. Mr. Gifford, no doubt, is the Evangelist of *The Pilgrim's Progress,* who points Christian to the Wicket Gate; but Bunyan was in the Slough of Despond for a whole year before he finally reached the Wicket Gate and before his burden rolled away at the foot of the cross.

During that time, although he was in awful despair, his conscience was so tender with regard to sin that he "dared not pick up a pin, or a stick, though it were not even as big as a straw," or do the least thing that he considered wrong. But the thought that he was reprobated to be lost made him wish that he had never been born.

He found peace and joy in Christ one evening as he sat by the fireside, musing on his miserable condition. The Lord brought Hebrews 2:14–15 vividly to his mind. "I thought," said he,

> that the glory of these words was then so weighty on me that I was, both once and twice, ready to faint away; yet not with grief and trouble, but with solid joy and peace.

Later on he said,

> But, oh, how my soul was led from truth to truth by God! Even from the birth and cradle of the Son of God to His ascension and second coming from heaven to judge the world.

His love for Christ now seemed to burn as "hot as fire."

After continuing for some time to enjoy peace and rest of soul, he had a great conflict, represented by the fight with Apollyon in *The Pilgrim's Progress*. Temptations to sell Christ for trifles came into his mind, and he imagined that he had actually yielded to them and that Christ had forsaken him. "Now for two years, nothing would abide with me but damnation and an expectation of damnation," he said. He felt that he had committed a worse sin than David, Judas, or Peter had, and that he had sinned against the Holy Spirit. So great was his despair, he found it hard to pray. "Then I was struck into a very great trembling," he said,

> insomuch that at times I could, for days on end, feel my very body, as well as my mind, shake and totter under the sense of the dreadful judgment

of God that should fall on those who have sinned
that most fearful and unpardonable sin. I felt
such a clogging and heat at my stomach, by reason of this terror, that I especially felt at times
as if my breastbone would split in two.

But with *"the sword of the Spirit, which is the
word of God"* (Eph. 6:17), Bunyan at last gave Satan
such a deadly thrust that he left him. Like Job, Paul,
Madame Guyon, and others, Bunyan went through
fiery trials. And then Scriptures such as, *"I have loved
you with an everlasting love"* (Jer. 31:3), *"The blood of
Jesus Christ His Son cleanses us from all sin"* (1 John
1:7), and, *"My grace is sufficient for you"* (2 Cor. 12:9),
brought sweet peace to his soul.

Bunyan's complete deliverance from his dreadful
doubts and despair came one day while he was passing
through a field. Suddenly the sentence fell upon his
soul: "Your righteousness is in heaven." By the eye of
faith, he seemed to see Jesus, his righteousness, at
God's right hand. He described what happened next:

> Now did my chains fall off my legs indeed,
> and I was loosed from my afflictions and irons;
> my temptations also fled away, so that, from that
> time, those dreadful Scriptures of God stopped
> troubling me! Now I went home rejoicing for the
> grace and love of God.

When he reached home, he tried to find the text,
"Your righteousness is in heaven," and was somewhat
discouraged to find that it was not in the Scriptures.
But his joy was restored and deepened when he found
the similar text, *"But of Him you are in Christ Jesus,
who became for us wisdom from God; and righteousness and sanctification and redemption"* (1 Cor. 1:30).

Bunyan still had many conflicts and trials, but after the above experience, he seemed to have been

passing through Beulah. Sometimes he was so overwhelmed with the sense of God's grace and power that
he could hardly bear up under it. He soon began to
preach in little meetings, and people were deeply convicted of sin and wept tears of penitence. The Lord
gave him "an awakening word," and so many were
brought to Christ under his preaching that he was astonished that the Lord should thus use him. He became very famous as a preacher, but his plain speaking
roused much opposition.

The story of his twelve years' imprisonment for
holding meetings separate from the Established
Church of England, and of the writing of his famous
books while in prison, does not belong to a narrative of
this kind. He had only the Bible and *Foxe's Book of
Martyrs* with him in prison when he wrote *The Pilgrim's Progress.* He was frequently allowed some freedom and sometimes used it in preaching the Gospel.

After his release, he traveled and preached in
many places, and he was so popular that he was nick-
named "Bishop Bunyan." King Charles was surprised
that the learned Dr. Owen would go to hear "an illiterate tinker" preach. "I would gladly give up all my
learning for that tinker's power of preaching," said Dr.
Owen. Being told one time that he had preached a
grand sermon, Bunyan replied, "Oh, you have no need
to tell me that, for the Devil whispered it to me before I
was well out of the pulpit." He became one of England's most famous men; but in the midst of his religious activity, he was smitten with a fever while on an
errand of mercy and died August 31, 1688. He was
buried in Bunhill Fields, London's famous Noncon-
formist cemetery, where tens of thousands of people
have visited his grave.

Chapter 9

John Wesley

⎯⎯⎯⎰⎯⎯⎯

*T*he life and teachings of John Wesley, the founder of Methodism, have probably had a greater
influence than those of any other man since the
days of the apostles in deepening the spiritual life of
the present time. The introduction to the Methodist
book of discipline states that Methodism was raised up
under God "for the spread of Scriptural holiness." Like
a mighty fire, it swept over the world until in less than
two centuries it numbered more adherents than almost
any other Protestant church. The secret of its success
was partly owing to the fact that its theology presented
a less fatalistic view of salvation than did that of the
old-school Calvinism so common among other Protestant denominations.

But Methodism probably owed its success still
more to the deep spiritual experiences of the Wesleys
and the other early Methodist preachers, many of
whom were so anointed with the Holy Spirit's power
that multitudes were brought under conviction of sin
while listening to their earnest sermons and exhorta-
tions. People often trembled and shook, and many in
the meetings were even struck down under the overwhelming sense of their sins received under the
preaching of these men of God.

Wesley's great-grandfather, his grandfather, and his father were all clergymen in the Church of England, in which church Wesley was himself an ordained minister and remained such until his death. The Methodist Societies in Britain did not become an independent church until 1793, or two years after John Wesley died. Susannah Wesley, the mother of John and Charles Wesley, was the daughter of the great Dr. Annesley, the "St. Paul of Nonconformity." Her grandfather and her father were ministers of the Gospel, and she was herself famous for her piety and prudence. John Wesley was born at Epworth, in Lincolnshire, England, on June 17, 1703, and was the fifteenth in a family of nineteen children, of whom only ten survived the period of infancy. At the age of six, John himself was barely rescued from the flames when his father's rectory burned down.

Wesley's mother was very careful in the training of the children, and they were all brought up *"in the training and admonition of the Lord"* (Eph. 6:4). They also received a good secular education. John was educated at the Charter House School in London until he was seventeen years of age, at which time he was sent to Christ Church College, Oxford University. He was a diligent student and made great progress in his studies. At the age of twenty-three, his accomplishments in the classics were so great that he was elected Fellow of Lincoln College and was also chosen as moderator of classes, and the following year he was made a Master of Arts. Before leaving Oxford University, he had become proficient in Latin, Greek, Hebrew, French, and logic, and he afterward obtained a knowledge of German.

Wesley followed the pious advice of his father and mother until after he was ten years of age, without consciously disobeying them in any way. "The next six or seven years were spent at school," he said, and with outward restraints being removed, I was much more negligent than before, even to outward duties. I was almost continually guilty of outward sins, which I knew to be such, though they were not scandalous in the eyes of the world. However, I still read the Scriptures and said my prayers, morning and evening.

For his salvation, he relied on these outward acts, on churchgoing, and also on the fact that he was not as bad as others. For about five years after going to Oxford, he constantly did things that he knew were sinful in the sight of God; but he still continued to pray, read his Bible, and go to church.

At about twenty-two years of age, his eyes were opened to some extent by reading the works of Thomas à Kempis, and he began to see that true religion had to do with the heart, and not with outward actions only. "I was, however, angry at Kempis for being too strict," said Wesley. But he also said,

> Yet I frequently had much comfort in reading him, such as I was an utter stranger to before. I also began meeting with a religious friend, which I had never done until now, and I began to alter the whole form of my behavior, and to set in earnest upon a new life.

Bishop Taylor's book, *Rules of Holy Living and Dying,* made a still deeper impression upon him, and his life became a very sincere one.

Wesley's friends now urged him to be ordained, and in 1725, in his twenty-second year, after much prayer and consideration, he was ordained by Bishop Potter. In 1727 he read William Law's *Christian Perfection* and *Serious Call,* and these books made him resolve more than ever to be wholly the Lord's. The writings of William Law seem to have influenced his life more than any other writings outside the Scriptures, just as the works of Aquinas influenced the life of Savonarola. It was probably William Law's books, more than any other human cause, that led Wesley to start the Methodist Societies.

In a letter to Mr. Morgan, written in later years, Wesley thus described the founding of the first Methodist society:

> In November 1729, at which time I came to reside at Oxford, your son, my brother, myself, and one other man agreed to spend three or four evenings a week together. Our plan was to read over the classics, which we had read before in private, and on Sunday some book on divinity.
>
> During the following summer, Mr. M—— told me he had visited a jail, to see a man who was condemned for killing his wife. He also told me that, from a talk he had with one of the debtors, he truly believed it would do much good if anyone would take the time to speak with them now and then. This he so frequently repeated, that on August 24, 1730, my brother and I walked with him to the castle. We were so well satisfied with our conversation there, that we agreed to go there once or twice a week. We had not done this for long before he desired me to go with him to see a poor woman in the town who was sick. In this employment, too, when we came to reflect upon it, we believed it would be worthwhile to spend an hour or two in a week, provided the minister of the parish was not against it.

In this humble manner, the first Methodist society was formed, and the great founder of Methodism was thus led to engage in active Christian service. The society increased in number, and when Whitefield joined them, there were fifteen members. They soon earned the nickname of "the Holy Club," and finally of

"Methodists." It is remarkable that God brought together in this little group two of the world's greatest preachers and one of the greatest hymnwriters—John Wesley, George Whitefield, and Charles Wesley. The society continued its good work until 1735, when Wesley left the University.

In 1735 John and his brother Charles sailed for America, intending to become missionaries to the American Indians. On the vessel were a number of Moravian missionaries, and their pious conduct so deeply impressed Wesley that he began to study German so that he would be able to converse with them. A great storm arose, and while the English were screaming and in great distress, the Moravians calmly and joyfully united in prayer and praise. Conversations with these godly people during the voyage, and later in Georgia, led the Wesleys to doubt their own conversion to Christ.

The Wesleys seemed to have accomplished very little in Georgia. They tried to bring the people to their own high standard of living, and they preached against the popular sins with such directness and personality as to provoke much opposition. Finally, they deemed it wise to return to England. Charles returned first, and John soon followed. John said, "I shook the dust off my feet (Matt. 10:14) and left Georgia, after having preached the Gospel there—not as I ought, but as I was able—one year and nearly nine months." During the voyage home, he wrote, "I went to America to convert the Indians, but oh, who shall convert me?"

Wesley preached in England in many places, but the results were generally not remarkable or encouraging. Much opposition was provoked, and little blessing seemed to attend his preaching. He conversed much with Peter Bohler and other Moravians and was surprised when they proved to him that almost all the conversions to Christ mentioned in the Bible were instantaneous. He now began to see that people do not grow into salvation, but that they are justified by faith the moment they believe in the Lord Jesus Christ. It was from the Moravians that the Methodists learned the doctrine of instantaneous conversion, also known as regeneration or justification by faith.

At first, Charles Wesley opposed what he called "the new doctrine," but he was soon convinced of his error, and in May 1738, through simple faith in Christ, he found a joy he had never known before. The news that Charles had obtained joy and peace in believing greatly deepened John Wesley's desire for a real assurance of salvation. After a ten-year struggle to find peace and rest in Christ, the light began to dawn upon him. On the morning of May 24, 1738, his eyes fell upon 2 Peter 1:4, and then on the words, *"You are not far from the kingdom of God"* (Mark 12:34). During the day, he was on the verge of receiving rest and joy through faith in Christ. "In the evening," said he,

> I went very unwillingly to a meeting on Aldersgate Street, where one was reading Luther's preface to the Romans. About a quarter before nine, while he was describing the change God works in the heart through faith in Christ, I felt my heart strangely warmed. I felt I did trust in Christ alone for salvation, and an assurance was given to me that He had taken away my sins, even mine, and had saved me, John Wesley, from the law of sin and death.

The same year that he obtained this blessing through faith in Christ, he visited the Moravian settlement of Herrnhut, on Count Zinzendorf's estate in Germany. This visit greatly strengthened his faith, and he returned to England to preach, with a new zeal, the doctrine of instantaneous conversion and justification through faith in Christ. Many were now converted to Christ in his meetings almost everywhere he went.

We learn from his journal on October 3 and 15, 1738, that Wesley had a great longing for a still deeper experience. "I was asking," he wrote in the latter entry, "that God would fulfill all His promises in my own soul." His longings seem to have been satisfied, in a measure at least, in a memorable dinner meeting in London, when he and Whitefield and other prominent Methodist ministers were present at a meeting of the Methodist Societies. Describing this meeting in his journal, Wesley wrote,

> Monday, January 1, 1739. Messrs. Hall, Kinchin, Ingham, Whitefield, Hutchins, and my brother Charles were present at our love feast in Fetterslane, with about sixty of our brothers in Christ. About three in the morning, as we were *"continuing steadfastly in prayer"* (Rom. 12:12), the power of God came mightily upon us, insomuch that many cried out for exceeding joy, and many fell to the ground. As soon as we recovered a little from the awe and amazement at the presence of His majesty, we broke out with one voice, "We praise You, O God; we acknowledge You to be the Lord."

Wesley must have received a powerful anointing of the Spirit at the time mentioned above, because after the experience he seemed to have preached with greater anointing and power. The Methodist Societies now began to multiply rapidly, many souls being converted to God. The state churches were closing rapidly against the Methodists, when Whitefield began to preach to gigantic audiences in the open air at Bristol. After continuing in Bristol for some time, Whitefield desired John Wesley to come and take the work there off his hands so that he could go elsewhere. After seeking to know the Lord's will in the matter, Wesley complied with his request.

Staid churchman that he was, Wesley had many misgivings about the propriety of preaching in the open air; but when he saw Whitefield preaching to the great multitudes in the open air at Bristol, his prejudices gradually melted away. He said,

> I could hardly reconcile myself at first to this strange way of preaching in the fields, of which Whitefield set me an example on Sunday. All my life, until very recently, I had been so tenacious of every point relating to decency and order, that I should have thought the saving of souls almost a sin if it had not been done in a church.

It was only after witnessing the marvelous results accompanying Whitefield's preaching in the open air that Wesley began to speak in open-air meetings, but he soon became famous as an open-air preacher. Until the day of his death, he exercised the greatest care to have everything *"done decently and in order"* (1 Cor. 14:40), and to avoid all fleshly excitement, hallucination, and delusion. But, on the other hand, he was careful to encourage every genuine work of the Holy Spirit. *"Do not quench the Spirit"* (1 Thess. 5:19) was to him a solemn warning that he scrupulously and conscientiously tried to follow.

Wesley preached for some time in Bristol, to immense audiences sometimes numbering many thousands of people. His open-air meetings were as large, if not larger, than those of Whitefield. Powerful conviction of sin rested upon the people, and multitudes turned to Christ. Three weeks after the remarkable love feast experience in London, while Wesley was preaching in Bristol, "a well-dressed, middle-aged woman suddenly cried out, as in the agonies of death. She continued to do so for some time," according to Wesley, "with all the signs of the sharpest anguish of

spirit." She was finally able to *"rejoice in the* LORD...
[and] *joy in the God of* [her] *salvation"* (Hab. 3:18).

On April 17, 1739, there was another remarkable
case of conviction of sin, in Bristol. Wesley had just ex-
pounded Acts 4, on the power of the Holy Spirit. "We
then called upon God to confirm His Word," said
Wesley.

> Immediately one who stood by, to our great
> surprise, cried out aloud with the utmost vehe-
> mence, even as the agonies of death. But we con-
> tinued in prayer until a new song was put in her
> mouth (Ps. 40:3), a thanksgiving unto God. Soon
> after, two other people who were well-known in
> this place for their labors to live in all good con-
> science toward all men, were seized with strong
> pain and were constrained to roar for the dis-
> quiet of their hearts.

These people also found peace.

Many other wonderful cases of conviction of sin
accompanied Wesley's preaching. It was a frequent oc-
currence for people to cry out or fall down as if dead in
the meetings, so great was their anguish of heart. This
was caused, no doubt, by the Holy Spirit convicting
them of sin. It is a well-known fact that great and sudden emotion of any kind will often cause people to
faint. This fact undoubtedly accounts for people drop-
ping down as if dead in revivals and other meetings.
The sudden realization of the enormity of their sins
and of the doom of the impenitent, when the Spirit of
God convicts them of sin, is so great that it absorbs all
their mental faculties, and they lose control of themselves and faint away.

Instances of this kind were frequently recorded by
Wesley. On April 21, 1739, at Weavers Hall, Bristol, "a
young man was suddenly seized with a violent trembling all over; and, in a few minutes, the sorrows of his

heart being enlarged, he sunk down to the ground." He also found peace. On the twenty-fifth day of the same month, while Wesley was preaching, one person after another "sank to the earth; they dropped on every side as if thunderstruck."

Day after day, Wesley preached to immense audiences in Bristol and Bath and suburbs of those cities. He then went to other places, preaching with the same anointing and power, and many Methodist societies sprang up as a result of his and Whitefield's preaching. Many found fault with the outcries of those brought under conviction of sin. Describing one meeting, Wesley said, "My voice could hardly be heard amid the groanings of some and the cries of others, calling aloud to Him who is mighty to save." He said, "A Quaker who stood by was quite displeased at what he considered the false appearances of these creatures, and was biting his lips and knitting his brows, when he dropped down as thunderstruck."

The next day, in a little prayer meeting, "just as we rose from giving thanks," said Wesley, "another person reeled four or five steps, and then dropped down." A certain J—— H——, a zealous Episcopalian, opposed the Methodists in every way possible. He went to his acquaintances, persuading them that people falling in the meetings and crying out in agony was "a delusion of the Devil." While sitting at the table one day, this same man "changed color, fell off his chair, and began screaming terribly and beating himself against the ground."

Almost everywhere that Wesley went, people were struck down in his meetings in the manner already described, but these cases were the exception, and the individuals usually found peace in Christ when prayed for. Most of the people had never heard such pointed and powerful preaching as Wesley's, and the suddenness with which they were brought face-to-face with their sinful and lost condition probably had much to do with the fact that many of them fainted away or cried out in agony. People who had entertained false hopes of salvation had the masks torn away by the plain preaching of Wesley and were stricken with great agony until they found peace with God.

In one place where Wesley was preaching, the Lord began to make bare His arm (Isa. 52:10). "One after another was struck to the earth, exceedingly trembling at the presence of His power. Others cried with a loud and bitter cry, 'What must we do to be saved?' (see Acts 16:30)." The same evening, while Wesley was preaching, a man cried out in agony of soul. Soon afterward,

> another person dropped down close to one who was a strong asserter of the contrary doctrine. While he stood astonished at the sight, a little boy near him was seized in the same manner. A young man, who stood up behind, fixed his eyes on him, and sunk down himself as one dead.

The plain and fearless preaching of Wesley caused much opposition, and he was often mobbed and came near to losing his life. But in the meetings, "the power of God came with His Word, so that no one scoffed or interrupted or opened his mouth." The scoffing and persecution came from those who had never been in the meetings or heard Wesley preach.

On his return to London, Wesley preached at Wapping, and 26 people were struck down under conviction of sin. "Some sunk down, and there remained no strength in them," Wesley reported,

> and others exceedingly trembled and quaked. Some were torn with a kind of convulsive motion in every part of their bodies....I immediately prayed that God would not permit those who were weak to be offended. But one woman was

offended greatly, and she went about three or four yards when she also dropped down, in as violent an agony as the rest.

In London, Wesley preached in the open air to vast audiences of many thousands of people, as Whitefield and he had done in Bristol; and he afterward held similar outdoor meetings all over Britain. Even when rain was falling or biting frost was on the ground, he sometimes preached to many thousands in the open air, and sometimes the sermons were two or three hours long. When the doors of his home church at Epworth were closed against him, he preached standing on his father's tombstone in the churchyard with an immense crowd around him. He often spoke with great liberty and power when preaching in these open-air meetings.

On December 23, 1744, while preaching at Snow-Fields, "I found," he said,

> such light and strength as I never remember to have had before. I had often wondered at myself—and sometimes mentioned it to others—how ten thousand cares of various kinds were no more weight to my mind than ten thousand hairs were to my head.

When worn-out with overwork, he often found new strength in answer to prayer. On March 17, 1740, writing in his journal concerning one of these occasions, he said, "I then thought, 'Cannot God heal either man or beast by any means, or without any?' Immediately my weariness and headache ceased, and my horses' lameness in the same instant."

Wesley was a great organizer and a strict disciplinarian. He expelled from the Methodist Societies everyone who was frivolous or trifling. He expelled them by the scores. He insisted upon modesty in dress, upon abstinence from worldly amusements, and upon daily holy living. It was his desire to have no one in the Methodist Societies except those who would adorn them by holy and consistent living. Concerning the society at Epworth he wrote, "The society here is not large, but God has worked upon the whole place. Sabbath breaking and drunkenness are no more seen in the streets; cursing and swearing are rarely heard."

Both John and Charles Wesley, as well as the other early Methodist preachers, were strong advocates of the doctrine of entire and instantaneous sanctification through faith. In his *Works,* Wesley said,

> Many years ago, I saw that without holiness no man will see the Lord. I began by following after it and inciting all with whom I had any acquaintance to do the same. Ten years after that, God gave me a clearer view than I had before of the way to attain it, namely, by faith in the Son of God. And immediately I declared to all, "We are saved from sin; we are made holy by faith." This I testified in private, in public, and in print; and God confirmed it by a thousand witnesses.

In his journal, September 28, 1762, Wesley wrote,

> Many years ago, my brother frequently said, "Your Day of Pentecost is not fully come, but I do not doubt that it will; and you will then hear of people being sanctified as frequently as you do now of people being justified." Any unprejudiced reader may observe that it was now fully come for me. And accordingly, we did hear of people being sanctified in London and most other parts of England, and in Dublin and in many other parts of Ireland, as frequently as of people being justified, although instances of the latter were far more frequent than they had been for twenty years before.

Wesley's famous sermon on Christian perfection was first published in 1733, and was often reprinted by him, without alteration, in later years. Deeming it complete, he simply reprinted it. Some have thought that he changed his mind with regard to the doctrine of Christian perfection, but in 1778, he wrote, "Forty years ago I knew and preached every Christian doctrine that I preach now."

On June 27, 1769, he defined what he meant by Christian perfection; and in his *Works,* he explained his ideas concerning inbred or original sin and its eradication. In his journal, November 1, 1762, he wrote concerning the views of a certain individual,

> I like your doctrine of perfection or pure love—love excluding sin. I also like your insisting that it is merely by faith, that consequently it is instantaneous (though preceded and followed by a gradual work), and that it may be now, at this instant.
>
> But I dislike your supposing that man may be as perfect as an angel, that he can be absolutely perfect, that he can be infallible or above being tempted, or that the moment he is pure in heart he cannot fall from it.
>
> I dislike the saying, "This was not known or taught among us until within two or three years ago." I grant you did not know it. You have over and over again denied instantaneous sanctification to me; but I have known and taught it (and so has my brother, as our writings show) for more than twenty years.

In his journal, May 14, 1765, Wesley explained how he came to believe in the doctrine of Christian perfection and what he believed the experience to be. He said,

> But how did this opinion come into my mind? I will tell you with simplicity. In 1725 I

read Bishop Taylor's *Rules of Holy Living and Dying*. I was struck particularly with the chapter on intention, and felt a fixed intention to give myself up to God. This was confirmed in my heart soon afterward, and I longed to give God my whole heart. This is just what I mean by perfection now. I sought it from that hour.

In 1727 I read William Law's *Christian Perfection* and *Serious Call*, and more explicitly resolved to be all devoted to God—in body, soul, and spirit. In 1730 I began to be *homo unius libri*, that is, to study (comparatively) no book but the Bible. I then saw in a stronger light than ever before that only one thing is needful: faith that brings about all inward and outward holiness by the love of God and man. I groaned to love God with all my heart and to serve Him with all my strength.

On January 1, 1733, I preached the sermon on the circumcision of the heart, which contains all that I now teach concerning salvation from all sin, and loving God with an undivided heart. In the same year I printed—this was the first time I ventured to print anything—for the use of my pupils, *A Collection of Forms of Prayer*. In this I spoke explicitly of giving the whole heart and the whole life to God. This was then, as it is now, my idea of perfection.

In 1735, I preached my farewell sermon at Epworth in Lincolnshire. In this, likewise, I spoke with the utmost clearness of having one plan, one desire, one love, and of pursuing the one end of our lives in all our words and actions.

In January 1738, I expressed my desires in these words:

> O grant that nothing in my soul
>   May dwell but Thy pure love alone;
> O may Thy love possess me whole,
>   My joy, my treasure, and my crown.

Strange flames far from my heart remove;
My every act, word, thought be love.

I am still persuaded that this is what the
Lord Jesus has bought me with His blood.

Wesley was almost constantly traveling and
preaching. "The world is my parish" was his famous
motto. In 1774 he wrote that he never traveled less
than 4,500 miles a year. For many years his annual
record was 8,000 miles, and during this period he seldom preached less than five thousand times a year. After he was thirty-six years of age, he traveled 225,000
miles as an itinerant preacher and preached more than
forty thousand sermons, some of them to congregations
of above 20,000 people. He rose at four o'clock in the
morning and preached at five nearly every day.

In 1789 Wesley's sight and strength were pretty
well exhausted, and he felt that he was an old man. But
he continued to preach and write until within a few
days of his death. With the power of God manifestly
present, he passed away triumphantly on March 2,
1791, his dying testimony being, "Best of all, God is
with us."

Chapter 10

George Whitefield

⤙⤚

The name of George Whitefield, the prince of open-air preachers, will ever rank high among those of great soulwinners. Perhaps no preacher was ever gifted with a more powerful voice for open-air work, or ever preached to larger outdoor congregations, than Whitefield. It is estimated that he preached to 100,000 people at Cambuslang in Scotland, and that 10,000 people professed conversion to Christ as the result of his sermon there. Although frail in body and having weak lungs, God seemed to endow him with supernatural strength for open-air work at a time when church doors were closed against him. Benjamin Franklin claimed to have tested the voice of Whitefield to find out how far he could hear him distinctly, and he heard him clearly for over a mile.

Whitefield's grandfather was a clergyman in the Church of England, and his father was a wine merchant and barkeeper. George was born in 1714. He was the youngest of a family of seven children. His father died when he was an infant, and his mother—like the mother of D. L. Moody—was left to struggle through poverty with a large family. When four years old, George had the measles, which through neglect left one of his lively blue eyes with a slight squint. This, however, did not mar the charm of his countenance.

His early life was stained with lying, cheating, evil speaking, small thefts, and other juvenile sins. In this he much resembled the celebrated Saint Augustine. He would sometimes run into the dissenting meetinghouse during services and shout the name of the minister— "Old Cole! Old Cole! Old Cole!"—and then he was off in a hurry. A member of the same chapel once asked him what he intended to be. "A minister," said he, "but I would take care never to tell stories in the pulpit like the old Cole," he added. The worthy old minister afterward rejoiced to hear Whitefield relate anecdotes and incidents with a vividness and power far exceeding his own capabilities.

Whitefield was a wild, unrestrained lad. His mother tried to keep him from taking part in the business at the saloon, but he sometimes sold drinks over the counter and kept the money. "It would be endless," said Whitefield, "to recount the sins and offenses of my younger days." He had many good thoughts and compunctions of conscience. Thus, he did not use all the money he stole from his mother, but gave some of it to the poor. Among the books that he stole from others were devotional books as well as romance books; he afterward restored them fourfold.

Whitefield had a disposition toward higher things, and once when some people had greatly provoked him, he went to his room, and on his knees, with tears in his eyes, prayed over Psalm 118. He was familiar with the Bible. Although he ridiculed sacred things, he was fond of the thought of someday being a clergyman, and he frequently imitated the clergyman's manner of reading prayers, or intoning them in the manner so common at that time. In the Church of St. Mary de Crypt, in Gloucester, Whitefield was christened as a baby, made fun of the minister as a boy of ten, and preached his first sermon as a deacon at the age of twenty-one.

When he was ten years of age, Whitefield's mother married again, but this did not seem to improve their condition, at least financially. At the public school of St. Mary de Crypt, young Whitefield's memory and public speaking powers won him great distinction in the amateur theatricals, of which he was very fond.

At fifteen years of age he gave up the public school and began helping his mother in the housework at Bell Inn. In the evenings he often read his Bible and even composed several sermons. Finally his brothers took charge of the saloon. George could not agree with the sister-in-law, and so he left and went to another brother's place in Bristol. Here he first felt the power of God's Spirit working upon his heart. He felt a great longing for the things of God. After two months he returned home, and these convictions and longings left him. His mother gave him the best she could: a bed on the floor. No business seemed to open up for him, and one day he said to his sister, "Sister, God intends something for me that we do not know about." His mother also seemed to have had presentiments of his coming greatness.

After remaining idle for some time, he found that there was opportunity for him to work his way, as a servant, through Oxford University. He went to school again to prepare for Oxford and was led off into atheism by sinful companions. This did not last long, and he finally made up his mind to prepare to take communion on his seventeenth birthday. A dream about God and a powerful impression that he was to preach the Gospel seem to have greatly sobered him. A brother also gave him a straight talk about his rapid changes from saint to sinner and from sinner to saint.

In 1732, when eighteen years of age, he went to Oxford. At Oxford, to his great delight and after long desiring it, he was taken into the group of Methodists, which then numbered fifteen. A book entitled *The Life of God in the Soul of Man,* lent to him by Charles

Wesley, opened Whitefield's eyes to see that outward works and outward forms and ceremonies would not save the soul. When he read that "true religion is a union of the soul with God, or Christ formed within us," a ray of light instantaneously darted in upon his soul, and from that moment, but not until then, he knew that he must be a new creature.

Whitefield was "born of God" long before the Wesleys, his devout companions, were brought out into the clear light of the new birth. He wrote to his acquaintances concerning his conversion, and they charitably supposed him to be insane. He shared great persecution with the other members of "the Holy Club," or the Methodists. The contempt and shame he suffered at Oxford helped to prepare him for the still greater persecutions of his later life.

Owing to the fact that the Wesleys did not yet understand regeneration, or the new birth, Whitefield got his eyes off Christ and began once more to look to external works for salvation. He went through many sore trials and temptations and spent whole days and nights in fasting and prayer for deliverance from the proud, hellish thoughts that used to crowd into his soul. He said, "I never ceased wrestling with God until He blessed me with victory over them." (See Genesis 32:24–26.) Before obtaining victory through faith, he sought it by means of severe fasting, eating coarse food, dressing poorly, and by practicing other severe austerities and penances. He prayed one night out under a tree in the coldest weather, and he lived for some time on sage tea, without sugar, and coarse bread. Finally, his strictness with himself so weakened his body that he could hardly crawl upstairs.

The Wesleys could only help him a little, but after seven weeks of self-centered seeking, his eyes were once more directed to Christ as his Savior, and peace and joy returned to his soul. He said,

> Oh, with what joy, joy unspeakable, even joy
> that was full of and big with glory, was my soul
> filled when the weight of sin went off! An abid-
> ing sense of the pardoning love of God, and a full
> assurance of faith, broke in upon my disconso-
> late soul!

Ever afterward he seemed to have had clearer views
concerning salvation through faith, and he was soon
the means of leading several of his companions into the
experience of the new birth, both at Gloucester and
Oxford.

He now began joyfully to read the Word of God, to
visit the sick, and to perform other services for the
Master. Soon his friends urged him to be ordained. His
great humility led him to decline; but being patient and
flexible in all matters regarding himself, though firm
as a rock in matters of conviction, he was persuaded to
go through the ceremony of ordination. As he had previously dreamed, the bishop sent for him and received
him kindly, gave him some gold as a present, and informed him that though he had previously made up his
mind not to ordain anyone under twenty-three years
old, still he was willing to ordain him whenever he desired.

It was at the moment of his ordination that Whitefield seemed to have made a complete consecration of
himself to God and to have received the anointing of
the Spirit and power that made him such a mighty
worker in God's harvest field. It was on June 20, 1736,
at the age of twenty-one, that he was ordained by the
good Bishop of Gloucester, Dr. Benson. In *Account of
God's Dealings*, Whitefield thus described what he experienced at that time:

> About three days before the time appointed
> for my ordination, the bishop came to town. The
> next day I sent his lordship an abstract of my

private examination on these two questions: Do you trust that you are inwardly moved by the Holy Spirit to take upon you this office and administration? and, Are you called according to the will of the Lord Jesus Christ and the laws of this realm? The next morning I called on the bishop. He received me with much love, telling me he was glad I had come, that he was satisfied with the preparation I had made and with the allowance given me by Sir John Phillips. "I had myself," said he, "made provision for you of two little parishes, but since you choose to be at Oxford, I am very well pleased. I do not doubt that you will do much good."

Upon this I took my leave, abashed with God's goodness to such a wretch like myself, but I exceedingly rejoiced that in every circumstance He made my way into the ministry so very plain before my face.

This, I think, was on Friday. On the following day I continued in fasting and prayer. In the evening I retired to a hill near the town and prayed fervently for about two hours on behalf of myself and those who were to be ordained with me.

On Sunday morning I rose early and prayed over Paul's epistle to Timothy, and more particularly, over that precept, *"Let no one despise your youth"* (1 Tim. 4:12). When I went up to the altar, I could think of nothing but Samuel standing as a little child before the Lord with a linen ephod. When the bishop laid his hands upon my head, my heart was melted down, and I offered my whole spirit, soul, and body to the service of God's sanctuary. At the bishop's command, I read the Gospel with power. Afterward I sealed *"the good confession"* (1 Tim. 6:12) I had made *"in the presence of many witnesses"* (v. 12) by partaking of the holy sacrament of our Lord's most blessed body and blood.

That God really touched the lips of Whitefield with the divine fire of His Holy Spirit at the time of his ordination seems proved by the fact that he began to preach with great anointing and power on the next Sunday after his ordination. His first sermon was delivered to an immense audience in his old home church at Gloucester. Complaint was afterward made to the bishop that 15 people were driven mad by this sermon. The good bishop replied that he hoped that the madness would not be forgotten before the next Sunday.

After his ordination, Whitefield returned to Oxford with great joy to complete his course at the university. While there, he was invited to occupy a friend's pulpit for two months in an obscure part of London. He accepted the invitation, and although his youth provoked sneers at first, great crowds flocked to hear him. At Oxford his rooms were often filled with praying students. He left the university full of fervor, zeal, and the constraining power of the Holy Spirit. After preaching a few sermons in England with great anointing and power, he sailed for the United States. His few sermons in Bristol, just before he left England, stirred the whole city.

On his second visit to Bristol, crowds of people flocked out to meet him on his way to the city. Although he was only twenty-two years of age, Bristol was completely under his spell. Quakers and Nonconformists generally left their own chapels to hear him preach. The new birth that was preached with power from on high seemed to attract all kinds of men. Every nook and corner of the church was crowded, and half the people who came had to be turned away. Many wept bitterly when Whitefield left the city, as did the people of Gloucester when he left that city.

In London, while waiting for his ship, he was compelled to preach, and the large churches could not hold his audiences. Thousands went away because there was no room. On Sunday the streets were crowded with people going to the meetings long before the break of day. The stewards could hardly carry the donations made for the orphanage he hoped to start in America, so heavy and so many were the large English pennies of that day, which formed the bulk of the collections. Soon the clergy became jealous, bitter opposition set in against Whitefield, and churches were closed against him.

Near Christmas 1737, Whitefield set sail for America, as weeping crowds bade him farewell. He left the charity schools of England £1,000 richer for his brief labors there. Everyone on board the vessel was greatly blessed by his ministering during the voyage. When Whitefield reached his destination in Georgia, he had little opportunity to preach to large crowds, as 200 people were a large congregation in the frontier settlements at that time. But he won his way to the hearts of the people, and scores were brought to Christ.

He returned to England in 1738, and began to work in cooperation with the Wesleys, who had been led out into the light concerning the new birth during his absence in America. God was greatly blessing them, but their preaching was too plain to suit lukewarm, worldly, and fashionable churches, and the doors of these churches were rapidly closing against them. Whitefield preached in one church where 1,000 people were unable to get inside, and this suggested to him the idea of outdoor preaching, but even his fellow Methodists at that time regarded this as "a mad idea." Soon after this, the people were so deeply moved by his preaching that they began to say aloud "Amen" to many things that he said. This seems to have been a new thing in those days.

Excluded from many of the state churches, Whitefield began his open-air preaching at Kingswood, Bristol, in 1739. There the rough coal miners gathered to hear him, and his audiences doubled and tripled until he found himself preaching to 20,000 people at a time.

Tears streamed down the cheeks of the coal-begrimed men, and hundreds and hundreds were convicted of sin and brought to Christ. Whitefield had now stopped using printed prayers and written sermons, and he prayed and preached extempore as he felt led by the Spirit of God. Wherever he went, the people flocked to hear him in such great crowds that the churches would no longer have contained them, had they been open to him. When Whitefield was saying farewell from Bristol, the crowd was so great at one of the Methodist societies that he had to leave by mounting a ladder and climbing over the roof of an adjoining house.

When evicted from a Church of England in London while preaching, Whitefield continued his sermon in the churchyard. He then began his open-air meetings at Moorfields, one of the largest, vilest, and most notorious pleasure resorts in London. Great was the astonishment of the London rowdies to see the tall, graceful young clergyman, with mild blue eyes and dressed in gown and cassock, standing on the wall addressing them on the second coming of Christ. That same day he addressed a more refined audience of 20,000 people on Kennington Common. After this he continued to preach to great audiences of from 20,000 to 40,000 in both of these places.

It is said that Whitefield received more than a thousand written requests for prayer at one of his meetings at Moorfields. The singing of the vast audiences could be heard for a distance of 2 miles. When the people at Kennington Common heard that he was to leave for America, their weeping was so loud as to almost drown his voice. A similar scene was enacted at Moorfields. At Hackney Marsh he preached at a horse race to about 10,000 people, and the horses got little attention.

On his second and subsequent trips to America, Whitefield had very great success. He preached to large audiences and won many souls to Christ. It was claimed that every student in Harvard University professed conversion to Christ during his meetings there. Benjamin Franklin was deeply impressed with his preaching, and the celebrated Jonathan Edwards wept while listening to his sermons.

On his return to England, Whitefield preached to great audiences in the tabernacle built for him at Moorfields, and also to vast audiences in many other parts of Britain. Perhaps his greatest meeting was at Cambuslang, near Glasgow, Scotland, where he is said to have preached to an audience variously estimated at from 30,000 to 100,000 people. Many were bathed in tears for an hour and a half while he was preaching, and it is claimed that 10,000 people professed conversion to Christ under this sermon. All of Britain seemed to be in a holy fervor over his preaching. The Vicar of Bideford warned the people against Whitefield's preaching one Sunday evening, but the next morning Whitefield preached to an audience of 10,000. Even the nobility gladly sat at his feet, and thousands of people would often stand in the rain listening to him.

The frailty of Whitefield's body was so great that the marvelous range of his voice seemed almost supernatural. The clearness and range of his voice has probably never been equaled by that of any other open-air preacher.

The vividness with which Whitefield preached also seemed to be almost supernatural. One time he was preaching to sailors, and he described a vessel wrecked in a storm at sea. He portrayed her as on her beam and just ready to sink, and then he cried aloud, "What next?" The picture was so real that the sailors sprang to their feet and cried out, "The longboat! Take the longboat!" At another time he pictured a blind man walking toward the edge of a precipice without knowing where he was going, until finally he was right on the edge of the precipice. The portrayal was so vivid and real that when he reached this point in his sermon,

Lord Chesterfield, who was present, sprang to his feet and cried aloud, "My God! He is gone!" Famous actors also loved to hear Whitefield preach. One actor was so deeply impressed with the oratorical powers of Whitefield that he declared he believed Whitefield could make people weep by the mere enunciation of a word.

Whitefield was not a theologian by nature, and he found little time for reading books. Most of the books he did find time to read were of the old-school Calvinistic type so prevalent at that time, and his mind became confirmed in the Calvinistic views of theology. This led to a controversy between him and the Wesleys, as the latter rejected the fatalistic teachings of old-school Calvinism. Their friendship for each other continued, but Whitefield did not work in such full accord and harmony with the Wesleys as before the controversy. But both the Wesleys and Whitefield were mightily used by God, each preaching the Gospel with the degree of light given to him. Whitefield probably did not have as logical a mind as John Wesley. He was sometimes accused of rambling in his sermons and of not keeping to his subject. His reply to this was, "If men will continue to ramble like lost sheep, then I will continue to ramble after them."

Like Wesley, Whitefield was a strenuous worker. When in his prime, he seldom preached less than fifteen times a week. It is estimated that he preached at least eighteen thousand sermons, or an average of ten times a week for thirty-four years. He often preached as many as four or five times in one day.

After intensely longing to be with the Master for over twenty years, he died in 1770, during his seventh visit to America, having preached up to and on the day preceding his death.

Chapter 11

Christmas Evans

⁓

*W*ales has had many famous preachers. Among them are Daniel Rowlands, Robert Roberts, John Elias, William Williams, Henry Rees, John Jones, and Davies of Swansea. But Christmas Evans, "the one-eyed preacher of Anglesea," seems to have exceeded all the others both in fame and spiritual power. He once said to Richard Rowlands, "Brother, the truths, the confidence, and the power I feel will cause some to dance for joy in parts of Wales." And so it was.

Christmas Evans, often called "the John Bunyan of Wales," was born on Christmas Day, 1766—hence his name. His parents were very poor. His father died when he was nine years of age, and little Christmas did chores for six years for a cruel, ungodly uncle. His education was neglected, and at the age of seventeen he could not read a word.

Many accidents and misfortunes befell him. Once he was stabbed in a quarrel, once he nearly drowned, once he fell from a high tree with an open knife in his hand, and once a horse ran away with him and dashed at full speed through a low and narrow passage. After his conversion to Christ, some of his former ungodly companions waylaid him at night and unmercifully beat him so that he lost one eye as a result. But God mercifully preserved him through all these trials.

He left his cruel uncle at the age of seventeen, and soon afterward, during a revival, he identified himself with the church. From an early age he had many religious impressions, but he did not decide for Christ until his seventeenth year. New desires then awoke in his soul, and he began to learn to read and to improve his mind. He soon felt a call to the ministry, and this feeling was deepened by a remarkable dream he had concerning the second coming of Christ. He felt that he was only a mass of sin and ignorance and was much discouraged by his early efforts to preach. He memorized the prayers and sermons of others and tried to pray and preach them.

In 1790 he was ordained by the Baptists and commenced work as a missionary among some of the humbler churches. For three years before joining the Baptists, he suffered much from doubts regarding his own conversion to Christ, but soon after uniting with them, all his doubts rolled away and he received *"the garment of praise for the spirit of heaviness"* (Isa. 61:3). He was surprised at first to see people brought to God through his ministry; but the Lord greatly blessed him, and his meetings began to attract widespread attention. He made a tour of South Wales on foot and sometimes preached as many as five times during one Sunday. Although he was shabbily dressed and awkward, large crowds came to hear him preach, and often there were tears and uncontrollable excitement. His sermons took great hold upon the people.

At twenty-six years of age, Evans began to preach among the churches on the island of Anglesea, and there he remained for twenty years, preaching the Gospel with much success. Here many of the churches had been carried away by the Sandemanian teachings, which seem to have been a form of extreme Calvinism, amounting to fatalism, depriving man of moral responsibility. The leader of the sect was a brilliant and cultured orator, and for years Christmas Evans labored and preached to counteract his teachings.

Evans' controversies with the Sandemanians brought him into a place where he had lost much of the spirit of prayer and sweetness so necessary for the enjoyment of a Christian life. He felt an intense need and longing for a closer fellowship with God. The following is his description of the manner in which he sought and obtained the richer, fuller Christian experience that he so much desired and that set his soul on fire with divine anointing and power such as he had never experienced before:

> I was weary of a cold heart toward Christ, His atonement, and the work of His Spirit. I was weary of a cold heart in the pulpit, in secret prayer, and in study, especially when I remembered that for fifteen years before, my heart had been burning within me as if I were on the way toward Emmaus with Jesus. A day came at last, a day ever to be remembered by me, when I was on my way from Dolgelly to Machynlleth. I felt it my duty to pray, though my heart was hard and my spirit worldly.
>
> After I had commenced praying in the name of Jesus, I soon felt as if the shackles were falling off, and as if the mountains of snow and ice were melting within me. This brought confidence in my mind for the promise of the Holy Spirit. I felt my whole spirit relieved of some great bondage, as if it were rising up from the grave of a severe winter. My tears flowed copiously, and I was constrained to cry aloud and pray for the gracious visits of God, for the joy of His salvation, and that He would again visit the churches in Anglesea that were under my care. I embraced in my supplications all of the churches, and prayed for most of the preachers of Wales by name.

This struggle lasted for three hours. It would come over me again and again, like one wave after another, like a tide driven by a strong wind, until my physical power was greatly weakened by weeping and crying. Thus I gave myself up wholly to Christ, body and soul, talents and labors—all my life, every day, and every hour that remained to me—and all my cares I entrusted into the hands of Christ.

The road was mountainous and lonely, so I was alone and had no interruption in my wrestlings with God. This event caused me to expect a new revelation of God's goodness to me and the churches. Thus the Lord delivered me and the people of Anglesea from being swept away by the evils of Sandemanianism.

In the first service I held after this event, I felt as if I had been removed from the cold and sterile region of spiritual ice into the pleasant lands of the promises of God. The former striving with God in prayer, and the longing for the conversion of sinners that I had experienced at Leyn, were now restored. I had a hold of the promise of God. When I returned home, the first thing that attracted my notice was that the Spirit was working in the believers in Anglesea, inducing in them a spirit of prayer, especially in two of the deacons, who were particularly praying that God would visit us in mercy and would render the Word of His grace effective among us in the conversion of sinners.

It was undoubtedly about the time of this remarkable experience of the anointing of the Holy Spirit that Christmas Evans wrote a solemn covenant with God, to every article of which he signed his initials. This covenant of consecration is as follows:

Covenant with God

1. I give my soul and body to You, Jesus, the true God and everlasting life. Deliver us from sin and from eternal death, and bring me into life everlasting. Amen. —C. E.

2. I call the day, the sun, the earth, the trees, the stones, the bed, the table, and the books to witness that I come unto You, Redeemer of sinners, that I may obtain rest for my soul from the thunders of guilt and the dread of eternity. Amen. —C. E.

3. I do, through confidence in Your power, earnestly entreat You to take the work into Your own hand, and give me a circumcised heart, that I may love You. Create in me a right spirit, that I may seek Your glory. Grant me the principle that You will acknowledge in the Day of Judgment, that I may not then assume pale-facedness and find myself a hypocrite. Grant me this, for the sake of Your most precious blood. Amen. —C. E.

4. I entreat You, Jesus, the Son of God in power, grant me, for the sake of Your agonizing death, a covenant interest in Your blood, which cleanses; in Your righteousness, which justifies; and in Your redemption, which delivers. I entreat an interest in Your blood, for Your blood's sake, and a part in You, for Your name's sake, which You have given among men. Amen. —C. E.

5. Jesus Christ, Son of the living God, take for the sake of Your cruel death my time, my strength, and the gifts and talents I possess, which with a full purpose of heart I consecrate to Your glory in the building up of Your church in the world, for You are worthy of the hearts and talents of men. Amen. —C. E.

6. I desire You, my great High Priest, to confirm, by Your power from Your high court, my usefulness as a preacher and my piety as a Christian—as two gardens near one another—that sin

may not have place in my heart to cloud my confidence in Your righteousness, and that I may not be left to any foolish act that may cause my gifts to wither and render me useless before my life ends. Keep Your gracious eye upon me, and watch over me, O my Lord and my God forever! Amen. —C. E.

7. I give myself in a particular manner to You, O Jesus Christ the Savior, to be preserved from the falls into which many stumble, that Your name may not be blasphemed or wounded, that my peace may not be injured, that Your people may not be grieved, and that Your enemies may not be hardened. Amen. —C. E.

8. I come entreating You to enter into a covenant with me in my ministry. Oh, prosper me as You prospered Bunyan, Whitefield, and others. Remove the impediments in the way of my prosperity. Work in me the things approved by You, so that I may attain this. Give me a heart that is "lovesick" (Song 2:5) for You and for the souls of men. Grant that I may feel the power of Your Word before preaching it, as Moses felt the power of his rod before he felt the effect of it on the land and waters of Egypt. For the sake of Your precious blood, Jesus, my all in all, grant me this. Amen. —C. E.

9. Search me now, and lead me in the paths of judgment. May I see in this world what I really am in Your sight, that I may not find myself otherwise when the light of eternity will dawn upon me and when I will open my eyes in the brightness of immortality. Wash me in Your redeeming blood. Amen. —C. E.

10. Give me power to trust in You for food and clothing, and to make known my requests to You. Oh, let Your care be over me as a covenant privilege between You and me, and not simply as a general care that You show in feeding the bird that perishes and clothing the lily that is

"thrown into the oven" (Matt. 6:30), but remember me as one of Your family and as one of Your unworthy brothers. Amen. —C. E.

11. Take upon Yourself, O Jesus, to prepare me for death, for You are God, and You need only to speak the word. If it be possible—but Your will be done—let me not linger in sickness or die a sudden death without saying good-bye to my brothers, but rather let me die with them around me, after a short illness. May everything be put in order, ready for that day of passing from one world to another, so that there may be no confusion or disorder, but a passing away in peace. Oh, grant me this for the sake of Your agony in the Garden. Amen. —C. E.

12. Grant, O blessed Lord, that no sin may be nourished or fostered in me that may cause You to cast me off from the work of Your sanctuary, like the sons of Eli. And for the sake of Your infinite merits, do not let my days be longer than my usefulness. Do not let me become, at the end of my days, like a piece of lumber, in the way of the usefulness of others. Amen. —C. E.

I beseech You, my Redeemer, to present these supplications of mine before the Father. Inscribe them in Your book with Your own immortal pen, while I am writing them with my mortal hand in my book on earth. According to the depths of Your merit, Your infinite grace, Your compassion, and Your tenderness toward Your people, attach Your name in Your upper court to these humble supplications of mine. Set Your amen to them, even as I set mine on my side of the covenant, Amen. —Christmas Evans, Llangevni, Anglesea, April 10, 18—.

After his entire consecration to God, and after receiving the anointing of the Holy Spirit while he wrestled in prayer, Christmas Evans began to preach with a new anointing and power. A great revival spread all over the island of Anglesea, and then over all of Wales. The people were often so affected by Evans' sermons that they literally danced for joy, and their actions obtained for them the nickname of "the Welsh jumpers." Often the audiences were moved to weeping and tears. Once when Evans preached concerning the demoniac of Gadara, and vividly portrayed the deliverance of the demoniac and especially the joy of the demoniac's wife and children when he returned home healed and saved, the audience laughed and wept alternately. Shouts of prayer and praise mingled together. One who heard this wonderful sermon said that, near the end, the people seemed like the inhabitants of a city that had been shaken by an earthquake, who rushed into the streets in their escape, falling upon the earth, screaming and calling upon God.

The powerful sermons, the breath of heaven, the weeping, the praising, and the return of sinners to God now characterized Evans' meetings wherever he went. This was especially true when he preached his famous "graveyard sermon," in which he described the world as dead and buried in the graveyard of Law, with Justice guarding the gates but Mercy coming to unlock them. This sermon has been widely published. The preaching of it brought conviction of sin like a deluge over the people.

Evans was a man whose very name could wake up all the sleepy villages of a town and cause their inhabitants to pour up by the hills and down by the valleys. These expectant crowds would watch his appearance with tears, sometimes hailing him with shouts. "It must be said, his are very great sermons," said the Reverend Paxton Hood. "I am almost disposed to describe them as the grandest gospel sermons of the last hundred years." One biographer described Evans' manner while preaching as follows:

Christmas Evans, meantime, is pursuing his way, lost in his theme. Now his eye lights up... like a brilliantly flashing star. His clear forehead expands, his form dilates in majestic dignity, and all that has gone before will be lost in the white-heat passion with which he prepares to sing of paradise lost and paradise regained.

The anointing of the Holy Spirit was the great secret of Evans' power. Writing to a young minister, Evans said,

You will observe that some heavenly ornaments and powers from on high are visible in many ministers when they are under divine inspiration. You cannot approach this by merely imitating their artistic excellence, without resembling them in their spiritual taste, fervency, and zeal that Christ and His Spirit work in them. This will not only cause you to be like them in gracefulness of action and propriety of elocution, but it will also induce prayer for the anointing of the Holy One, which works mightily in the inward man. This is the mystery of effective preaching. We must be filled with power from on high.

Evans collected much money for the building of churches, the Baptist churches of Anglesea being more than doubled under his ministry. In one place where he was raising money to build a chapel, the money came very slowly, although the audiences were very large. There had been much sheep-stealing in the neighborhood, and Evans decided to use this fact to advantage in collecting money. He told the people that undoubtedly some of the sheep-stealers must be present in the congregation, and he hoped that they would not throw any money into the collection. A big collection was taken. Those who did not have any money to give borrowed from their neighbors to put in the collection.

"Dear old Christmas," as he was familiarly called in his old age, finished his course with joy. He fell asleep in Christ on July 23, 1838, with a song of victory on his lips.

Chapter 12

Charles Finney

❦

I am inclined to regard Charles Finney as the greatest evangelist and theologian since the days of the apostles. It is estimated that during the years 1857–58, over 100,000 people were led to Christ as the direct or indirect result of Finney's labors, while 500,000 people professed conversion to Christ in the great revival that began in his meetings. Another remarkable fact—and this was found by actual research—is that over 85 of every one 100 people professing conversion to Christ in Finney's meetings remained true to God, whereas 70 percent of those professing conversion in the meetings of even as great an evangelist as Moody afterward became backsliders. Finney seemed to have had the power of impressing the consciences of men with the necessity of holy living in such a manner as to procure the most lasting results.

The Autobiography of Charles G. Finney is perhaps the most remarkable account of the manifestations of the Holy Spirit's power since apostolic days. It is crowded with accounts of spiritual outpourings that remind one of the Day of Pentecost. Finney's *Systematic Theology* is considered to be one of the greatest works on theology outside the Scriptures. The wonderful anointing of God's Spirit, combined with Finney's remarkable reasoning powers and his legal training, enabled him to present clearer views of Christian doctrine than any other theologian since the days of early Christianity. His views with regard to the difference between physical and moral law and physical and moral depravity, on the reasonableness of the moral law and the Atonement, and on the nature of regeneration and sanctification are the clearest of any I have had the privilege of reading or hearing. Finney's teachings probably did more than all other causes combined to bring the old-school Calvinists over to a belief in man's free will and moral responsibility, or the views commonly known as new-school Calvinism.

Charles Grandison Finney was a descendant of the New England Puritans and was born in Connecticut in 1792. He moved to western New York with his parents when he was two years of age. This part of New York was then a frontier wilderness, with few educational or religious privileges. Finney had a good public school education, however, and at twenty years of age he went to New England to attend high school, but soon afterward went to New Jersey to teach school and to continue his studies. He became quite proficient in Latin, Greek, and Hebrew, and in other college studies. In 1818 he commenced the study of law in the office of Squire Wright, of Adams, a town near his old home in western New York.

At Adams, Finney had his first religious privileges. During the three years he taught school in New Jersey, about the only preaching in his neighborhood was in German, and the preaching he heard while at high school in New England was not of a kind calculated to grab his attention. The old preacher who spoke there read old manuscript sermons in a monotonous, humdrum way that made no serious impression on the mind of Finney. Finney's parents were not professing Christians, and in his childhood days in western New York, the only preaching he heard was during an occasional visit from some itinerant preacher. At Adams, while studying law, he attended the Presbyterian Church. The pastor, George W. Gale, was an able and highly educated man. His preaching, though of the old-school Calvinistic type, grabbed the attention of Finney, although to his keen and logical mind it seemed like a mass of absurdities and contradictions.

It was while studying law and attending church at Adams that Finney became interested in Bible study. He found so many references to the Scriptures in his law books, he decided to buy himself a Bible, and he soon became deeply absorbed in studying it. He had many conversations with Mr. Gale, who frequently dropped into the office to talk with him, but they could scarcely agree on any point of doctrine. This fact probably led Finney to study the Scriptures much more diligently than if he had agreed with Mr. Gale in everything.

The fact that the church members were constantly praying prayers that seemed to expect an answer was a great drawback to Finney. But he became more and more concerned about his own soul. He felt that if there was a life beyond, he was not prepared for it. Some of the church members wanted to pray for him, but he told them that he did not see that it would do any good because they were continually asking without receiving.

Finney remained in a skeptical yet troubled frame of mind for two or three years. At last he came to a decision that the Bible was the true Word of God and that it was the fault of the people if their prayers were not answered. He was then brought face-to-face with the question as to whether or not he would accept Christ. "On a Sabbath evening, in the autumn of 1821," he said, "I made up my mind that I would settle the question of my soul's salvation immediately, that if it were possible I would make my peace with God." He was obliged to be in the office, however, and could not devote the entire time to seeking his soul's salvation, although on the following Monday and Tuesday he spent most of his time in prayer and reading the Scriptures.

Pride was the great obstacle that hindered him from accepting Christ as his Savior. He found that he was unwilling to have anyone know that he was seeking salvation. Before praying, he plugged the keyhole of the door and then only prayed in a whisper for fear that someone would hear him. If he was reading the Bible when anyone came in, he would throw his law books on top of it to create the impression that he had been reading them instead of the Bible.

During Monday and Tuesday, his conviction of sin increased, but his heart seemed to grow harder. Tuesday night he had become very nervous and imagined that he was about to die and sink into hell, but he quieted himself as best he could until morning. Next morning, on the way to the office, he had as clear a view of the atonement of Christ as he ever had afterward. The Holy Spirit seemed to present Christ hanging on the cross for him. The vision was so clear that, almost unconsciously, he stopped in the middle of the street for several minutes when it came to him. North of the village and over a hill lay a wooded area, and he decided to go there and pour out his heart in prayer. So great was his pride, he kept out of sight as far as possible for fear that someone would see him on the way to the woods and would think that he was going there to pray.

Finney penetrated far into the woods to where some large trees had fallen across each other, leaving an open space between. He crept into this space to pray. "But when I attempted to pray," said he, "I found that my heart would not pray." He was in great fear, lest someone would come and find him praying. He was on the verge of despair, having promised God not to leave the spot until he settled the question of his soul's salvation, and yet it seemed impossible to him to settle the question. "Just at this moment," said Finney,

> I again thought I heard someone approach me, and I opened my eyes to see if it were so. But just then the revelation of my pride of heart, as the great difficulty that stood in the way, was distinctly shown me. An overwhelming sense of my wickedness in being ashamed to have a human being see me on my knees before God, took such powerful possession of me, that I cried at the top of my voice and exclaimed that I would not leave that place if all the men on earth and all the devils in hell surrounded me.

Finney was completely humbled by the thought of his pride. Then the most comforting verses of Scripture seemed to pour into his soul. He saw clearly that faith was not an intellectual state but a voluntary act, and he accepted the promise of God.

Promises of salvation, from both Old and New Testaments, continued to pour into his soul, and he continued to pray. "I prayed," said he, "until my mind became so full that, before I was aware of it, I was on my feet and tripping up the hill toward the road." On reaching the village, he found that it was noon, although he had gone into the woods immediately after an early breakfast. He had been so absorbed in prayer that he had no idea of the time. There was now a great calm in his soul, and the burden of sin had completely rolled away, yet he was tempted to believe that he was not yet born of God. He went to his dinner, but found that he had no appetite. He then went to the office and took down his bass viol and began to play some hymns, but his soul was so overflowing that he could not sing without weeping.

On the evening of the same day in which Finney received this pardon of his sins, he received a mighty,

overwhelming baptism of the Holy Spirit, which
started him immediately to preaching the Gospel. Continuing the narrative of his conversion, he described
this filling of the Spirit:

> After dinner we [Squire Wright and him-
> self] were engaged in moving the books and fur-
> niture to another office. We were very busy in
> this and had but little conversation the whole af-
> ternoon. My mind, however, remained in that
> profoundly tranquil state. There was a great
> sweetness and tenderness in my thoughts and
> feelings. Everything appeared to be going right,
> and nothing seemed to disturb me or ruffle me in
> the least.
>
> Just before evening the thought took pos-
> session of my mind, that as soon as I was left
> alone in the new office, I would try to pray
> again—that I was not going to abandon the sub-
> ject of religion and give it up, at any rate; and
> therefore, although I no longer had any concern
> about my soul, still, I would continue to pray.
>
> By evening we got the books and furniture
> adjusted; and I built a fire in the open fireplace,
> hoping to spend the evening alone. Just at dark
> Squire Wright, seeing that everything was ad-
> justed, bid me goodnight and went to his home. I
> had accompanied him to the door; and as I closed
> the door and turned around, my heart seemed to
> be liquid within me. All my feelings seemed to
> rise and flow out; and the utterance of my heart
> was, "I want to pour my whole soul out to God."
> The rising of my soul was so great that I rushed
> into the room behind the front office, to pray.
>
> There was no fire, and no light, in the room;
> nevertheless, it appeared to me as if it were per-
> fectly light. As I went in and shut the door after
> me, it seemed as if I met the Lord Jesus Christ
> face-to-face. It seemed to me that I saw Him as I
> would see any other man. He said nothing, but

looked at me in such a manner as to break me right down at His feet. I have always since regarded this as a most remarkable state of mind, for it seemed to me a reality, that He stood before me, and I fell down at His feet and poured out my soul to Him. I wept aloud like a child and made such confession as I could with my choked speech. It seemed to me that I bathed His feet with my tears, and yet I had no distinct impression that I touched Him, that I recall.

I must have continued in this state for a good while, but my mind was too much absorbed with the interview to recall anything that I said. But I know, as soon as my mind became calm enough to break off from the interview, I returned to the front office and found that the fire that I had made of large wood was nearly burned out. But as I turned and was about to take a seat by the fire, I received a mighty baptism of the Holy Spirit.

Without any expectation of it, without ever having the thought in my mind that there was any such thing for me, without any recollection that I had ever heard the thing mentioned by any person in the world, the Holy Spirit descended on me in a manner that seemed to go through me, body and soul. I could feel the impression, like a wave of electricity, going through and through me. Indeed, it seemed to come in waves and waves of liquid love, for I could not express it in any other way. It seemed like the very breath of God. I can recall distinctly that it seemed to fan me, like immense wings.

No words can express the wonderful love that was shed abroad in my heart. I wept aloud with joy and love, and I literally bellowed out the unutterable gushings of my heart. The waves came over me and over me, one after the other, until I recall I cried out, "I will die if these waves continue to pass over me." I said, "Lord, I cannot bear any more," yet I had no fear of death.

Finney continued for some time under this re-markable manifestation of the Holy Spirit's power. Wave after wave of spiritual power rolled over him and through him, thrilling every fiber of his being. Late in the evening, a member of his choir—for Finney was the leader of the choir—came into the office. He was a member of the church, but was astonished to see Fin-ney weeping under the power of the Spirit. After ask-ing a few questions, he went out to find an elder of the church who was a very serious man, but who laughed with joy when he saw Finney weeping under the Spirit's power. A young man who had associated much with Finney came into the office while Finney was trying to relate his experience to the elder and the member of the choir. He listened with astonishment to what Finney was saying and suddenly fell upon the floor, crying out in the greatest agony of mind and saying, "Do pray for me!"

Although he had experienced such a remarkable baptism of the Holy Spirit, Finney was tempted the same night to believe that he had been deluded in some way or other, and that he had not received the real baptism of the Spirit. "I soon fell asleep," said he,

> but almost as soon woke again on account of the great flow of the love of God that was in my heart. I was so filled with love that I could not sleep. Soon I fell asleep again and awoke in the same manner. When I awoke, this temptation would return upon me, and the love that seemed to be in my heart would abate; but as soon as I was asleep, it was so warm within me that I would immediately awake. Thus I continued un-til, late at night, I obtained some sound sleep.
>
> When I awoke in the morning, the sun had risen and was pouring a clear light into my room. Words cannot express the impression that the sunlight made upon me. Instantly, the bap-tism that I had received the day before returned

upon me in the same manner. I arose upon my knees in the bed and wept aloud with joy, and I remained for some time too much overwhelmed with the baptism of the Spirit to do anything but pour out my soul to God. It seemed as if this morning's baptism was accompanied with a gentle reproof, and the Spirit seemed to say to me, "Will you doubt? Will you doubt?" I cried, "No! I will not doubt; I cannot doubt." The Spirit then cleared the subject up so much in my mind that it was impossible for me to doubt that the Spirit of God had taken possession of my soul.

On the morning just described, Finney went to his office, and the waves of power continued to flood his soul. When Squire Wright came into the office, Finney said a few words to him about the salvation of his soul. He made no reply but dropped his head and went away. Finney said, "I thought no more of it then, but afterward I found that the remark I made pierced him like a sword; and he did not recover from it until he was converted."

Almost every person Finney spoke to during the day was stricken with conviction of sin and afterward found peace with God. His words seemed to pierce their hearts like arrows. Although he had been fond of law, Finney now lost all taste for it and for every other secular business. His whole desire now was to preach the Gospel and to win men to Christ. Nothing else seemed of any consequence. He left the office and went out to talk to individuals concerning the salvation of their souls. Among those brought to Christ through his efforts that day were a Universalist and a distiller.

During the day, there had been much conversation and excitement concerning Finney's conversion, and in the evening most of the people in the village gathered at the church, although no meeting had been appointed as far as Finney knew. All the people seemed to be waiting for him to speak, and he arose and related what the Lord had done for his soul. A certain Mr. C——, who was present, was so convicted of sin that he arose and rushed out and went home without his hat. Many others were also deeply convicted of sin. Finney spoke and prayed with liberty, although he had never prayed in public before. The meeting was a wonderful one, and from that day, meetings were held every night for some time. The revival spread among all classes in the village and to many surrounding places. All of Finney's former companions, with one exception, were brought to Christ.

Finney soon visited his home at Henderson, New York, and his parents were brought to Christ. On his return to Adams, he continued his meetings and spent much time in fasting and prayer. One time, as he approached the meetinghouse, "a light perfectly ineffable" shone in his soul and almost prostrated him to the ground. It seemed greater than the light of the noonday sun, as did the light that prostrated Saul on the way to Damascus. (See Acts 26:12–14.) Many were brought to Christ, and some were healed in body, in answer to Finney's prayers. He now learned what it was to have real travail of soul for the unsaved. "When Zion travails she shall bring forth" (see Isaiah 66:8) became a precious promise to him.

Soon after receiving the anointing of the Holy Spirit, Finney had a lengthy conversation with his pastor, Mr. Gale, concerning the advisability of preparing for the ministry. Mr. Gale was a graduate of Princeton University but was a full believer in the old-school Calvinistic doctrines, which to Finney's mind seemed very absurd and contradictory. Mr. Gale and he could scarcely agree on any point of doctrine. Mr. Gale believed in the doctrine of a limited atonement, or that Christ died only for the elect, while Finney believed that He died for all. Mr. Gale believed that men were so depraved by nature that they had no free will, while Finney believed that all men had the power to accept or reject salvation. Mr. Gale believed that Christ paid the exact penalty of the sinner, while Finney believed that He did not bear the exact penalty but that He bore sufficient penalty to enable God to forgive sin without mankind thinking that He was allowing sin to go unpunished.

Notwithstanding their differences, Finney, in 1822, placed himself under the care of the Presbytery as a candidate for the ministry. Some of the ministers urged him to go to Princeton, but he declined. They then appointed Mr. Gale to superintend his studies. His studies, as far as Mr. Gale was concerned, were only a series of controversies, but he made good use of Mr. Gale's library. He felt that he would rather not preach than teach the doctrines held by Mr. Gale, but a good elder in the church who held similar views to Finney gave him much encouragement and prayed with him frequently.

During the few months that Finney studied under Mr. Gale, a Universalist minister came to Adams and greatly disturbed the faith of many. Finney replied to his arguments and completely overthrew them.

In 1824 the Presbytery was finally called together at Adams, and Finney was licensed to preach. The two written sermons he prepared for them were, with two other exceptions, the only written sermons he ever prepared. He tried one other time to preach from a written sermon but believed that it hindered the Spirit of God from speaking through him.

Finney's first regular meetings were held at Evans Mills, Oneida County, New York. The people praised his sermons, but for two or three weeks no one decided for Christ. Then Finney urged all who were willing to accept Christ to rise to their feet and all who were willing to reject Him to remain on their seats. This was very unusual in those days and made the people so angry that they were almost ready to mob Finney. The next day, he spent the day in fasting and prayer, and in

the evening preached with such anointing and power
that a great conviction of sin swept over the people. All
night long they were sending for him to come and pray
with them. Even hardened atheists were brought to
Christ.

He continued to preach the Gospel with increasing
power and results, visiting many of the leading cities of
America and Great Britain. Sometimes the power of
God was so manifest in his meetings that almost the
entire audience fell on their knees in prayer or were
prostrated on the floor. When in the pulpit, Finney
sometimes felt almost lifted off his feet by the power of
the Spirit of God. Some people believe that the work of
the Holy Spirit is not accompanied by any physical
manifestations, but both in Bible times and in Finney's
meetings remarkable physical manifestations seemed
to accompany the work of the Holy Spirit when the
work was deep and powerful. At times, when Finney
was speaking, the power of the Spirit seemed to de-
scend like a cloud of glory upon him. Often a hallowed
calm, noticeable even to the unsaved, seemed to settle
down upon cities where he was holding meetings. Sinners were often brought under conviction of sin almost
as soon as they entered these cities.

Finney seemed so anointed with the Holy Spirit
that people were often brought under conviction of sin
just by looking at him. When holding meetings at
Utica, New York, he visited a large factory there and
was looking at the machinery. At the sight of him, several of the workers broke down and wept under a sense
of their sins, and finally so many were sobbing and
weeping that the machinery had to be stopped while
Finney pointed them to Christ.

At a country place named Sodom, in the state of
New York, Finney gave one address in which he described the condition of Sodom before God destroyed it.
"I had not spoken in this strain more than fifteen minutes," said Finney,

when an awful solemnity seemed to settle upon them. The congregation began to fall from their seats in every direction, and they cried for mercy. If I had had a sword in each hand, I could not have cut them down as fast as they fell. Nearly the whole congregation were either on their knees or prostrate, I should think, in less than two minutes from the first shock that fell upon them. Everyone prayed who was able to speak at all.

Similar scenes were witnessed in many other places. In London, England, between 1,500 and 2,000 people were seeking salvation in one day in Finney's meetings. Enormous numbers inquired the way of salvation in his meetings in New York, Boston, Rochester, and many other important cities of America. The great revival of 1858–59, one of the greatest revivals in the world's history, was the direct result of his meetings. "That was the greatest work of God and the greatest revival of religion the world has ever seen," said Dr. Lyman Beecher. It is estimated that 600,000 people were brought to Christ in this revival.

In 1833 Finney became a Congregationalist and later a founder and first president of Oberlin College, Ohio. The great objective in founding this college was to train students for the ministry. The remainder of Finney's time was divided between his work at Oberlin and holding meetings in different parts of the country.

Finney's writings have had an enormous circulation and have greatly influenced the religious life of the world. This is especially true of his *Autobiography,* his *Lectures on Revivals,* his *Lectures to Professing Christians,* and his *Systematic Theology.* These books have all had a worldwide circulation.

Finney continued to preach and to lecture to the students at Oberlin until two weeks before he was eighty-three years of age, when he was called up higher to enjoy the reward of those who have turned many to righteousness.

Chapter 13

Billy Bray

⟡

G od sometimes uses weak vessels in a most marvelous way. Billy Bray, the famous Cornish miner, was perhaps one of the quaintest vessels ever used by God to accomplish a great work of any kind. Before his conversion to Christ, he was a drunken, profligate miner; but after the Spirit of the Lord took possession of him, he became such a burning, shining light for Christ that his name is now known all over the world. From one end of Cornwall, England, to the other, scarcely any name is better known than that of Billy Bray.

Billy Bray was born in 1794, at Twelveheads, a village near Truro, in Cornwall, England. His grandfather had joined the Methodists under the preaching of John Wesley. Billy's father was also a Christian but died when his children were all quite young. Billy lived with his grandfather until he was seventeen years of age and then went to Devonshire, where he lived a very wicked and sinful life. He was both drunken and lascivious. One night he and a companion were going home drunk from Tavistock when they met a big horse and climbed on his back. The horse threw them and nearly killed them.

Billy had many other narrow escapes from death. After his conversion to Christ, he often said, "The Lord was good to me when I was the servant of the Devil or I would have been down in hell now." Once he was nearly killed in a mine. He ran out just about a minute before the mine caved in. He became so great a drunkard that his wife had to bring him away from the saloons night after night. "I never got drunk without feeling condemned for it," he afterward said.

Billy was led to Christ, or rather, was convicted of sin, through reading Bunyan's *Visions of Heaven and Hell*. When he was seeking the Lord, he went a mile one Sunday morning to attend a meeting of the Bible Christians. It was a wet day, and no one came. This had a discouraging effect on him. After he had been seeking salvation for a long time, the Devil strongly tempted him to believe that he would never find mercy. "But," said Billy, "I said to him 'You are a liar, Devil,' and as soon as I said so, I felt the weight gone from my mind, and I could praise the Lord."

In the evening on the same day, after he had gone home from work, he went into his room alone and said, "Lord, You have said, *'Ask, and it will be given to you; seek, and you will find; knock, and it will be opened to you'* (Matt. 7:7), and I have faith enough to believe it." This brought joy to his soul. "In an instant," said he, "the Lord made me so happy that I cannot express what I felt. I shouted for joy." This was in 1823.

After his conversion, Billy became a very happy Christian and also a very earnest worker for the salvation of others. This was especially true after he was led into a deeper, richer, and fuller Christian experience than he had received when he converted to Christ. The following account of how he was led into this deeper experience is from *The King's Son: A Memoir of Billy Bray*, by F. W. Bourne:

> It is more important to speak of his deep piety, his abiding sense of the divine favor, the secret of his great usefulness, the source of his

constant and perpetual joy. The *"much fruit"* (John 15:5) that is so pleasing to God cannot come unless the roots have struck deep into the soil. Religion is not shallow in its nature. *"The water that I shall give* [you]," said the Savior, *"will become in* [you] *a fountain of water springing up into everlasting life"* (John 4:14).

Very early in his religious history, Billy felt it was both his duty and his privilege to be sanctified wholly, to use an apostolic phrase. "I remember being at a meeting," he said, "at Hick's Mill Chapel one Sunday morning, when a stranger led the class. The leader asked one of our members whether he could say that the Lord had cleansed him from all sin, and he could not. 'That,' I said in my mind, 'is sanctification; I will have that blessing by the help of the Lord.' And I went on my knees at once, and cried to the Lord to sanctify me wholly—body, spirit, and soul. And the Lord said to me, *'Ye are clean through the word which I have spoken unto you'* (John 15:3 KJV). And I said, 'Lord, I believe it.' When the leader came to me, I told him, 'Four months ago I was a great sinner against God. Since that time I have been justified freely by His grace, and while I have been here this morning, the Lord has sanctified me wholly.' When I had finished telling what the Lord had done for me, the leader said, 'If you can believe it, it is so.' Then I said, 'I can believe it.' When I had told him so, such joy filled my heart that I cannot find words to tell of it. After the meeting was over, everything around me seemed so full of glory that it dazzled my sight. I had a *'joy inexpressible and full of glory'* (1 Pet. 1:8)."

Some may not agree with the way in which Billy came to be sanctified. It seems unwise, to say the least, to tell a believer that he is sanctified if he believes he is, or to tell a penitent that he is saved if he only believes he is. There is a more excellent way. But from that time, Billy did not live for himself, but for Him who died for him and rose again.

Billy set the Lord always before him. (See Psalm 16:8.) His path was like the light that shines more and more to the perfect Day (Prov. 4:18). *Justified, sanctified,* and *sealed* were successive steps in Christian experience, clearer to him perhaps than to others. His faith did not become feeble, but became stronger and stronger; his love for the Savior grew in intensity until it became the absorbing passion of his soul; and his hope brightened into heavenly radiance and splendor. The freshness, the delicacy, and the fragrance of richest Christian experience seemed always to be his.

After the experience related above, Billy often felt the love of God overflowing his soul, so much so that he frequently shouted aloud or danced for joy. His Christian experience was so happy, so bright, so trustful, and so sunshiny that many of the great individuals of the world have been highly interested in the story of his life. Among these were Queen Victoria, Charles Spurgeon, and many leading ministers of Britain and America. His name is a household word throughout Cornwall, where he labored so earnestly for the salvation of others.

Billy did not have the gloomy, dismal, sorrowful religion that so many professing Christians seem to have. His was the joyous, victorious Christian experience that attracts sinners to Christ as honey attracts the bees. Sinners want a religion that will give them victory over sin, and wherever this kind of religion is preached, souls are won to Christ. But the gloomy, dismal testimony does not attract souls to Christ. In the Methodist church at St. Blazey, Billy heard the people telling about their many trials and difficulties. He arose, smiling and clapping his hands, and said,

"Well, friends, I have been taking vinegar and honey, but, praise the Lord, I've had the vinegar with a spoon and the honey with a ladle." His testimony was always one of joy and victory.

Speaking concerning the Lord, Billy said,

> He has made me glad, and no one can make me sad. He makes me shout, and no one can make me doubt. He makes me dance and leap, and there is no one who can keep down my feet. I sometimes feel so much of the power of God that, I believe, if they were to cut off my feet, I would heave up the stumps.

Billy often literally danced for joy. One time he became so happy on his way home from the market that a new garment for his little girl fell out of the basket in which he was carrying it. It was found later and was returned to him. Some objected to his dancing and shouting, but Billy justified himself by referring to how Miriam and David danced before the Lord, and to the example of the cripple at the gate Beautiful who, after he was healed, leaped and walked and praised God. Billy also said that it was prophesied that *"the lame shall leap like a deer"* (Isa. 35:6). "I can't help praising God," he once said.

> As I go along the street, I lift up one foot, and it seems to say, "Glory!" and I lift up the other, and it seems to say, "Amen"; and so they keep on like that the entire time I am walking.

Even when his wife died, Billy jumped around the room with joy, exclaiming, "Bless the Lord! My dear Joey has gone up with the bright ones! My dear Joey has gone up with the shining angels! Glory! Glory!" He believed that afflictions were a special mark of God's favor and that Christians ought to rejoice in them.

To those who objected to his shouting so much, Billy once said, "If they were to put me in a barrel, I would shout glory out through the bunghole! Praise the Lord!" Someone asked him one time, when he was praising the Lord, if he did not think that people sometimes got in such a habit of praising the Lord that they did not know what they were saying. He very coolly replied that he did not think that the Lord was much troubled with that class of people. At a meeting at Hick's Mill in 1866, a Mr. Oliver told how triumphantly a dying woman expired shouting victory. "Glory!" shouted Billy. "If a dying woman praised the Lord, I should think a living man might do the same." When Billy heard the news of a certain preacher's death, he said, "So he has finished with the doubters and has gone up with the shouters."

"Some can only eat out of the silent dish," said Billy, "but I cannot eat only out of that. I must eat out of the shouting dish, the jumping dish, and every other dish." He often spoke of his determination to enjoy the abundance of his Father's house. "My comrades used to tell me," said he, "that dancing, shouting, and making so much fuss was no religion, but I was born in the fire and could not lie in the smoke."

When Billy met people, he often urged them to say "amen," and if they did not do so, he was not satisfied with their Christian experience. The first thing he inquired when meeting anyone was about their soul, and if he got an assuring answer, he would shout for joy. He would shout for joy when he heard of souls being saved anywhere. He would sometimes pick people up and carry them around because he was so happy. He picked up several ministers and carried them around in this way when he became very happy in the meetings. Such actions caused some people to criticize him. "They said I was a madman, but they meant I was a *glad* man," said he.

Like all great soulwinners, Billy spent much time in prayer. Before going anywhere, he would ask the Lord to keep the Devil from scratching him while he was traveling. The Devil was very real to him.

When tempted by Satan at one time, Billy said, "What an old fool you are; I have been battling with you for twenty-eight years, and I have always beat you, and I always will." One time, when Billy's potato crop was very poor, Satan tempted him to believe that God did not love him, or He would have given him a better potato crop. Billy recognized this as a temptation from the Devil, and he said, "I have a written description of your character at my house, and it does say that you are 'a liar from the beginning' (see John 8:44)." Billy then recounted God's blessings until the Devil "went off as if he'd been shot."

Some of the ruffians of the town, knowing that Billy had a very strong belief in Satan and a very wholesome fear of him, thought they would frighten him by hiding near the road at night and making unearthly noises. Billy paid no attention to their noises but went on his way singing. At last one of them near the road said, "But I'm the Devil up here in the hedge, Billy Bray." "Bless the Lord! Bless the Lord!" exclaimed Billy. "I did not know you were so far away."

Not only did Billy pray much, but like all others who pray much, he also had great faith in the Lord, and his prayers were often answered in a most remarkable manner. One time his child was very sick, and his wife feared it would die and urged him to go for a doctor. Billy took all the money he had, which was 18 pence, and went out to find a doctor. On the way, he met a poor man who had lost a cow and who was trying to get enough money to purchase another. His story touched Billy's heart so much that he gave him the 18 pence. Not having any money left, he could not go for a doctor. He then went behind a hedge and told his heavenly Father all about it and asked for the child's healing. The child soon became well.

One day when Billy had no money, not having received his wages for some time, he took the matter to the Lord in prayer. He had bacon and potatoes but no bread in the house. He went to the captain of the mine and borrowed 10 shillings. On the way home, he found two families more destitute than himself. He gave them each 5 shillings and went home without any money. His wife felt blue, but Billy affirmed that the Lord would not remain in their debt very long. Soon a sovereign was given to them by a lady.

Billy said that he was working for a big firm—the Father, Son, and Holy Spirit—and that he had great confidence in them. Once he said,

> If Billy gets work, he praises the Lord; when he gets none, he sings all the same. Do you think that He will starve Billy? No, no, there is sure to be a bit of flour in the bottom of the barrel for Billy. I can trust in Jesus, and while I trust Him, He'd as soon starve Michael the Archangel as He'd starve Billy.

Billy was a hard worker. He often worked twenty hours out of the twenty-four, building meetinghouses with his own hands after working his regular shift in the mines. One time he went to the town of St. Ives to get money for one of his chapels. But the fish had been so few that season that the fishermen did not have any money to give him. Billy and others prayed earnestly for fish, and the fishermen caught thousands upon thousands.

Billy worked and prayed earnestly for the salvation of souls and won many to Christ. About a year after his conversion, his name was placed on the local preachers' list at the Bible Christian Church, a branch of the Methodists. But he was more of an exhorter than a preacher, although he often conducted and spoke in meetings. His principal work in soulwinning was probably done outside the pulpit, for he was always busy trying to win souls for Christ. He would pray for his fellow miners before they went to work in the mornings. "Lord," he would say, "if any of us must be killed, or die today, let it be me; do not let one of these men die, for they are not happy, and I am. If I die today I will go to heaven."

He often visited the sick and dying. When ministering to the dying, he often expressed a wish that he might "see them in heaven, dressed in robes of glorious brightness; for," he would add in his quietest vein of humor, "if I saw them there, I must be there, too. They say that every man has a little of self, and so have I."

One time when Billy was walking over a certain hill, the Lord seemed to say to him, "I will give you all who dwell on this mountain." He prayed for and visited the people in the three houses on the hill until they were all brought to the Lord. Then he complained to the Lord that there were only three houses on the hill, and the Lord showed him there would be more. Long after this, an Episcopal church and parsonage were built on the hill. Billy heard of it and visited the church. He was disgusted to find the preacher a "Puseyite," or extreme High Churchman. This made him unhappy until he reflected that he had visited the place before the Lord told him to do so.

After some time, the clergyman's gardener, who was also a ritualist, was converted to Christ. His pastor was displeased but was afterward deeply convicted of sin and was himself converted to Christ. One night, about 11:30 P.M., as Billy was going to bed, the Lord showed him that he could now visit the hill. He hitched up the donkey cart and started, reaching the hill the next morning. The pastor heard someone coming through the hallway praising the Lord and guessed that it was Billy Bray. He and his wife and servants and Billy Bray had a great time of rejoicing together. Billy then visited the other houses on the hill and found the people all converted, and he was almost beside himself with joy.

Billy used some very original illustrations in his sermons. Before his conversion, he was an inveterate smoker. He would sooner have gone into the mine without his dinner than without his pipe. But the Lord so thoroughly saved him from this habit that he threw away his pipe and became an opponent of the use of tobacco in every form. He frequently said that if the Lord had intended people to snuff, He would have turned their noses upside down, and that if He had intended them to smoke, He would have put a chimney in the back of their heads. He said that an architect who would build a house so that all the smoke had to come out at the front door was in his opinion a very poor architect, and surely the Lord could not be a worse architect than man.

Not only did Billy oppose the use of tobacco, but he was also a strong advocate of temperance. "Men set lime-twigs to catch birds," said he, "and Satan sets wine bottles and beer mugs to catch fools."

Worldly dress and extravagance were also things of which Billy did not approve. "I would rather walk to heaven than ride to hell in a fine carriage," he said. Speaking concerning fasting, Billy said, "If the members of the churches would mortify the flesh more, and not gratify it, they would be much happier than they are." When someone asked Billy how the world was getting on now, he said, "I don't know, for I haven't been there for twelve years."

Billy was a poor singer but was often singing. He affirmed that the Lord liked to hear him sing. "Oh, yes, bless the Lord! I can sing," he would say. "My heavenly Father likes to hear me sing as well as those who can sing better than I can. My Father likes to hear the crow as well as the nightingale."

After a nice meetinghouse was built in one place, Billy was called upon with others to speak at the dedication. "I told the people," said Billy,

> that the dear Lord had given them a pretty chapel to worship in; and now He wanted good furniture, for bad furniture looks disgraceful in a good house. I told them that the good furniture for the house of the Lord was sanctified souls. We must be pardoned, sanctified, and sealed, and then we will not only be fit for the Lord's house on earth, but we will also be good furniture in heaven.

Billy had one illustration that always appealed very forcibly to the miners. He portrayed himself as working all week at a poor mine, where the pay was very poor, and then on payday going to a good mine, where the wages were good, to get his pay. He asked if that would not be a very foolish thing to do, and then pointed out how that many people are working for Satan and expecting God to save them in the end.

When Billy lay dying, and the doctor told him that he was going to die, he said, "Glory! Glory be to God! I will soon be in heaven." He then added, in his own peculiar way, "When I get up there, may I give them your compliments, doctor, and tell them you will be coming, too?" This made a deep impression on the doctor. Billy's dying word was "Glory!" A little while before dying, he said,

> What? Can I fear death? Could I be lost? Why, my Savior conquered death. If I were to go down to hell, I would shout glory to my blessed Jesus until I made the bottomless pit ring again, and the miserable old Satan would say, "Billy, Billy, this is no place for you; go back!" Then up to heaven I would go, shouting glory and praise to the Lord!

Billy fell asleep in Christ in 1868.

The following verse is from one man's poetical tribute to Billy:

> His fare was sometimes scanty,
>   And earnest was the fight;
> But his dear Lord provided,
>   And with him all was right.
> His dress was always homely—
>   His dwelling somewhat poor,
> But the presence of his Savior
>   Made up for that and more.

Chapter 14

George Müller

⁓

A mong the greatest monuments of what can be accomplished through simple faith in God are the great orphanages covering thirteen acres of ground at Ashley Downs, Bristol, England. When God put it into the heart of George Müller to build these orphanages, he had only 2 shillings in his pocket. Without making his needs known to any man, but to God alone, over £1,400,000 was sent to him for the building and maintaining of these orphan homes. When I first visited them, near the time of Müller's death, there were five immense buildings of solid granite, capable of accommodating 2,000 orphans. In all the years since the first orphans arrived, the Lord had sent food in due time, so that they had never missed a meal.

Although George Müller became famous as one of the greatest men of prayer known to history, he was not always a saint. He wandered very deeply into sin before he was brought to Christ. He was born in Prussia in 1805. His father was a revenue collector for the government and was a worldly-minded man. He supplied George and his brother with plenty of money when they were boys, and they spent it very foolishly. George deceived his father about how much money he spent, and also as to how he spent it. He also stole the government money during his father's absence.

At ten years of age, George was sent to the cathedral classical school at Halberstadt. His father wanted to make a Lutheran clergyman of him, not that he might serve God, but that he might have an easy and comfortable living from the state church. "My time," said Müller,

> was now spent in studying, reading novels, and indulging, though so young, in sinful practices. Thus it continued until I was fourteen years old, when my mother suddenly fell ill and died. The night she was dying, I, not knowing of her illness, was playing cards until two in the morning, and on the next day, a Sunday, I went with some of my companions in sin to a tavern, and then, being filled with strong beer, we went about the streets half intoxicated.
>
> I grew worse and worse. Three or four days before I was confirmed (and thus admitted to partake of the Lord's Supper), I was guilty of gross immorality. And the very day before my confirmation, when I was in the vestry with the clergyman to confess my sins (according to the usual practice), I defrauded him, for I handed over to him only a twelfth of the fee that my father had given me for him.

A few solemn thoughts and desires to lead a better life came to him, but he continued to plunge deeper and deeper into sin. Lying, stealing, gambling, licentiousness, extravagance, and almost every form of sin was indulged in by him. No one would have imagined that the sinful youth would ever become eminent for his faith in God and for his power in prayer. He robbed his father of certain monies that he had been entrusted to collect, falsifying the accounts of what he had received and pocketing the balance. His money was spent on sinful pleasures, and once he was reduced to such poverty that, in order to satisfy his hunger, he stole a piece of bread, the allowance of a soldier who was quartered in the house where he was.

In 1821 Müller set off on an excursion to Magdeburg, where he spent six days in much sin. He then went to Brunswick and stayed at an expensive hotel until his money was exhausted. He then stayed at a fine hotel in a neighboring village, intending to defraud the hotel keeper. But his best clothes were taken in lieu of what he owed. He then walked six miles to another inn, where he was arrested for trying to defraud the landlord. He was imprisoned for this crime when he was sixteen years of age.

After his imprisonment, young Müller returned to his home and received a severe thrashing from his angry father. He remained as sinful in heart as ever, but in order to regain his father's confidence he began to lead a very exemplary life outwardly, until he had the confidence of everyone around him. His father decided to send him to the classical school at Halle, where the discipline was very strict, but George had no intention of going there. He went to Nordhausen instead, and by using many lies and entreaties, persuaded his father to allow him to remain there for two years and six months, until Easter of 1825.

At Nordhausen he studied diligently, was held up as an example to the other students, and became proficient in Latin, French, history, and his own language (German). "But while I was outwardly gaining the esteem of my fellow creatures," said he,

> I did not care in the least about God, but lived secretly in much sin, in consequence of which I became ill, and for thirteen weeks was confined to my room. All this time I had no real sorrow of heart, yet being under certain natural impressions of religion, I read through Friedrich Klopstock's

poetic works without weariness. I cared nothing about the Word of God.

Now and then I felt I ought to become a different person, and I tried to amend my conduct, particularly when I went to the Lord's Supper, as I used to do twice every year, with the other young men. The day previous to attending that ordinance, I used to refrain from certain things, and on the day itself I was serious. Once or twice I vowed to God, with the emblem of the broken body in my mouth, that I would become better, thinking that for the oath's sake I would be induced to reform. But after one or two days were over, all was forgotten, and I was as bad as before.

Müller entered the University of Halle as a divinity student, with good character references. This qualified him to preach in the Lutheran state church. While at the university, he spent all his money in profligate living. "When my money was spent," said Müller,

I pawned my watch and part of my linen and clothes, or borrowed in other ways. Yet in the midst of all this, I had a desire to renounce this wretched life, for I had no enjoyment in it, and had sense enough left to see that the end one day or other would be miserable, for I would never be able to make a living. But I had no sorrow of heart on account of offending God.

At the university, he formed the acquaintance of a miserable backslider named Beta, who was trying by means of worldly pleasures to drown out his conviction of sin. They plunged into sin together, and in June 1825, George again became sick. After his recovery, they forged letters purporting to be from his parents. With these they obtained passports and set out to see Switzerland. Müller stole from the friends who accompanied him, and the journey did not cost him as much as it did them. They returned home to finish up the vacation and then went back to the university, Müller having lied to his father about the trip to Switzerland.

At the University of Halle, there were about nine hundred divinity students. All of these were allowed to preach, but Müller estimated that not even nine of them feared the Lord. "One Saturday afternoon, about the middle of November 1825," said Müller,

> I had taken a walk with my friend Beta. On our return he told me that he was in the habit of going on Saturday evenings to the house of a Christian, where there was a meeting. On further inquiry he told me that they read the Bible, sang, prayed, and read a printed sermon. As soon as I heard this, it was as if I had found something I had been seeking all my life. I immediately wished to go with my friend, who was not immediately willing to take me; for, knowing me as he did, he thought I would not like this meeting. At last, however, he said he would call for me.

Describing the meeting, Müller said,

> We went together in the evening. As I did not know the manners of believers, and the joy they have in seeing poor sinners even in any measure caring about the things of God, I made an apology for coming. I will never forget the kind answer of one dear brother. He said, "Come as often as you please; house and heart are open to you."

After a hymn was sung, they fell upon their knees. A man named Kayser, who afterward became a missionary to Africa, asked God's blessing on the meeting. "This kneeling down made a deep impression upon me," said Müller, for I had never either seen anyone on his knees, nor had I ever prayed on my knees. He then read a chapter and a printed sermon, for no regular meetings for expounding the Scriptures were allowed in Prussia, unless an ordained clergyman was present. At the close we sang another hymn, and then the master of the house prayed.

The meeting made a deep impression upon Müller. "I was happy," he said,

> though if I had been asked why I was happy, I could not clearly have explained it.
>
> When we walked home, I said to Beta that everything we had seen on our journey to Switzerland, and all our former pleasures, were nothing in comparison with this evening. Whether I fell on my knees when I returned home, I do not remember, but this much I know: I lay peaceful and happy in my bed. This shows that the Lord may begin His work in different ways. I have not the least doubt that on that evening He began a work of grace in me, though I obtained joy without any deep sorrow of heart, and with scarcely any knowledge.
>
> But that evening was the turning point in my life. The next day, and Monday, and once or twice more in that week, I went again to this brother's house, where I read the Scriptures with him and another believer, for it was too long for me to wait until Saturday came again.
>
> Now my life became very different, though not so that my sins were all given up at once. My wicked companions were given up; the going to taverns was discontinued; the habitual practice of telling falsehoods was no longer indulged in, but still a few more times I spoke a lie. I now no longer lived habitually in sin, though I was still often overcome—sometimes even by open sins— though far less frequently than before, and not

without sorrow of heart. I read the Scriptures, prayed often, loved other believers, went to church out of the right motives, and stood on the side of Christ, though I was laughed at by my fellow students.

For a few weeks after his conversion, Müller made rapid advancement in the Christian life, and he was greatly desirous of becoming a missionary. But he fell in love with a Roman Catholic girl, and for some time the Lord was nearly forgotten. Then Müller saw a young missionary giving up all the luxuries of a beautiful home for Christ. This opened his eyes to his own selfishness and enabled him to give up the girl who had taken the place of Christ in his heart. "It was at this time," said he,

> that I began to enjoy the peace of God *"which surpasses all understanding"* (Phil. 4:7). In this joy of mine, I wrote to my father and brother, entreating them to seek the Lord and telling them how happy I was. I thought that if the way to happiness were set before them, they would gladly embrace it. To my great surprise, an angry answer was returned.

George could not enter any German missionary training institution without the consent of his father, and this he could not obtain. His father was deeply grieved that after educating him so that he could obtain a comfortable living as a clergyman, he turned to the life of a missionary. George felt that he could no longer accept any money from him. The Lord graciously sent him means with which to complete his education. He taught German to some American college professors at the university, and they handsomely repaid him for his services. He was now the means of winning a number of souls to Christ. He gave away thousands of religious tracts and papers, and he spoke to many people concerning the salvation of their souls.

Although before his conversion Müller had written to his father and told him about sermons he had preached, he never really preached a sermon until some time after his conversion. He thought to please his father by making him believe that he was preaching. His first sermon was a printed one that he had memorized for the occasion. He had little liberty in preaching it. The second time he preached extemporaneously and had some degree of liberty. "I now preached frequently," he said,

> both in the churches of the villages and towns, but I never had any enjoyment in doing so, except when speaking in a simple way; though the repetition of sermons that had been committed to memory brought more praise from my fellow creatures. But from neither way of preaching did I see any fruit. It may be that the Last Day will show the benefit even of those feeble endeavors. One reason why the Lord did not permit me to see fruit, it seems to me, was that I probably would have been lifted up in pride by success. It may also be because I prayed exceedingly little in regard to the ministry of the Word, and because I walked so little with God, and was so rarely *"a vessel for honor, sanctified and useful for the Master"* (2 Tim. 2:21).

The true believers at the university increased from six to about twenty in number before Müller left. They often met in Müller's room to pray, sing, and read the Bible. He sometimes walked 10 or 15 miles to hear a really pious minister preach.

In 1827 Müller volunteered to go as a missionary pastor to the Germans at Bucharest, but the war between the Turks and Russians prevented this. In 1828, at the suggestion of their agent, he offered himself to the London Missionary Society as a missionary to the Jews. He was well versed in the Hebrew language and had a great love for it. The Society asked him to come to London so that they might see him personally. Through the providence of God, he finally secured exemption for life from serving in the Prussian army, and he went to England in 1829, at twenty-four years of age. He was not able to speak the English language for some time after he landed in England, and then only in a very broken manner at first.

Soon after coming to England, Müller received a deeper Christian experience that entirely revolutionized his life. "I came weak in body to England," said he,

> and in consequence of much study, I suppose, I became ill on May 15. I was soon apparently beyond recovery, at least in my own estimation. The weaker I got in body, the happier I was in spirit. Never in my whole life had I seen myself so vile, so guilty, so altogether what I ought not to have been, as at that time. It was as if every sin of which I had been guilty was brought to my remembrance; but at the same time I could realize that all my sins were completely forgiven, that I was washed and made clean, completely clean, in the blood of Jesus. The result of this was great peace. I longed exceedingly to depart and to be with Christ.
>
> After I had been ill for about two weeks, my doctor unexpectedly pronounced me better. This, instead of giving me joy, bowed me down, so great was my desire to be with the Lord. Almost immediately afterward, however, grace was given to me to submit myself to the will of God.

Müller always regarded the above experience as one that deepened his whole spiritual life. This is clearly shown by a letter of his that appeared in the

British *Christian,* on August 14, 1902. In this letter
Müller wrote,

> I became a believer in the Lord Jesus in the
> beginning of November 1825, now sixty-nine
> years and eight months ago. A good part of the
> first four years afterward were spent in great
> weakness, but in July 1829, now sixty-six years
> ago, I came to an entire and full surrender of
> heart. I gave myself fully to the Lord. Honors,
> pleasures, money, my physical powers, my men-
> tal powers—all were laid down at the feet of Je-
> sus, and I became a great lover of the Word of
> God. I found my all in God, whether my trials
> were of a temporal or spiritual character, and it
> has remained so for sixty-six years. My faith is
> not merely exercised regarding temporal things,
> but also regarding everything, because I cleave to
> the Word. My knowledge of God and His Word is
> what helps me.

Being advised to go into the country for his health,
he prayed about it and finally decided to go. He went to
Devonshire, where the great blessing he had already
received was greatly augmented by his conversations
and prayers with a Spirit-filled minister whom he first
heard preach at Teignmouth. Through the conversations and sermons of this minister, he was led to see as
never before

> that the Word of God alone is our standard of
> judgment in spiritual things; that it can be ex-
> plained only by His Holy Spirit; and that in our
> day, as well as in former times, He is the teacher
> of His people. I had not experientially under-
> stood the office of the Holy Spirit before that
> time. The result of this was that the first evening
> that I shut myself into my room to give myself to
> prayer and meditation over the Scriptures, I

learned more in a few hours than I had during a
period of several months previously. In addition
to these truths, it pleased the Lord to lead me to
see a higher standard of devotedness than I had
seen before.

On his return to London, Müller sought to lead his
friends in the seminary into the deeper truths he had
been brought to realize. "One brother in particular,"
said Müller,

was brought into the same state in which I was;
and others, I trust, were more or less benefited.
Several times, when I went to my room after
family prayer, I found communion with God so
sweet that I continued in prayer until after
twelve, and then being full of joy, went into the
room of the brother just referred to. Finding him
also in a similar frame of heart, we continued
praying until one or two, and even then I was a
few times so full of joy that I could scarcely sleep,
and at six in the morning again called the group
together for prayer.

Müller's health declined in London, and his soul
was also now on fire for God in such a way that he
could not settle down to the routine of daily studies.
His newly acquired belief in the near coming of Christ
also urged him forward to work for the salvation of
souls. He felt that the Lord was leading him to begin at
once the Christian work he was longing to do, and as
the London Missionary Society did not think it proper
to send him out without the prescribed course of
training, he decided to go at once and trust the Lord
for the means of support. Soon after this, he became
pastor of Ebenezer Chapel, Teignmouth, Devonshire.
His marriage to Miss Mary Groves, a Devonshire lady,
followed. She was always of the same mind as her husband, and their married life was a very happy one.

Not long after his marriage, Müller began to have conscientious scruples about receiving a regular salary, and also about the renting of pews in his church. He felt that the latter was giving the "man with the ring on his finger" the best seat, and the poorer brother the footstool (see James 2:1–4), and the former was taking money from those who did not give as the Lord had prospered them. (See 1 Corinthians 16:2.) These two customs were discontinued by him. He and his wife told their needs to no one but the Lord. Occasionally, reports were spread that they were starving; but though at times their faith was tried, their income was greater than before. He and his wife freely gave away all that they had above their present needs, and they trusted the Lord for their daily bread.

Müller preached in many surrounding towns, and many souls were brought to Christ in his meetings. In 1832 he felt profoundly impressed that his work was ending in Teignmouth, and when he went to Bristol the same year, he felt that the Lord wanted him to work there. When the Spirit, the Word, and the providence of God agree, we may be quite certain that the Lord is leading us, for these three are always in harmony and cannot disagree. Not only did Müller feel led by the Lord to work in Bristol, but the providence of God also opened the way, and it seemed in harmony with the Word of God.

Müller began his labors in Bristol in 1832, as co-pastor with his friend Mr. Craik, who had been called to that city. Without salaries or rented pews, their labors were greatly blessed at Gideon and Bethesda Chapels. The membership more than quadrupled in numbers in a short time. Ten days after the opening of Bethesda, there was such a crowd of people inquiring the way of salvation that it took four hours to minister to them. Subsequently, Gideon Chapel was relinquished, and in the course of time two neighboring chapels were secured. These churches, though calling themselves non-sectarian, were usually classed with the people commonly known as Plymouth Brethren. Müller continued to preach to them as long as he lived, even after he began his great work for the orphans. At the time of his death, he had a congregation of about 2,000 people at Bethesda Chapel.

In 1834 Müller started the Scripture Knowledge Institution for Home and Abroad. Its purpose was to aid Christian day schools, to assist missionaries, and to circulate the Scriptures. This institution, without worldly patronage, without asking anyone for help, without contracting debts, without committees, subscribers, or memberships, but through faith in the Lord alone, had obtained and disbursed no less a sum than £1,500,000 at the time of Müller's death. The bulk of this was spent on the orphanages. At the time of Müller's death, 122,000 people had been taught in the schools supported by these funds, and about 282,000 Bibles and 1,500,000 Testaments had been distributed by means of the same fund. Also, 112 million religious books, pamphlets, and tracts had been circulated; missionaries had been aided in all parts of the world; and no less than 10,000 orphans had been cared for by means of this same fund.

At the age of seventy, Müller began to make great evangelistic tours. He traveled 200,000 miles, going around the world and preaching in many lands and in several different languages. He frequently spoke to as many as 4,500 or 5,000 people. Three times he preached throughout the length and breadth of the United States. He continued his missionary or evangelistic tours until he was ninety years of age. He estimated that during these seventeen years of evangelistic work he addressed 3 million people. All his expenses were sent in answer to the prayer of faith.

Greatest of all Müller's undertakings was the building and maintenance of the great orphanages at Bristol. He began the undertaking with only 2 shillings in his pocket; but in answer to prayer and without making his needs known to human beings, he received the means necessary to erect the great buildings and to feed the orphans day by day for sixty years. In all that time, the children did not have to go without a meal, and Müller said that if they ever had to go without a meal he would take it as evidence that the Lord did not desire the work to continue. Sometimes the mealtime was almost at hand and they did not know where the food would come from, but the Lord always sent it in due time, during the twenty thousand or more days that Müller had charge of the homes.

When Müller began to trust the Lord for money, he found it as difficult to trust the Lord for a shilling as it was afterward to trust Him for £1,000. The more his faith was exercised, the stronger it became. Funds for one immense building after another were sent in answer to prayer, until Müller had received more than a £100,000 for this purpose alone. Six hundred pounds a week was required for the support of the orphans at the time of Müller's death, and yet day by day the Lord sent them their daily bread.

When he was a youth, Müller had seen the great orphanage at Halle, in Prussia, supported by Professor Francke in answer to the simple prayer of faith. After going to Bristol, Müller felt that the Lord was laying it upon his heart to begin a similar work in that city, as a monument and testimony to the world that the Lord still hears and answers prayer. When he had accomplished this great work, the Lord gently removed him. He died in his room on the night of March 10, 1898. One of his helpers informed me that every feature of his countenance showed that he had died in peace.

Chapter 15

Frances Ridley Havergal

❦

ew lives have left behind them a sweeter fragrance or holier influence than that of beautiful, talented, consecrated Frances Ridley Havergal, who wrote "Take My Life and Let It Be" and other popular hymns. Countless multitudes have received blessing through her hymns and devotional works. Her little booklets, *My King, Royal Commandments and Royal Bounty, Daily Thoughts on Coming to Christ, Kept for the Master's Use,* and so on, have been the means of deepening the spiritual life of many of God's children. To Miss Havergal, Christ was indeed "a living bright reality, more dear, more intimately near, than even the sweetest earthly tie." One of her last whispers was, "I did so want to glorify Him in every step of my way." Many Christians sincerely desire to know the secret of a life such as hers, and to attain its lofty heights of joy and peace.

Frances Ridley Havergal was the youngest child of Christian parents. She was born in 1836, at Astley, in Worcestershire, England, where her father was rector at the time. She was a very beautiful child, fond of romping and climbing trees. She was so full of life and vivacity that her father called her his "Little Quicksilver." She was very precocious, and she could read simple books easily at three years of age. At four years of age, she could write well and could read the Bible correctly. Her father was a composer and musician of notable merit, and at nine years of age Frances wrote long letters to her friends in perfect rhyme.

As a little girl, Frances sang hymns sweetly, and she often sat upon her father's knee while he read the Scriptures; but she did not remember having any serious impressions about religion until she was six years old. At that age, she was deeply convicted of sin by hearing a sermon concerning the terrors of hell and of the Judgment Day. She told no one, but the sermon was on her mind day and night, and she sought relief in prayer. She remained in great distress about her soul for two years without telling anyone about it.

She then ventured to tell a certain curate of the Church of England, in which she was raised and of which she continued as a member. But the curate attributed her feelings to a recent change of residence that her parents had made in moving from one rectory to another. He thought that she was simply homesick for the old home and friends, and advised her to be a good child and to pray. After this she did not open her heart to anyone for about five years, although she was under deep concern about her soul most of the time.

Frances' mother died when Frances was twelve years of age, and this was a great blow to her. When she was between thirteen and fourteen years of age, she went to the school of a Mrs. Teed, who was a godly woman, so filled with the Spirit that a great revival broke out in her school, and most of her pupils were converted to Christ. Many of the girls were so happy that "their countenances shone with a heavenly radiance." This deepened Frances' conviction of sin, and she prayed more earnestly than ever for pardon.

After much anxious seeking, she ventured to tell a Miss Cooke—who afterward became her stepmother— how willing she was to give up everything if she could only find Christ as her Savior. Miss Cooke said, "Why can't you trust yourself to your Savior right now?" Miss Havergal recalled,

> Then came a flash of hope across me, which made me feel literally breathless. I remember how my heart beat. "I could, surely," was my response; and I left her suddenly and ran upstairs to think it out. I flung myself on my knees in my room and strove to realize the sudden hope. I was very happy at last. I could commit my soul to Jesus. I could trust Him with my all for eternity.

She then received a definite assurance of salvation. "Then and there," said Frances,

> I committed my soul to my Savior. I do not mean to say that I did so without any trembling or fear, but I did it—and earth and heaven seemed bright from that moment. I did trust the Lord Jesus.

From the time of her conversion, Frances lived a very earnest Christian life. She was in schools and colleges in England and Germany, and afterward visited different parts of England, Switzerland, Wales, Ireland, and Scotland, but everywhere she went she took a bold stand for Christ. She received a splendid education both in England and in Germany and grew into a very beautiful and accomplished young lady. She won many of the highest honors and became proficient in several languages, including Latin, Greek, French, German, and Hebrew. She was a talented musician and a gifted singer, and she wrote many poems of considerable merit. She was the only truly converted person among the 110 young ladies in her school in Germany, but she took a firm stand for Christ. She suffered much persecution on that account, but she won the hearts of some of her schoolmates.

Returning to England in 1854, she was confirmed in Worcester Cathedral. When the bishop laid hands on her and prayed, "Defend, O Lord, this Your child with Your heavenly grace, that she may continue as Yours forever, and daily increase in Your Holy Spirit more and more, until she come into Your everlasting kingdom," her heart entered into the prayer. "If ever my heart followed a prayer, it did then," she said. "If ever it thrilled with earnest longing mixed with joy, it did at the words, 'Yours forever.'" She always observed the anniversary of her confirmation by spending the day in prayer and holy retirement.

Although Miss Havergal lived a very earnest Christian life and sought to glorify God and serve Him by teaching in Sunday school, singing in churches and elsewhere, visiting the needy, and so on, she felt that she was only a little child in the spiritual life, and she longed for a deeper Christian experience. Her writings began to attract much attention, and her sweet Christian spirit was noticed on every hand. She was a great student of the Word of God, and at the age of twenty-two knew all of the Gospels, Epistles, Revelation, Psalms, and Isaiah by heart, and the Minor Prophets she learned in later years. She asked the Lord to direct her writing and to give her every word, even the rhymes of her poetry. Still she longed for a deeper, richer, fuller Christian experience.

She had many longings to be filled with the Spirit and to have a closer walk with God. In "Gleams and Glimpses," written in 1858, she wrote, "Gleams and glimpses—but oh, to be filled with joy and the Holy Spirit! Oh, why can I not trust Him fully?" Later she wrote, "I still wait for the hour when I believe He will reveal Himself to me more directly, but it is the quiet waiting of present trust, not the restless waiting of anxiety and danger." It was in 1858, at the age of twenty-two, that she wrote the well-known hymn, "I Gave My Life for Thee," which reveals the deep longings of her heart to be more fully consecrated to Christ.

Miss Havergal often encountered dark places in seeking a deeper spiritual experience. In 1865, she wrote,

> I had hoped that a kind of plateau had been reached in my journey, where I might walk a while in the light, without the weary succession of rock and hollow, crag and morass, stumbling and striving. But I seem to be carried back into all the old difficulties of the way, with many sin-made aggravations. I think that the great root of all my trouble and alienation is that I do not now make an unconditional surrender of myself to God, and until this is done I will know no peace. I am sure of it.

Later she said, "Oh, that He would indeed purify me and make me white at any cost!" She prayed regularly three times a day, and every morning she prayed especially for the Holy Spirit. After a season of sickness, she wrote,

> Oh, that He may make me a *"vessel... sanctified and useful for the Master"* (2 Tim. 2:21)! I look at trial and training of every kind in this light, not its effect upon me for myself, but in its gradual fitting of me to do the Master's work. So, in every painful spiritual darkness or conflict, it has already comforted me to think that God might be leading me through strange dark ways so that I might afterward be His messenger to some of His children in distress.

She often wondered why others obtained so easily the blessing she had agonized and prayed for so long.

Perhaps the Lord was letting her learn what trial was, so that her sweet songs might better comfort others in distress. She said,

> I suppose that God's crosses are often made of the most unexpected and strange material. Perhaps trial must be felt keenly, or it would not be powerful enough as a medicine in the hands of our beloved Healer; and I think it has been a medicine to me recently.
>
> I have learned a real sympathy with others walking in darkness, and sometimes it has seemed to help me to help them.

Concerning her trials she also wrote,

> Did you ever hear of anyone being very much used for Christ who did not have some special waiting time, some complete upset of all his or her plans first? Paul was sent off into the desert of Arabia for three years, when he must have been boiling over with the glad tidings.

Miss Havergal traveled much throughout the British Isles and made numerous trips to Switzerland, but wherever she was, her soul still longed for a deeper experience. She spent much time in studying and marking her Bible, and this increased her longings to lay hold of the *"exceedingly great and precious promises"* by which we are made *"partakers of the divine nature"* (2 Pet. 1:4). At this time she wrote, "I have been taking hold of all the promises with a calm sort of twilight happiness, waiting for a clearer light to show me their full beauty and value."

At last the long-awaited experience came, and it lifted her whole life into sunshine and gladness. The following account of how she was brought into a Beulah experience is from the pen of her sister Maria, who also enjoyed the same experience.

We now reach a period in Frances' life that was characterized by surpassing blessing to her soul. The year 1873 was drawing to a close, and she was again visiting Winterdyne.

One day she received in a letter from N—— a tiny book with the title, *All for Jesus*. She read it carefully. Its contents captured her attention. It set forth a fullness of Christian experience and blessing exceeding what she had as yet attained. She was gratefully conscious of having for many years loved the Lord and delighted in His service; but there was in her experience a falling short of the standard, not so much of a holy walk and behavior, as of uniform brightness and continuous enjoyment in the divine life.

All for Jesus went straight to this point of the need and longing of her soul. Writing in reply to the author of the little book, she said, "I do so long for deeper and fuller teaching in my own heart. *All for Jesus* has touched me very much. I know I love Jesus, and there are times when I feel such intensity of love for Him that I do not have words to describe it. I rejoice, too, in Him as my Master and Sovereign, but I want to come nearer still, to have the full realization of John 14:21, and to know *'the power of His resurrection'* (Phil. 3:10), even if it is with *'the fellowship of His sufferings'* (v. 10). And all this is not exactly for my own joy alone, but for the joy of others, too. So I want Jesus to speak to me, to say *'many things'* (Matt. 13:3) to me, so that I may speak for Him to others with real power. It is not knowing doctrine, but being with Him, that will give this."

God did not leave her long in this state of mind. He Himself had shown her that there were *"regions beyond"* (2 Cor. 10:16) of blessed experience and service; had kindled in her soul the intense desire to go forward and possess them; and now, in His own grace and love, took her by the hand and led her into the good land. A few words from her correspondent on the power of Jesus to keep those who abide in Him from falling, and on the continually present power of His blood (1 John 1:7), were used by the Master in bringing this about. Very joyously she replied, "I see it all, and I have the blessing."

The "sunless ravines" were now forever passed, and her peace and joy flowed onward, deepening and widening under the teaching of God and the Holy Spirit. The blessing she had received had (to use her own words) "lifted her whole life into sunshine, of which all she had previously experienced was like pale and passing April gleams compared with the fullness of summer glory."

The practical effect of this was most evident in her daily, truehearted, wholehearted service for her King, and also in the increased joyousness of the unswerving obedience of her home life, the surest test of all.

To the reality of this, I do most willingly and fully testify. Some time afterward, when we were talking quietly together, Frances said, "Yes, it was on Advent Sunday, December 2, 1873, that I first saw clearly the blessedness of true consecration. I saw it as a flash of electric light, and what you see, you can never *un*see. There must be full surrender before there can be full blessedness. God admits you by the one into the other. He Himself showed me all this most dearly. You know how I have been withheld from attending all conventions and conferences; man's teaching has, consequently, had little to do with it. First, I was shown that *"the blood of Jesus Christ...cleanses us from all sin"* (1 John 1:7), and then it was made plain to me that He who had thus cleansed me had power to keep me clean. So I just utterly yielded myself to Him, and utterly trusted Him to keep me."

In a letter to her sister Maria, written several months after the experience just described, Frances said, regarding her experience,

> First, I would distinctly state that it is only while a soul is under the full power of the blood of Christ that it can be cleansed from all sin. Give the soul one moment's withdrawal from that power, and it is again actively sinning. It is only while we are kept by the power of God Himself that we are not sinning against Him; one instant of standing alone is certain fall!
>
> But have we not been limiting the cleansing power of the precious blood when applied by the Holy Spirit, and also the keeping power of God? Have we not been limiting 1 John 1:7 by practically making it refer only to *"remission of sins that are past"* (Rom. 3:25 KJV), instead of taking the grand simplicity of *"cleanses us from all sin"* (1 John 1:7, emphasis added)? *"All"* includes everything, and as we may trust Him to cleanse us from the stain of past sins, so we may trust Him to cleanse us from all present defilement— yes, all! If not, we take away from this most precious promise. And by refusing to take it in its fullness, we lose the fullness of its application and power. Then we limit God's power to keep; we look at our frailty more than His omnipotence.
>
> Where is the line to be drawn, beyond which He is not able? The very fact of His keeping us implies total helplessness without it, and His cleansing us most distinctly implies our defilement without it. It was that one word, *"cleanses,"* that opened the door of a glory of hope and joy to me. I had never seen the power of a continual present tense—always a present tense, not a present that the next moment becomes a past. It goes on cleansing, and I have no words to tell how my heart rejoices in it. We do

not come only to be cleansed in the fountain, but also to remain in the fountain, so that it may go on cleansing.

Why should we pare down the promises of God to the level of our previous experiences of what God is *"able to do"* (Eph. 3:20), or even of what we have thought He might be able to do for us? Why not receive God's promises, with no doubting, just as they stand? Take *"the shield of faith with which you will be able to quench all the fiery darts of the wicked one"* (Eph. 6:16). *"God is able to make all grace abound toward you, that you* [may] *always* [have] *all sufficiency in all things"* (2 Cor. 9:8), through all the promises, which surely mean what they say.

One arrives at the same conclusion starting from almost anywhere in the Scriptures. Take Philippians 4:19, which talks about *"your need."* Well, what is my great need and craving of soul? Surely, after having been justified by faith and having assurance of salvation, it is to be made holy by the continually sanctifying power of God's Spirit, to be kept from grieving the Lord Jesus, and to be kept from thinking or doing whatever is not in accord with His holy will. Oh, what a need this is! And it is said that He *"shall supply all your need"* (v. 19). Now, will we turn around and say *"all"* does not mean quite all? In regard to both the commands and promises, it seems to me that everything short of believing them as they stand is just another form of *"Has God indeed said...?"* (Gen. 3:1), the very words that the Devil used to tempt Eve.

By thus accepting God's commands and promises with a simple and unquestioning faith, one seems to be immediately brought into intensified views of everything. Never, oh never before, did sin seem so hateful, so really intolerable. Nor did watchfulness seem so necessary, and a keenness and uninterruptedness of watchfulness too, beyond what one ever thought of; only this time it is a happy sort of watchfulness. It is the watchfulness of a sentinel when his captain is standing by him on the ramparts, when his eye is more than ever on the alert for any sign of the approaching enemy, because he knows they can only approach to be defeated.

This is where the "all for Jesus" comes in: one sees there is no halfway; one must be absolutely all yielded up, because the smallest unyielded or doubtful point is sin, let alone the great fact of owing all to Him. And one cannot, dares not, compromise with sin. I know, and have found, that even a momentary hesitation about yielding, obeying, trusting, or believing tarnishes everything; the communion is broken; the joy is vanished. Thank God, this condition never has to continue even five minutes. Faith may plunge instantly into the fountain that is open for sin and uncleanness, and again find its power to cleanse and restore.

Then one desires to have more and more light; one does not shrink from painful discoveries of evil, because one so wants to have the unknown depths of it cleansed as well as what comes to the surface. One begins to pray, *"Wash me thoroughly from my iniquity, and cleanse me from my sin"* (Ps. 51:2). But insofar as one does see, one must *"put away sin"* (Heb. 9:26) and obey entirely. Here again, His power is our resource, enabling us to do what we could not do without it.

One of the most intense moments of my life was when I saw the force of that word *"cleanses"* (1 John 1:7). The utterly unexpected and altogether unimagined sense of its fulfillment to me, on simply believing it in its fullness, was just indescribable. I expected nothing like it short of heaven.

Referring to the same experience, in a letter to a friend, she said, "The year 1873 has been a time of unprecedented blessing to me."

Miss Havergal's whole life was now lifted to a higher plane, and the few remaining years were the richest of her life, richest in Christian experience and richest in service for her King. Wherever she went, her life was full of service, and her words were elevated with a new spiritual power. It was at this time, too, that she wrote her great consecration hymn, "Take My Life and Let It Be." She said,

> Perhaps you will be interested to know the origin of the consecration hymn, "Take My Life." I went for a little visit of five days. There were ten people in the house, some unconverted and long prayed for, some converted but not rejoicing Christians. God gave me the prayer, "Lord, give me all in this house." And He did exactly that! Before I left the house, everyone had gotten a blessing. The last night of my visit I was too happy to sleep, and I spent most of the night in praise and renewal of my consecration. These little couplets formed themselves and chimed in my heart one after another, until they finished with, "Ever, only, all for Thee!"

She now refused to sing anything except sacred songs and hymns. Her voice, like her pen, was "always, only, for her King," and many hearts were touched by her consecrated singing and writing. She considered every moment of her time as belonging to the Lord, and sought to use it to His glory. She was very fond of romping over the mountains in Switzerland, and her Alpine guide said that in climbing them she "went up like an antelope." But these rambles were for the benefit of her health, and in her writings she embodied the thoughts concerning God that were suggested to her by His handiwork in nature. Frances also sought to win souls for Christ during her numerous visits to Switzerland.

Not only did she consider every moment of her time as wholly the Lord's, but she also regarded every penny of her money as belonging to Him. "I forget sometimes," she said, "but as a rule I never spend a sixpence without the distinct feeling that it is His and must be spent for Him only, even if indirectly." She did not feel free to spend her money for fine clothing. She gave her jewelry to the missionary cause and dressed plainly but neatly. Her idea of the proper way for a Christian to dress was so as not to attract attention either by slovenliness or extravagance. "The question of cost I view very strongly," said she,

> and do not consider myself at liberty to spend on clothing what might be spared for God's work. But it costs no more to have a thing as well and prettily made, and I would only feel justified in getting a costly dress if it would last proportionately longer.

Miss Havergal's time was now occupied with her writing, in giving Bible readings and addresses, in visiting the poor, and in doing needlework for the Zenana missions and for the poor. In 1877 she took up temperance work as well. She spent much time in visiting from house to house, to read the Bible and point souls to Christ. She often gave Bible readings or addressed meetings, and she frequently led consecration meetings. The first consecration meeting she was ever in was conducted by herself, and it was a time of rich blessing. Deeply spiritual and full of trust were her Bible readings and addresses. She often sang in churches, hospitals, and other places.

Every morning she spent much time in studying and marking her Bible, sitting at her table to do so. Sometimes, on bitterly cold mornings, her sister would beg her to study with her feet to the fire. "But then," Frances would reply, "I can't draw my lines neatly; just see what a discovery I've made! If one only searches, there are such extraordinary things in the Bible!" She sent many letters of comfort and consolation to all parts of the earth. Her books also carried a blessing with them wherever they went. Children flocked to her in crowds, and adults corresponded with her from all quarters. From morning to night she was occupied in the Master's service.

Miss Havergal often referred to the experience of 1873, which made the closing years of her life such a blessing to others. In 1875 she said to her sister, "It's no mistake, Maria, about the blessing God sent me December 2, 1873. It is far more distinct than my conversion; I can't date that. I am always happy, and it is such peace." The same year she wrote, "He has granted me to rejoice fully in His will; I am not conscious of even a wish crossing it. I do really and altogether desire that His will may be done, whatever it is." Even when suffering from poor health, or after some great temporal loss, she could still *"rejoice in the LORD...*[and] *joy in the God of* [her] *salvation"* (Hab. 3:18).

When her American publishers went under, and she did not receive the money due for her books, Frances wrote, "I have not a fear or a doubt or a care or a shadow upon the sunshine of my heart." Later, when many valuable stereotype plates of her music and songs were destroyed by fire, she was still happy, believing that God had a purpose in allowing adversities.

She suffered much from poor health, and as the years went on, her health was more and more broken. She literally wore herself out ministering to others. When her friends sympathized with her sufferings in her last illness, she whispered, "Never mind! It's home the faster! God's will is delicious; He makes no mistakes." Shortly before she died, she requested that her favorite text, *"The blood of Jesus Christ His Son cleanses us from all sin"* (1 John 1:7), be placed on her tombstone. On her deathbed she frequently exclaimed, "So beautiful to go!" Near the end she said, "Oh, I want you all to speak bright, bright words for Jesus! Oh, do, do! It is all perfect peace. I am only waiting for Jesus to take me in."

Perhaps Miss Havergal's experience is best described in her own words, quoted by her sister:

There were strange soul depths,
Restless, vast, and broad,
Unfathomed as the sea.
An infinite craving for some infinite stilling;
But now Thy perfect love is perfect filling,
Lord Jesus Christ, my Lord, my God,
Thou, Thou art enough for me.

Chapter 16

A. J. Gordon

◅◦►

One of the most famous Spirit-filled ministers of
modern times was Dr. Adoniram Judson
Gordon. His deeply spiritual books, especially
The Ministry of the Spirit, have been a means of deepening the faith and experience of many of the Lord's
children.

Gordon was born in New Hampshire on April 13,
1836. His parents were devout Christians of the old-
school Baptist type. Adoniram was a "thoughtless,
somewhat indifferent, unresponsive lad" until about
fifteen years of age. There were twelve children in the
family, and his life, like that of the others, was little
out of the ordinary. He helped his father in the family's
little wooden mill, and he worked on the farm.

At about fifteen years of age, Adoniram became
interested in the salvation of his soul. His conviction of
sin became very deep until finally it was almost unen-
durable. He spent a whole night in such anguish of soul
that his father was obliged to sit up with him until
daybreak. "Calm as the sunshine that flooded the hills
the next day was the boy's spirit, which had found
peace with God through our Lord Jesus Christ," said
his son, in the biography of his father Adoniram.

Soon after his conversion to Christ, Adoniram
was baptized and received into the church. Before his

conversion, he cared little for books. Studying was a very unpleasant task to him. But after his conversion, new desires and ambitions took possession of him, and he applied himself diligently to his studies. Soon after his sixteenth year, he openly confessed to the church his desire and determination to prepare for the ministry. An old deacon remarked to someone, "Judson is a good boy and would make a good minister if he only had energy." Little did he foresee the life of incessant toil and consecrated energy awaiting the seemingly sluggish lad.

Young Gordon was sent to a preparatory school, and he worked during all his spare hours to help pay his tuition and other expenses. He was very eager to master the Greek language, so that he would better understand the New Testament. In 1856 he went to Brown University. He took only medium rank as a scholar, but his reading was extensive. In 1860 he entered the Newton Theological Seminary. The Civil War then broke out, and he was fired with a desire to go to the front with many of his comrades. But his parents were so thoroughly opposed to his going that he finally gave up the cause.

Before leaving the seminary, he preached a number of times in surrounding villages. In 1863 he graduated, and he accepted a call to become pastor of the little church at Jamaica Plain, near Boston. He spent six years at this little church in the suburbs of Boston. The church prospered and increased in number under his ministry, and the people were reluctant to part with him when he received a call from a larger church in Boston in 1867. He declined the new call over and over again, but the Boston church would take no denial. He wrote out a letter of acceptance but tore it up immediately. At last the pressure became so great that, in 1869, he accepted the position at the Clarendon Street Baptist Church, in Boston, the church where he was destined to become famous.

Boston was full of skepticism and unbelief, and Clarendon Street Church was in a very sluggish spiritual condition when Gordon became the pastor. It was a very wealthy and exclusive church, and there was little room for the poor in it. "A line of substantial merchants and bankers ran up and down the ends of the most desirable pews."

Dr. Gordon remained pastor of Clarendon Street Church for more than a quarter of a century. By persevering in preaching the plain, unvarnished truths of the Gospel, he at last saw the church completely transformed. It became one of the most spiritual and aggressive churches of the time.

The great secret of Dr. Gordon's wonderful success in the ministry was undoubtedly in his own personal experience of the baptism and anointing of the Holy Spirit, which he seems to have received at one of Moody's conferences at Northfield, sometime after he began his ministry at the Clarendon Street Church. The deepening of his spiritual experience seems to have been brought about through two great agencies: the prayers and labors of the famous Uncle John Vassar, and the great meetings that D. L. Moody held in Boston close to Dr. Gordon's church in 1877. Of Uncle John Vassar, Gordon wrote,

> Far beyond any man whom I ever knew, it was true of him that his citizenship was in heaven. (See Philippians 3:20.) He was so filled with the glory and power of the heavenly life that to many he seemed like a foreigner speaking an unknown tongue. I have never been so humbled and quickened by contact with any living man as with him. Hundreds of Christians, while sorrowing that they would see his face no more for the present, will bless God as long as they live for the inspiration that they received from his devoted life.

Ernest B. Gordon, son of Dr. Gordon, said concerning Uncle John Vassar,

> For five successive years, off and on, Uncle
> John labored with the Clarendon Street Church
> in his peculiar work of "spiritual census taking,"
> going through the streets of proud, cultivated,
> self-righteous Boston, ringing every doorbell,
> and confronting every household with the great
> question of the new birth. He was inclined to de-
> scribe himself as "only a shepherd dog, ready to
> run after the lost sheep and bring them back to
> the Shepherd," and he always refused the honors
> and emoluments of the ministry.
>
> Uncle John would literally travail in prayer
> for the unconverted. "The nights that he spent
> at my home," wrote A. J. Gordon, "were nights
> of prayer and pleading for my congregation and
> my ministry. Again and again would I hear him
> rising in the midnight hours to plead with God
> for the unsaved, until I frequently had to ad-
> monish him that he must not lose his sleep."
> And so he worked and prayed and instructed the
> young minister, who was meekly teachable be-
> fore such a master of spiritual things, in those
> hard-learned and rarely acquired secrets that
> open the way to the heart of sinful humanity.
>
> The inspiration this faithful man brought
> with him increased chiefly in the pastor of
> Clarendon Street. The influence of Mr. Moody's
> meetings in 1877 affected both pastor and peo-
> ple. Indeed, this year was the turning point that,
> after seven years of lethargic religious life,
> opened a new period of spiritual health. When
> the revival meetings were finished, Gordon real-
> ized that the crest of the hill had been passed
> and that the crisis in the struggle for a spiritual
> church was over.
>
> These meetings, which were organized and
> carried on by Moody with all the executive ability

and religious fervor for which he is distinguished, were held in a large tabernacle—a great "tent" of brick and wood, with nothing around it to attract people besides the Gospel of Christ preached therein. This building stood within three hundred feet of the Clarendon Street Church, which was used from the beginning for overflow and inquiry meetings [attended by sinners who wanted to learn about salvation]. The tabernacle was thronged night after night by audiences of from 5,000 to 7,000 people. Men and women of all ranks and conditions attended. Trains brought in thousands from all parts of New England. Seventy thousand families in Boston were personally visited. Great noon prayer meetings were held daily in Tremont Temple by businessmen. Meetings were organized for young men, for boys, for women, for the intemperate—in short, for all classes in the community that were ready to help or be helped.

And at the center of all these operations stood the Clarendon Street Church, like a field temporarily occupied by troops in battle. What a shattering and overwhelming of weather-stained, moss-grown traditions followed! What experiences of grace, what widening vistas of God's power, what instruction in personal religion resulted from these six months of revival! A window was built into the religious life of the church, letting in floods of light. The true purpose of a church's existence began to be emphasized. Drunkards and outcasts were daily reclaimed and brought into fellowship. Christian evidences of the best sort, evidences that had to do with the potency of a saving Christ, were multiplied, strengthening the faith of believers. The duties and opportunity of everyone in the work of the inquiry room were asserted. A great education in methods of practical religious work resulted.

It seems to have been in 1882, during the first of Moody's Northfield conventions, that Gordon received the anointing of the Holy Spirit. The following account is from the biography written by his son:

> The letters that follow touch closely upon Northfield, and illustrate from Dr. Gordon's personal experience the doctrine of enduement for service, which he preached with so much power at the conferences.
>
> "Dr. Gordon," writes Mr. George C. Needham, "unlike some Christians, believed there was something always beyond. This he ever sought to attain. Fifteen years ago, during the first Northfield convention, he was desirous to secure what he yet needed as a saint and servant of Christ. Toward the close of those memorable ten days, spent more in prayer than in preaching, my beloved friend joined me in a midnight hour of great heart searching and infilling of the Spirit. He read with special tenderness our Lord's intercessory prayer of John 17. The union of the believer with Christ and the Father, as taught by our Lord in that chapter, caused fervent exclamations, while with deep passion he continued reading.
>
> "During united prayer that followed, the holy man poured out his soul with a freedom and anointing that were indescribable. I never heard him boast of any spiritual attainment reached during the midnight hour. Soul experiences were to him very sacred, and not to be repeated on every ordinary occasion. But I have no doubt he then received a divine touch that further ennobled his personal life and made his ministry one of ever increasing spirituality and of ever widening breadth of sympathy."

Immediately after the conference referred to above, Dr. Gordon went to Seabright, New Jersey, to preach one Sunday. The following is from a letter of one who heard him preach at this seaside resort:

> I remember his once coming from North-field after the August conference. He seemed filled with the Spirit; he could not talk common-places. He said he had had a great blessing. He went to his room and came out shortly after, saying he was going down to the fishing village and asking the way. He did not come back until we were at dinner that hot afternoon. He had visited the saloons and prayed with the men there, and had been among the shanties. I know more than one family saved that day.

Dr. Gordon's Spirit-filled life and deeply spiritual books have had a powerful influence for good throughout the world, and his memory has the sweet savor of a saintly life. He was one of the most prominent leaders and speakers in Moody's great Northfield conventions, and one year Moody left the convention entirely in his charge. Dr. Arthur T. Pierson, speaking concerning Gordon's addresses at these conventions, said,

> He taught with authority, but it was with a derived and representative authority. Among all the renowned speakers at the Northfield conference, he was *facile princeps,* or, easily first. The address he gave there last summer on the Holy Spirit has been pronounced by competent judges the most complete ever given, even from that platform of great teachers.

In his *Ministry of the Spirit,* which is perhaps his greatest work, Dr. Gordon presented the work of the Holy Spirit in three parts—sealing, filling, and anointing. The sealing is accomplished with assurance, the filling with power, and the anointing with knowledge. In his well-known book on *The Ministry of Healing,* Dr.

Gordon opposed the so-called Christian Science, which had its headquarters in Boston, the city where his church was located; but he advocated the power of the Lord to heal disease or to keep His children well without the use of medicines.

Dr. Gordon was also a firm believer in the premillenial coming of Christ. He preached much on these deeper spiritual themes in the many conventions he visited. His services were in great demand in religious gatherings throughout the country, and great multitudes eagerly listened to his sermons. His missionary training school in Boston also became a great factor in spreading the Gospel. His church became so spiritual and energetic that it undertook many different forms of Christian work, including the missionary training institute, a mission to the Jews, a mission to the Chinese, a mission to the African Americans, an industrial home, rescue work for fallen women, and evangelistic work on the wharves, in hospitals, in streetcar stables, and in weak churches. From 10 to 20 missionaries and evangelists were also working in connection with Clarendon Street Church.

Often the church was crowded to the doors with eager listeners. Jews and the Chinese were often brought to Christ in the meetings.

Dr. Gordon felt that he could not consistently denounce going to the theater if he allowed the house of prayer to be turned into one itself. He sometimes quoted a returned missionary as saying, "For the honor of Christ I pray that the heathen may never learn how the American Christians raise money for missions." No questionable forms of raising money were ever resorted to in Gordon's church. He sought to follow the Scriptures implicitly and would not allow the use of leavened bread or fermented wine in the Communion.

The Life of David Brainerd, the consecrated missionary, had a wonderful influence in deepening the spiritual life of Gordon. He declared that he had never received such spiritual help from any other book of human origin. He used to visit the graves of John Eliot, David Brainerd, and Jonathan Edwards, and there received fresh inspiration to devote his life fully to the service of God.

On the morning of Feb. 2, 1895, Dr. Gordon, with "victory" as the last clearly audible word on his lips, fell asleep in Jesus, so far as the mortal body was concerned. But his spirit is undoubtedly with the *"great... cloud of witnesses"* mentioned in the twelfth chapter of the book of Hebrews (v. 1). His life will continue to exert a hallowed influence in this world.

Chapter 17

D. L. Moody

❧

*U*ndoubtedly one of the greatest evangelists of all time was D. L. Moody. The meetings held by Moody and Ira Sankey were among the greatest the world has ever known. Along with the power of God Himself, the meetings were the means of arousing the church to new life and activity and sweeping tens of thousands of people into the kingdom of God.

Moody was one of the weak instruments that God has chosen to put the mighty to shame. (See 1 Corinthians 1:27.) Like Christmas Evans, he had very little education before his conversion to Christ. At seventeen years of age, he could barely read or write, and in a Bible class he could not turn to the book of John but searched for it in the Old Testament. After his conversion, he became a proficient scholar. Few men have learned so much in the school of observation.

Dwight Lyman Moody was of old New England Puritan stock. For seven generations, or two hundred years, his ancestors lived the quiet lives of farmers in the Connecticut Valley. Moody inherited the vigorous constitution and hardy common sense of the typical New Englander. He was the sixth child in a family of nine children and was born February 5, 1837, in the town of Northfield, Massachusetts, where he afterward founded his famous Bible schools. His hometown was always very dear to him, and it was one of the greatest pleasures of his life to return to it after a long and arduous evangelistic campaign.

Moody's father died at the early age of forty-one and left his widow in poverty with a mortgage on the home and seven children to support. The creditors seized everything they could, even the firewood, and the children had to stay in bed until it was time to leave for school in order to keep warm. A brother of the widowed mother then came to their rescue and helped to relieve their immediate needs. In their extremity, Reverend Everett, the Unitarian minister, was very kind to them, and all the Moody children became members of his Sunday school and were enlisted as workers to bring in other children. It was here that young Moody began his successful career as a Sunday school worker.

Moody's mother had sought to bring up her children as a Christian mother should, and Dwight never wandered into gross sins as so many young men have done. Lying, complaining, breaking of promises, or talking evil about others was never allowed in the home. One evening, when the children had very little to eat, they divided their scant supply with a beggar. When Dwight was eight years of age, he and an older brother were crossing the river in a skiff with a boatman who was too drunk to row the boat, and who would not let them touch the oars. They were drifting with the current, but Dwight urged his brother to trust in the Lord, and they came safely to land. Dwight was mischievous but not wicked as a boy.

The Moody family was so poor that the boys would carry their shoes and socks in their hands on their way to church, to save them from wear, and would put them on when in sight of the church. Dwight thought it hard, after working all week, to have to go to church and listen to a sermon he did not understand. Once the preacher had to send someone to the balcony to awaken him. But he got in such a habit of going that he could not stay away, and he afterward said that he thanked his mother for making him go when he did not feel like going.

At ten years of age, Dwight left home with another brother to work at a place about 13 miles away. This nearly broke his mother's heart, as she had striven so hard to keep the family together. He was fondly attached to his mother and sorrowed over leaving her. When he arrived at the new place, an aged man gave him a penny and urged him to trust the Lord. "That old man's blessing has followed me for fifty years," said Moody.

At seventeen years of age, Moody, tired of farm life and ambitious to work his way upward in the world, decided to go to Boston. He arrived there without any money and tried in vain to find work until he was almost in despair. He then found employment with an uncle who was in the shoe business. He succeeded well as a salesman and became a regular attendant at the Mount Vernon Congregational Sunday school. Having little schooling, he took little part in the discussions in the class in Sunday school. But he gradually became deeply interested in the study of the Bible and finally took part in the discussions in the class. His teacher, Mr. Kimball, took great interest in him and gradually led him to see the plan of salvation, until all that was necessary was a personal interview to lead him to Christ. Mr. Kimball prayerfully sought for a proper time for this interview.

"I determined to speak to him about Christ and about his soul," said Mr. Kimball,

and started down to Holton's shoe store. When I was nearly there, I began to wonder whether I ought to go in during business hours or wait until later. I thought that possibly my call might embarrass the boy, and that when I went away the other clerks would ask who I was and would taunt him with my efforts in trying to make him a good boy. In the meantime, I had passed the store, and, discovering this, I determined to have it over with.

I found Moody in the back part of the building, wrapping up shoes. I went up to him immediately, and, putting my hand on his shoulder, I made what I afterward thought was a very weak plea for Christ. I don't know just what words I used, nor could Moody tell. I simply told him of Christ's love for him and the love Christ wanted in return. That was all there was. It seemed the young man was just ready for the light that then broke upon him, and there, in the back of the store in Boston, he gave himself and his life to Christ.

Moody's whole life was now changed and became one of joyful Christian service. "Before my conversion," said Moody, "I worked toward the Cross, but since then I have worked from the Cross; then I worked to be saved, now I work because I am saved." Again, he said,

I remember the morning on which I came out of my room after I first trusted Christ. I think the sun shone a good deal brighter than it ever had before—I thought that it was just smiling upon me. And as I walked out on Boston Common and heard the birds singing in the trees, I thought they were all singing a song to me.

Moody was now running over with zeal and love for the Master, but he did not seem to have received much help and encouragement from the conservative deacons and members in the church that he was attending. The year after his conversion, he was denied church membership because he was "not sufficiently instructed in Christian doctrine." Three of the committee who examined him were appointed to instruct him in the way of God more perfectly.

In 1856, the second year after his conversion, Moody went to Chicago, where he united with the Plymouth Congregational Church and became a very active Christian worker, putting his soul and energy into the work of winning men to Christ. He rented a pew in the church and filled it with young men every Sunday. Then he rented another and another, until he had rented and filled four pews. Meanwhile, Moody was prospering in his business and was such a good shoe salesman that his employer sent him out as a traveling salesman.

He found a little mission Sunday school in Chicago where they had 16 teachers and only 12 students. Here he applied to become a teacher. They consented on the condition that he would find his own students. This just suited his taste, and the next Sunday he arrived with 18 little hoodlums whom he had gathered from the streets. He soon had the building crowded. In the fall of 1858, he began another mission school on a larger scale in another part of the city. The large hall was soon overcrowded. He then procured a larger hall, which afterward developed into one of the leading churches of Chicago. This big hall he soon had filled with street urchins.

The children loved him and crowded in by the hundreds and sang the hymns with great enjoyment. Moody also enticed them in with prizes, free pony rides, picnics, candles, and other things dear to the hearts of children. Students were allowed to transfer to any class they desired by simply notifying the superintendent, and this plan resulted in the survival of the fittest teachers. The school soon numbered 1,500 students. Moody decided to build a church and issued share certificates at 25 cents each in order to raise the

$10,000 needed for construction. The Sunday school grew to such proportions that parents were drawn in, and then meetings were held almost every night of the week.

Many prominent men assisted Moody in the Sunday school and in the meetings, but so much responsibility fell on him that he sometimes had to be both janitor and superintendent. This practical training contributed much to his success as a preacher. Undoubtedly he needed such training, as at first he seemed to have spoken very awkwardly in public. When he first arose to speak in a prayer meeting, one of the deacons assured him that, in his opinion, he would serve God best by keeping quiet. Another critic, who praised Moody for his zeal in filling the pews at Plymouth Church, said that he should realize his limitations and not attempt to speak in public. "You make too many mistakes in grammar," said he. "I know I make mistakes," was Moody's reply, "and I lack many things, but I'm doing the best I can with what I've got." He then paused, and looking at the man searchingly, inquired in his own inimitable way, "Look here, friend, you've got enough grammar—what are you doing with it for the Master?"

Moody's great Sunday school work was accomplished before he was more than twenty-three years of age. With all his work for Christ, he had no thought of entering the ministry until he found that souls were being led to Christ through his efforts. He then decided to give up the business in which he had been engaged, and in which he had already made over $7,000, and to devote all his time to Christian work.

During the Civil War, Moody became a prominent member of the Christian Commission. He did a great work by holding meetings and distributing gospels and tracts among the soldiers and prisoners of war quartered in Chicago and on many leading battlefields of the southern states. After the war, he returned to Chicago

and again devoted himself to Sunday school and Young
Men's Christian Association (Y.M.C.A.) work. His Sunday school was so great a success that it made him famous all over the country. Inquiries concerning his
methods of work came from all directions, and people
traveled thousands of miles to learn them. He was
called to many places to address Sunday school conventions and to help organize Sunday school work.
Through his efforts, many Sunday schools were led to
agree to use the same lessons each Sunday, and thus
the International Sunday School lessons were started.

Moody became one of the most prominent
Y.M.C.A. workers in America, and it was at a Y.M.C.A.
convention in Indianapolis, Indiana, in 1870, that he
first met Ira David Sankey, who was destined to become his great song leader. Moody was so impressed
with his singing that he asked him to come with him
and sing for him, and in Indianapolis they held their
first meeting together, in the open air. Several months
afterward, Sankey gave up his business and joined
Moody in his work.

In 1867 Moody made up his mind to go to Great
Britain and study the methods of Christian work employed in that country. He did so, accompanied by Mrs.
Moody, who was suffering from asthma. He was particularly eager to hear Charles Spurgeon, the great
English preacher, and George Müller, who had the
large orphanages at Bristol. Moody was then unknown
in England except to a few prominent Sunday school
leaders, but he spoke a number of times in London and
Bristol with good results.

It was during this first visit to Britain that Moody
heard the words that set him hungering and thirsting
after a deeper Christian experience and that marked a
new era in his life. The words were spoken to him by
Mr. Henry Varley, a well-known evangelist, as they sat
together in a public park in Dublin. The words were
these: "The world has yet to see what God will do with

and for and through and in and by the man who is fully consecrated to Him."

"He said a man," thought Moody,

> but he did not say a great man or a learned man or a smart man, but simply a man. I am a man, and it lies with each man himself whether he will or will not make that entire and full consecration. I will try my utmost to be that man.

The words kept ringing in his mind and burning their way into his soul, until finally he was led into the deeper, richer, fuller experience for which his soul yearned.

The impression the words made was deepened soon afterward by words spoken by Mr. Bewley, of Dublin, Ireland, to whom he was introduced by a friend. "Is this young man all O-and-O?" asked Mr. Bewley. "What do you mean by 'O-and-O'?" said the friend. "Is he out-and-out for Christ?" was the reply. From that time forward, Moody's desire to be "O-and-O" for Christ was supreme.

Moody's hunger for a deeper spiritual experience was increased by the preaching of Henry Moorehouse, the famous English boy preacher, who visited Moody's church in Chicago soon after Moody returned to America. For seven nights, Moorehouse preached from the text of John 3:16: *"For God so loved the world that He gave His only begotten Son, that whoever believes in Him should not perish but have everlasting life."* Every night Moorehouse rose to a higher and higher plane of thought, beginning at Genesis and going through the Bible to Revelation, showing how much God loved the world. He pointed out how God loved the world so much that He sent patriarchs and prophets and other holy men to plead with the people; and then He sent His only Son; and when they had killed Him, He sent the Holy Spirit. In closing the seventh sermon from the text, Moorehouse said,

My friends, for a whole week I have been trying to tell you how much God loves you, but I cannot do it with this poor stammering tongue. If I could borrow Jacob's ladder and climb up into heaven and ask Gabriel, who stands in the presence of the Almighty, to tell me how much love the Father has for the world, all he could say would be, *"God so loved the world that He gave His only begotten Son, that whoever believes in Him should not perish but have everlasting life."*

Moody's heart melted within him as he listened to the young preacher describing the love of God for lost mankind. It gave him a vision of the love of God such as he had never seen before, and from that time forward Moody's preaching was of a more deeply spiritual character.

Moody continued to hunger for a deepening of his own spiritual life and experience. He had been greatly used by God, but he felt that there were much greater things in store for him. The year 1871 was a critical one with him. He realized more and more how little he was equipped with personal skills for his work, and how much he needed to be qualified for service by the Holy Spirit's power. This realization was deepened by conversations he had with two ladies who sat in the front pew in his church. He could see by the expression of their faces that they were praying. At the close of the service they would say to him, "We have been praying for you."

"Why don't you pray for the people?" Moody would ask.

"Because you need the power of the Spirit," was the reply.

"I need the power! Why," said he, in relating the incident afterward,

I thought I had power. I had the largest congregation in Chicago, and there were many conversions.

I was, in a sense, satisfied. But all along those two godly women kept praying for me, and their earnest talk about anointing for special service set me thinking. I asked them to come and talk with me, and they poured out their hearts in prayer so that I might receive the filling of the Holy Spirit. There came a great hunger into my soul. I did not know what it was. I began to cry out as I never did before. I really felt that I did not want to live if I could not have this power for service.

"While Mr. Moody was in this mental and spiritual condition," said his son,

Chicago was laid in ashes. A great fire swept out of existence both Farwell Hall and Illinois Street Church. On Sunday night after the meeting, as Mr. Moody went toward home, he saw the glare of flames and knew it meant ruin to Chicago. About one o'clock Farwell Hall was burned, and soon his church went down. Everything was scattered.

Moody went east to New York City to collect funds for the sufferers from the Chicago fire, but his heart and soul were crying out for the power from on high. "My heart was not in the work of begging," said he.

I could not appeal. I was crying all the time that God would fill me with His Spirit. Well, one day, in the city of New York—oh, what a day!—I cannot describe it; I seldom refer to it; it is almost too sacred an experience to name. Paul had an experience of which he never spoke for fourteen years. I can only say that God revealed Himself to me, and I had such an experience of His love that I had to ask Him to hold back His hand.

> I went back to preaching again. The ser-
> mons were not different; I did not present any
> new truths, and yet hundreds were converted. I
> would not now be placed back where I was before
> that blessed experience if you should give me all
> the world—it would be like dust in the balance.

Moody's church was soon rebuilt in Chicago, thousands of Sunday school scholars contributing 5 cents
each to place a brick in the new edifice. But the
anointing of the Spirit that he received while walking
along the streets of New York set his soul on fire in
such a way that his work soon became worldwide.

Desiring to learn more of the Scriptures from
English Bible students, he visited England again in
1872. He did not expect to hold any meetings during
this visit, but he accepted an invitation to preach at the
Sunday morning and evening services at Arundel
Square Congregational Church in the north part of
London. In the evening, the power of the Spirit seemed
to fall upon the congregation, and the inquiry room
was crowded with people seeking salvation. The next
day he went to Dublin, Ireland, but an urgent telegram
called him back to continue at Arundel for ten days.
Four hundred people were added to the church in that
time.

The next year, at the invitation of two English
friends, he started again for England, accompanied by
Mr. Sankey. His English friends had promised funds
for the visit; but the money did not come, and Moody
borrowed enough to enable him to go to England. On
arriving there, he learned that both of his friends had
died. No door seemed open for him. But before leaving
America he had received a letter from the secretary of
the Y.M.C.A. in York, England, inviting him to address
the young men there if he ever came to England. He
and Mr. Sankey went to York and began a series of
meetings there that lasted for five weeks. Interest

gradually increased until the meeting places were crowded half an hour before the time of service, and many souls decided for Christ.

The evangelists went from York to Sunderland, where they had still greater meetings than in York. The largest halls in the city had to be secured for the services. Their next series of meetings was in Newcastle. The meetings were like gigantic, special trains bringing people from surrounding cities and towns. Here the evangelists published their first hymnbook, which soon became popular all over Britain. On their return to America, in 1875, they published a similar hymnbook entitled *Gospel Hymns, No. 1,* which was followed by five more hymnals. These books have been a means of blessing to multitudes throughout the world. They marked a new era in the history of the Christian church. The royalties on them were at first devoted to a number of benevolent purposes, but afterward to the founding and operation of Moody's great Bible schools at Northfield.

From the north of England, the evangelists went to Scotland and began a series of meetings in Edinburgh. Here they had one of the greatest series of meetings ever known in the world's history. No building was large enough to accommodate the immense throngs that flocked to their meetings. "Never, probably," said Professor Blaikie, "was Scotland so stirred; never was there so much expectation."

In Glasgow, Scotland, the evangelists had similar meetings to those at Edinburgh. At the closing service at the Crystal Palace, in the Botanic Gardens, the building was packed so tightly with people that Moody could not enter, and there were still 20,000 or 30,000 people on the outside. Moody spoke to the great throng from the seat of a carriage, and the choir led the singing from the roof of a nearby shed. When the Crystal Palace was filled with inquirers seeking salvation, there were still about 2,000 inquirers on the outside of the building. Moody probably addressed as many as 30,000 people at one time in Edinburgh and as many as 40,000 in Glasgow.

Other great meetings were held in Liverpool and many other British cities, and finally in London. When the evangelists left Britain in 1875, after a campaign of two years and one week, the whole country had been stirred religiously as it had not been stirred since the days of Wesley and Whitefield. About 14,000 children attended the children's meeting in Liverpool. Over 600 ministers attended the closing services in London. Moody said that he had such a consciousness of the presence of God in the London meetings that "the people seemed as grasshoppers." Professor Henry Drummond said that Moody spoke to exactly "an acre of people" every meeting during his campaign in the East End of London.

On their return to America, Moody and Sankey held great meetings in Brooklyn, Philadelphia, New York, Boston, Chicago, and many other cities of the United States. In 1881 they again visited Great Britain and conducted another gigantic evangelistic campaign. After this, Moody made repeated trips to Britain, and once he visited the Holy Land. He devoted much time to building up his great Bible schools at Northfield and in Chicago. During the World's Fair in Chicago in 1893, he conducted great meetings in the largest halls in the city and in Forepaugh's Circus tent, with the assistance of famous preachers from all over the world. Millions heard the Gospel preached during this campaign.

Moody continued his evangelistic campaigns until his death in 1899. His last great series of meetings was in a gigantic hall in Kansas City. While there, he was seized with heart trouble and rushed home to die. Among his last words were, "This is my triumph; this is my coronation day! I have been looking forward to it for years." This old world had lost its charms for him, and for a long time he had been "homesick for heaven." He was laid to rest in his beloved Northfield. By his special request, there were no emblems of mourning at his funeral services. It is estimated that no less than a 100 million people heard the Gospel from his lips, and his schools are training many others to carry the Glad Tidings throughout the world.

Chapter 18

General Booth

One of the greatest religious leaders and reformers of all time was General William Booth, founder and head of the Salvation Army. During his lifetime, the discipline of the Salvation Army was so rigorous, its standards so high, and its methods so strenuous, it never did attract the great mass of professing Christians. But, like the Friends, the Salvation Army had a tremendous influence in the deepening of spiritual life and in opening up new channels of Christian service and blessing. Israel was a small nation, but to that people God gave the adoption, the covenants, the oracles, and the law. He made Israel the husbandmen, or teachers, of the world. In a similar manner, He taught the world many great lessons through the Salvation Army.

Perhaps all other denominations of Christians have been more one-sided than the Salvation Army. The Roman Catholic Church placed too much stress on outward works, forms, and ceremonies. The Protestant churches probably went to the other extreme and emphasized the act of faith to the neglect of insisting on good works and holy living. But the Salvation Army of the nineteenth century gave the world a new and greater vision of how saving faith should lead to a life of consecration and service. No other denomination of

Christianity seems to have realized so fully the duty of going out into the highways and byways to minister to the lost and suffering. The Army was "the church of the black sheep."

The Salvation Army gave the world a new idea of Christianity and won the confidence of the masses. Its members did not spend their time in discussing creeds and theories, but clothed the naked, fed the hungry, visited the sick and those in prison, and thus won the people for Christ. On the great Day of Judgment, the sheep are separated from the goats, not by an examination of their theories, but by an examination of whether or not they have really loved their neighbors and ministered to the sick, suffering, and needy as the divine Master did when He was here on earth.

Booth's Salvation Army probably measured up to this real test of love better than others who bear the name of Christ. Their original creed was a brief one. It has been summed up in three words: *soap, soup,* and *salvation.* They believed in *soap* to clean men outwardly and better their physical condition, in *soup* to satisfy their hunger and prepare them to receive the message of salvation, and in a full and free *salvation* for all mankind who meet the conditions.

While "less creed and more deed" was the fundamental basis of Booth's Salvation Army, they did not neglect the great essential doctrines of repentance, faith, and the necessity of holy living. To them, repentance was not mere sorrow for sin, but a real turning away from sin. Faith is not a mere intellectual act completed in a few seconds; but it is a real reliance of the soul upon Christ, beginning instantly but continuing through time and eternity. In every Salvation Army corps throughout the world, a Holiness Meeting was held every week to lead Christians into an experience of holiness, sanctification, or the filling of the Spirit. With them, holiness was not only imputed, but it was really imparted by the indwelling Spirit.

Every Salvation Army soldier was expected to be at his post and to take part in every meeting if possible. This was a strenuous life and required spiritual strength. General Booth realized this fact and made sanctification, or the filling of the Spirit, a fundamental doctrine of the Salvation Army. Not only the Salvation Army, but also most of the workers in mission halls and open-air meetings, learned the necessity of being filled with the Spirit in order to carry on an effectual work for Christ.

Few individuals have so emphasized and experienced the Holy Spirit's power as did General Booth and Mrs. Catherine Booth, the "father and mother" of the Salvation Army. Before her death, Mrs. Booth was universally regarded as one of the saintliest and most spiritual of women. Her influence both in and outside of the Salvation Army was tremendous. Thousands and tens of thousands have been won for Christ or led into a deeper spiritual experience through the influence of her life.

It was no unusual sight to see scores and scores, and sometimes hundreds, of people seeking salvation or sanctification at the close of one of General Booth's addresses, so manifest was the power of the Spirit in his meetings. He probably visited more countries, spoke more frequently, won more souls for Christ, and rescued more fallen men and women than did any other person. The Salvation Army spread to fifty-five different countries, and their shelters, rescue homes, farm colonies, and emigration bureaus did more to reclaim the fallen than any other agency. We might truthfully say that they did more to rescue the fallen than all other agencies combined.

William Booth, destined to become the founder of the Salvation Army and one of the greatest of social reformers, was born at Sneinton, a suburb of Nottingham, England, on April 10, 1829. His parents were members of the Established Church, and his mother was a very devout Christian. His father made considerable money but had the misfortune to lose it. William was brought up in poverty and realized much of the sorrow and suffering that afterward made his heart bleed for the poor. His father died at an early age, and William was left to struggle on in poverty with his widowed mother. He was thus deprived of the advantages of a good public school education.

As a boy of thirteen, William was a social reformer and longed to do something to alleviate the sufferings of the poor. At an early age he deserted the Church of England and became a regular attendant at the Wesleyan chapel. At the age of thirteen, he yielded his heart and life to God. Describing this event, he said,

> The Holy Spirit had continually shown me that my real welfare for time and eternity depended upon the surrender of myself to the service of God. After a long controversy, I made this submission, cast myself on His mercy, received the assurance of His pardon, and gave myself up to His service with all my heart. The hour, the place, and many other particulars of this glorious transaction are recorded indelibly on my memory.

Soon after young Booth's conversion, James Caughey, the famous Spirit-filled American evangelist, visited Nottingham. Caughey was a Methodist and preached the Wesleyan theory of sanctification with great anointing and power. His preaching made a deep impression on William Booth and kindled in his heart a great desire to win souls for Christ. But for a long time, he was too timid to hold religious meetings. Finally, after much time spent in prayer and the study of the Scriptures, he ventured to read the Bible and deliver some comments on the street corners of Nottingham. He was jeered at, ridiculed, and had to dodge the bricks that were thrown at him, but this did not discourage him. Later he joined some Christian companions in holding meetings in cottages and in the open air.

William's early efforts to speak in public were often very discouraging, but they laid the foundation of his future usefulness. He was apprenticed to a firm where he had to work hard until eight o'clock in the evening, and then he hurried to the cottage meetings, which lasted until ten o'clock, after which he was sometimes called to visit the sick or dying.

Young Booth soon became the leader of his companions in these religious services, and then he began to conduct meetings in country places, stumbling home in the dark, late at night, after holding the meetings. At seventeen years of age, he was made a local preacher. Two years later, his superintendent wanted him to become a regular minister, but the doctor advised him that his health was so poor that he was totally unfit for the strain of the life of a Methodist minister.

In 1849, when twenty years of age, Booth moved to London. Here he was without a friend and almost without money. He found work as a clerk and spent most of his leisure time working among the poor. Finally he devoted all his time to preaching and preached in many parts of London with varying success. Sometimes he was severely criticized for his style of preaching, but frequently souls were brought to Christ in his meetings. He thought of offering himself for the regular ministry, but his superintendent discouraged him.

In 1851 a controversy arose in the Wesleyan church over the question of layman representation, and a large number of ministers who favored layman representation and other reform movements either seceded or were expelled from the conference and formed a new movement and became known as Reformers. Because of his supposed sympathy with the Reformers— although he took no part in the controversy—Booth's name was dropped by the minister in charge of his circuit. The Reformers then offered him a position as pastor of one of their chapels in London. This he accepted, and here he met Catherine Mumford, the talented and consecrated young woman who several years afterward became his wife.

For two or three years, Booth preached in London and various other cities of England, and in many places met with great success. Many souls were won for Christ in his meetings. But his life was unsettled. The Reformers had no settled policy or organization, and they had many differences of opinion among themselves. Booth tried to induce them to unite with the Methodist New Connexion, which believed in layman representation and most of the reforms they advocated.

Finally, he and a number of other Reformers joined the New Connexion. He now met with great success in many cities, and his fame as a revivalist began to spread all over England. Hundreds of people now professed conversion to Christ in almost every series of meetings held by him. At last his financial prospects were good enough to enable him to marry Catherine Mumford, who had advised and helped him in so many ways. Their courtship and marriage was an ideal one, and few couples have been so fully joined in heart and life.

For four years, or until he was thirty-two years of age, Booth preached for the Methodist New Connexion in a number of leading cities, and many thousands of people professed conversion to Christ. Nearly 2,000 people claimed conversion in his meetings in less than four months' time, and so people continued to flock to the altar for prayer everywhere he went. He repeatedly urged the Conference to allow him to leave the regular circuit work and devote all his time to evangelistic work, but this they refused to do.

In 1861 he and Mrs. Booth decided to launch out into evangelistic work and trust the Lord for their support. Booth therefore sent in his resignation.

It was shortly before launching out on an independent course that Booth was led into a deeper Christian experience. Both he and Mrs. Booth were diligent students of the writings of John Wesley, and they accepted his views on sanctification, or holiness, as well as on other theological questions. General Booth wrote much on the question of sanctification, heart purity, and so on, but wrote little concerning his own experience of sanctification. In a letter written by Mrs. Catherine Booth, she briefly described how Mr. Booth and herself were led into the experience of holiness. Writing to her parents, she said,

> My soul has been much called out of late on the doctrine of holiness. I feel that until now we have not put it in a sufficiently definite and tangible manner before the people—I mean as a specific and attainable experience. Oh, that I had entered into the fullness of the enjoyment of it myself! I intend to struggle after it. In the meantime, we have commenced already to bring it specifically before our dear people.

In another letter, speaking concerning the doctrine of sanctification, she said,

> William has preached on it twice, and there is a glorious quickening among the people. I am to speak again next Friday night and on Sunday afternoon. Pray for me. I only need perfect consecration and Christ as my all, and then I might be very useful, to the glory of His great and boundless love—not of myself, the most unworthy of all who ever His grace received. May the Lord enable me to give my wanderings over and to find in Christ perfect peace and full salvation!
>
> I have much to be thankful for in my dearest husband. The Lord has been dealing very graciously with him for some time past. His soul

has been growing in grace, and its outward developments have been proportionate. He is now on full stretch for holiness. You would be amazed at the change in him. It would take me all night to detail all the circumstances and convergings of providence and grace that have led up to this experience, but I assure you it is a glorious reality, and I know you will rejoice in it.

Describing how she herself earnestly sought and obtained the experience of holiness, she said,

I struggled through the day until a little after six in the evening, when William joined me in prayer. We had a blessed season. While he was saying, "Lord, we open our hearts to receive You," that word was spoken to my soul: *"Behold, I stand at the door and knock. If anyone hears My voice and opens the door, I will come in to him and dine with him"* (Rev. 3:20). I felt sure He had been knocking, and oh, how I yearned to receive Him as a perfect Savior! But oh, the inveterate habit of unbelief! How wonderful that God should have borne so long with me!

When we got up from our knees, I lay on the sofa, exhausted with the effort and excitement of the day. William said, "Don't you lay everything on the altar?" I replied, "I am sure I do!" Then he said, "And isn't the altar holy?" I replied in the language of the Holy Spirit, "The altar is most holy, and whatever touches it is holy." (See Exodus 29:37.) Then William said, "Are you not holy, then, because God accepts your sacrifice?" I replied with my heart full of emotion and with some faith, "Oh, I think I am."

Immediately the word was given me to confirm my faith: *"You are already clean because of the word which I have spoken to you"* (John 15:3). And I took hold of it—true, with a trembling hand, and not unmolested by the

Tempter—but I held fast the beginning of my confidence, and it grew stronger. From that moment, I have dared to consider myself *"dead indeed to sin, but alive to God in Christ Jesus* [my] *Lord"* (Rom. 6:11).

It is evident from the above account of their deeper Christian experience that both Mr. and Mrs. Booth were led into this experience by means of the teaching that when our all is placed on the altar of consecration, the gift is sanctified by God's acceptance of it. They now became burning, shining lights for the Master.

After their decision to engage in evangelistic work, they waited for some time before receiving a call, and their faith was painfully tried. They then received a call to Cornwall, where a great revival broke out under their labors. Here Mr. Booth introduced the altar in his meetings, which has always been a regular feature of Salvation Army warfare. Perhaps no Salvation Army meeting was held by Booth in which there was not a bench, chair, drumhead, or some kind of place where inquirers could kneel for prayer. In the Cornish meetings, the people were so influenced that they exclaimed, "Glory!" "Hallelujah!" and so on, and such exclamations were always common in Salvation Army meetings. The crowds in Cornwall were too great to be accommodated in any building, and great open-air meetings were held. Open-air work was always a leading feature of Booth's Salvation Army warfare.

After their Cornish campaign, Mr. and Mrs. Booth held many other great evangelistic campaigns in which multitudes were won for Christ. In 1865 they began their work in East London that developed into the Salvation Army. A large tent was erected in a disused burying ground belonging to the Friends, and meetings were held in it every night for two weeks. Open-air meetings were held on Mile End Waste, and the workers marched in procession from the open-air meetings to the tent where another service was held. The tent blew down, and an old dancing hall was engaged for the meetings.

From this small beginning, a regular chain of missions was gradually formed, and this work was known as The Christian Mission. In 1877 Booth changed the name to The Salvation Army, and the work was gradually organized like a well-disciplined army, with uniforms, officers, and regulations resembling those of a regular army.

In the early days of the Salvation Army, when it was known as The Christian Mission, the power of God was wonderfully manifested in the meetings. According to Commissioner Booth-Tucker, one of the ablest officers of the Salvation Army, people were frequently struck down in the meetings, overwhelmed with a sense of the presence and power of God. After the Salvation Army name, uniform, and discipline were adopted, the work grew by leaps and bounds. In little more than a quarter of a century, its flag was unfurled in no less than fifty-five different countries, embracing almost every corner of the earth, and hundreds of thousands of souls had professed conversion to Christ in the meetings.

In 1890 General Booth published his great book, *In Darkest England,* which produced a sensation throughout the world. It was the most far-reaching and practical scheme ever proposed for the uplift of fallen humanity, the down-and-out portion of mankind, or "the submerged tenth," as General Booth called them. He proposed three things: the building of shelters and industrial homes in the cities, the establishing of farm colonies in the country, and the emigration of the poor to more promising parts of the world. The industrial homes and shelters would give immediate relief to the destitute, the farm colonies would provide temporary employment, and emigration would provide a permanent home. In this way, the people would be sent back to the land, so to speak, and the congestion in the cities would be relieved.

These schemes were carried out on a gigantic scale. Salvation Army shelters were started in most great cities of the world and saved multitudes from despair. Successful farm colonies were established in several different countries, and tens of thousands of individuals were assisted to emigrate to Canada, Australia, and South Africa.

General Booth believed in "going to the people with the message of salvation," and this led to the many forms of open-air work, factory work, slum work, and other work of the Salvation Army. He believed in "attracting the people," and this led to the use of the many musical instruments, lively tunes, and striking notices employed by the Army. He believed in "saving the people," and this led to the teaching of a victorious, conquering, sanctifying, cleansing religion that will really save the people from their sins. He also believed in "employing the people," and this led to the many meetings, the testifying, singing, and praying on the part of every soldier. It also led to the different officers and also to all the varied social work of the Salvation Army.

Chapter 19

Other Famous Christians

◦───∞

Thomas à Kempis

Those who are acquainted with the well-known book, *Of the Imitation of Christ,* have undoubtedly been impressed with the thought that the author of such a deeply spiritual book must have had such trials of faith, such self-crucifixion, and such fellowship with God as is only known to those who dwell *"in the secret place of the Most High"* (Ps. 91:1). Such was true of Thomas à Kempis, whose book has been published in every major language and has been a means of blessing for centuries.

À Kempis was born in Cologne in 1380, and was very pious from his early youth. He was brought up in a religious school and at nineteen years of age became a monk of the Augustinian order. He filled many of the highest offices in this order before his death, which occurred when he was ninety-two years of age. His conversion to Christ took place during his time as a novice, after he was deeply convicted of sin and after he had suffered many inward struggles. After this, he had many fierce conflicts of soul, as is very apparent from his writings. "O, how great," he exclaimed,

> has been the mercy of God toward me! How often, when I was almost overcome, has He been my deliverer! Sometimes my passions assailed me as a whirlwind, but God sent forth His arrows and dissipated them. The attack was often renewed, but God was still my support. Gradually I was weaned from everything earthly, and adhered to God alone. Then, I experienced how sweet, how full of mercy, God is to those who truly love Him.
>
> O my God, how merciful You have been to me! Many have been forsaken by You, and are lost, who were less guilty than I am. But Your mercies are unspeakable. You have said, "Let the worthless one draw near to Me, that he may be made worthy; the wicked one, that he may be converted; the imperfect one, that he may be made perfect. Let all draw near to Me and taste the living waters of salvation. It is My delight to be with the children of men."

ᑐᕫ

William Penn

William Penn, the famous Quaker who founded Pennsylvania, who wrote *No Cross, No Crown,* and who won many souls for Christ, was qualified by birth, talents, and education to be one of the leading noblemen of Great Britain. Like Moses, however, he renounced all worldly honors to suffer bitter persecution with the children of God. He even suffered imprisonment with the then-despised Quakers.

William Penn was under deep religious impressions as a child and was converted to Christ at twelve years of age. He made a full consecration of everything to God in 1666, when twenty-two years of age, after hearing the Quaker preacher Thomas Lee preach about the faith that overcomes the world. In his book, *The Guide Mistaken,* written in defense of the Quakers, William Penn thus described their teaching regarding the doctrine of Christian perfection:

> Perfection from sin they hold to be attainable, because he who is born of God does not sin, and nothing that is unclean can enter the kingdom of God. There is no crown without victory; the little leaven leavens the whole lump; the strong man must be cast out. Paul prayed that others might be sanctified wholly, that they might be perfect as God is perfect.
>
> As my faithful testimony, I declare—and may it be known to all who ever knew me—that when the unspeakable riches of God's love visited me, by the call of His glorious light, my heart was influenced thereby to leave off the dark practices, wandering notions, and vanity of this polluted world. Consequently, those very habits that I once judged impossible to have relinquished while here on earth, and those in which I allowed myself a great deal of liberty because they were not openly gross or scandalous, became not only burdensome, but by that light were also shown to be of another nature than what I was now called to. By this holy counsel and instruction, I was immediately filled with a power that gave dominion over them.

ᑕᗯ᧞

Dr. Adam Clarke

Dr. Adam Clarke, the great commentator and preacher, was one of the most famous of the early Methodist ministers, and he is ranked as one of the greatest of Bible scholars. He insisted on preachers urging people to seek an experience of entire sanctification, and he preached frequently on the same theme with great anointing and power. His powerful treatise on *Purity of Heart* was written to show Christians their privilege of being *"filled with all the fullness of God"* (Eph. 3:19).

Dr. Clarke is widely known as a writer of great learning, but it is not so generally known that he preached to immense audiences and was one of the most successful preachers in the early Methodist Church. That he enjoyed a very deep Christian experience himself is very evident from all his writings. In *Purity of Heart* he said,

> As there is no end to the merits of Christ incarnated and crucified, no bounds to the mercy and love of God, no hindrance to the almighty energy and sanctifying influence of the Holy Spirit, no limits to the improvability of the human soul, so there can be no bounds to the saving influence that God will dispense to the heart of every genuine believer. We may ask and receive, and our joy will be full! Well may we bless and praise God, who has called us into such a state of salvation, a state in which we may be thus saved, and, by the grace of that state, continue in the same to the end of our lives.
>
> As sin is the cause of the ruin of mankind, so the gospel system that holds its cure is aptly called the Good News, or the Glad Tidings. It is good news because it proclaims Him who saved His people from their sins, and it would indeed be dishonorable to that grace, and to the infinite merit of Him who procured it, to suppose, much more to assert, that sin had made wounds that grace could not heal. Of such a triumph Satan shall ever be deprived.

ᴄᴇᴥ

William Bramwell

Reverend William Bramwell, who lived at the same time as John Wesley, sang as a choirboy in the Church of England during his earlier years. After suffering under conviction of sin for many months, he was brightly converted to Christ and became an earnest worker for the salvation of souls. Later he became a class leader and finally a minister in the Methodist Church. He was full of zeal, and many souls were led to Christ under his work. Yet he yearned for a still deeper Christian experience. This is his account:

I was for some time deeply convinced of my need of purity and sought carefully with tears, entreaties, and sacrifice, thinking nothing was too much to give up, nothing was too much to do or suffer, if I might attain this *"pearl of great price"* (Matt. 13:46). Yet I did not find it, nor did I know the reason why, until the Lord showed me I had erred in the way of seeking it. I did not seek it by faith alone, but as it were, by the works of the law.

Being now convinced of my error, I sought the blessing by faith alone. Still it tarried a little, but I waited for it in the way of faith. In the house of a friend at Liverpool, where I had gone to settle some temporal affairs before traveling, while I was sitting on a chair, my mind was engaged in various meditations concerning my present affairs and future prospects. My heart now and then lifted up to God, but not particularly about this blessing. Heaven came down to earth; it came to my soul. The Lord, for whom I had waited, came suddenly to the temple of my heart, and I had an immediate evidence that this was the blessing I had for some time been seeking. My soul was then all wonder, love, and praise.

After receiving the above experience, great power was given to him. Thousands were converted to Christ in his meetings. Many of the sick were healed in answer to his prayers, and remarkable discernment was given to him to see and know the spiritual condition of others.

ᘓᗉ

William Carvosso

One of the most striking examples of what God can do for a man without natural talents, without education, and without worldly advantage of any kind, is found in the *Memoirs of William Carvosso*.

Truly converted from a life of sin at twenty-one years of age, Carvosso soon afterward sought and obtained a still deeper Christian experience, after which he became a great means of blessing to thousands of individuals with whom he prayed and conversed personally. He was one of the greatest soulwinners of the early Methodist Church. He served as class leader in the Methodist Church in England for over sixty years. He did not learn to write until after he was sixty-five years of age.

Of his deeper experience, Carvosso said,

What I now desired was inward holiness, and for this I prayed and searched the Scriptures. Among the number of Bible promises that brought me to see it was my privilege to be saved from all sin, my mind was particularly directed to Ezekiel 36:25–27. This is the great and precious promise of the eternal Jehovah, and I laid hold of it, determined not to stop short of my privilege, for I saw clearly that my sanctification was the will of God.

Finally, one evening while I was engaged in a prayer meeting, the great deliverance came. I began to exercise faith by believing, "I will have the blessing now." Just at that moment, a heavenly influence filled the room, and no sooner had I spoken the words from my heart, "I will have the blessing now," than refining fire went "through my heart, illuminated my soul, scattered its life through every part, and sanctified the whole." I then received the full witness of the Spirit that the blood of Jesus Christ had cleansed me from all sin. I cried out, "This is what I wanted! I now have a new heart." Oh, what boundless, boundless happiness there is in Christ, and all for such a poor sinner as I am! This happy change took place in my soul on March 13, 1772.

✍

David Brainerd

David Brainerd, the consecrated missionary, endured almost incredible hardships while laboring among the American Indians, but he lived so close to God that his life has been an inspiration to many. His biography was written by Jonathan Edwards, was revised by John Wesley, and influenced the life of Dr. A. J. Gordon more than any other book outside of the Bible.

The kind of intense longings and prayers after holiness that we read of in the journals of Brainerd are scarcely recorded anywhere else. "I long for God, and a conformity to His will, in inward holiness, ten thousand times more than for anything here below," said Brainerd. On October 19, 1740, he wrote,

In the morning I felt my soul hungering and thirsting after righteousness. In the forenoon, while I was looking on the sacramental elements and thinking that Jesus Christ would soon be *"set forth, crucified"* (Gal. 3:1 KJV) before me, my soul was filled with light and love so that I was almost in ecstasy. My body was so weak I could hardly stand. I felt at the same time an exceeding tenderness and fervent love toward all mankind, so that my soul and all the powers of it seemed, as it were, to melt into softness and sweetness. This love and joy cast out fear, and my soul longed for perfect grace and glory.

Brainerd experienced many manifestations of the Spirit in his meetings and during his numerous seasons of fasting and prayer and longings for holiness of life. He seemed to have risen above the things of this world to a remarkable degree. In his journal of March 10, 1743, he wrote,

I felt exceedingly dead to the world and all its enjoyments. I was ready to give up life and all its comforts, as soon as I was called to it; and yet I had as much comfort of life as almost ever I had. Life itself appeared as just an empty bubble; the riches, honors, and enjoyments of it extremely tasteless. I longed to be entirely crucified to all things here below. My soul was sweetly resigned to however God wished to use me, and I saw that nothing had happened to me but what was best for me.

It was my meat and drink to be holy, to live to the Lord, and die to the Lord. And I then enjoyed such a heaven that far exceeded the most sublime conceptions of an unregenerate soul; it was even unspeakably beyond what I could conceive at any other time.

ৎఞ

Edward Payson

Edward Payson was the most illustrious of the great Congregational preachers of New England. "His pulpit utterances," said McClintock and Strong,

> were of the most startling and uncompromising character. It may be truly said of Edward Payson that he labored not to please men, but God, and his pulpit thundered like another Sinai against every form of ungodliness and iniquity.

Over 700 people were received into the church at Portland, Maine, under the pastorship of Payson.

Payson was born in 1783, was precocious as a child, and at three years of age wept under the preaching of a sermon. He was a good reader when four years old. In 1803 he graduated from Harvard. He was definitely converted to Christ in 1804. After completing a theological course, he was ordained in 1807.

On September 19, 1827, Payson wrote from his sickbed, in a letter to his sister,

> Were I to adopt the figurative language of Bunyan, I might date this letter from the land of Beulah, of which I have been for some weeks the happy inhabitant. The Celestial City is full in my view. Its glories beam upon me, its odors are wafted to me, its sounds strike upon my ears, and its spirit is breathed into my heart. Nothing separates me from it besides the river of death, which now appears as but an insignificant rill that may be crossed at a single step whenever God will give permission.
>
> The Sun of Righteousness has gradually been drawing nearer, appearing larger and brighter as He approached, and now He fills the

whole hemisphere, pouring forth a flood of glory, in which I seem to float like an insect in the beams of the sun. I have been exulting, yet almost trembling, while I gaze on this excessive brightness, and wondering, with unutterable wonder, why God should stoop thus to shine upon a sinful worm like myself. A single heart and a single tongue seem altogether inadequate for my needs. I need a whole heart for every separate emotion, and a whole tongue to express that emotion.

Not long before he died, he said, "My soul is filled with joy unspeakable. I seem to swim in a flood of glory, which God pours down upon me."

ᥴ᠊᠊ᦡ

Dorothea Trudel

Marvelous are the answers to prayer recorded in the book entitled, *Dorothea Trudel, or The Prayer of Faith*. Dorothea had such faith that hundreds were healed in answer to her prayers, and her name became known all over the world. Travelers in Switzerland often heard about the marvelous cures brought about in the remote village of Mannendorf in answer to Dorothea Trudel's prayers.

Dorothea Trudel was born in 1813 and died in 1862. She was converted to Christ at twenty-two years of age, after being so deeply convicted of sin that many thought she was dying. Some years after this, she was led into a still deeper Christian experience, which she described as follows:

I persevered in working at my trade for a year, during which time the Lord continued to show me much that led to my self-abasement. I

learned that bodily suffering cannot produce conformity to God, even when it is borne with pa-
tience; that the only way in which grace can be
attained is by the outpouring of the love of God
in the heart. I did not know before what was
meant by being nothing, and yet I had considered myself converted.

But now the Lord opened my eyes and
showed me that the annoyance I felt to this hour,
when tried by any difficulty, arose from the presence of the *"old man"* (Rom. 6:6), and that if I
possessed the love described in 1 Corinthians 13,
which *"is not provoked"* and *"does not seek its
own"* (v. 5), I would no longer be provoked to
such irritation. From that time, the Lord has so
strengthened me night and day that the wonders
that have taken place in accordance with God's
Word will be less of a marvel than the fact that I
am still spared and strengthened to labor.

ᵕᵉ

Pastor Blumhardt

Almost identical with the great miracles of healing
brought about through the prayers and faith of
Dorothea Trudel in Switzerland, were those brought
about in answer to the prayers of the German pastor
John Christolph Blumhardt, who was born in 1805 and
died in 1880. Hundreds of invalids flocked to him at
Mott-lingen, and then at Bad Boll, and after being
prayed for they left with complete healing.

Pastor Blumhardt began preaching at Mott-
lingen in 1828, soon after graduating from the University of Tubingen. A remarkable case of deliverance of a
woman who seemed to be possessed by demons took
place in answer to his prayers. The whole village was
stirred, and a great revival followed. His home was

besieged all day by inquirers after the way of salvation. "Notwithstanding all this," said he,

> the feeling that this work of God would, according to the usual course of things, lose its vigor and freshness in the long run, made me more and more familiar with the thought that the church of Christ as a whole needs a new outpouring of the Spirit of Pentecost, and that without this, nothing would be durable. This led me to pray for a new outpouring of the Spirit, and that the Spirit would be poured out more and more as the signs seemed to indicate that we are not far from the last times. The clearer I begin to see the corruption and manifold defects of present Christendom, the more unavoidable to me is supplication for its renewal, which can only be accomplished through a special movement of the Spirit of God from above.

Blumhardt's special pleading for the Holy Spirit was answered with an outpouring of power from on high. After this, he had so much power in preaching the Gospel and in praying for the sick, and his work grew to such an extent, that he was compelled to procure the large government building at Boll. In this way he could accommodate the sick who flocked from all over Europe, and even from America, so that he might pray for their healing. The government sold the building to him at less than cost, and the king made a special donation to help him start his work at Boll.

ॐ

Phoebe Palmer

Inseparably connected with the doctrine of entire consecration and sanctification are the names of Dr. and Mrs. Phoebe Palmer. After obtaining a deeper

Christian experience themselves, the lives of these two consecrated evangelists were devoted to leading others to the same experience. The influence of their teachings can be traced in the lives of many noted Christians of both America and Britain.

Mrs. Palmer is well-known for her teaching, "Put all upon the altar, and God's acceptance of the gift sanctifies it." This illustration was drawn from the fact that in Old Testament times, the fire was always burning on the altar, and the sacrifice was consumed as soon as it was placed on the altar. Likewise, Mrs. Palmer taught, the fire of the Holy Spirit is always burning on the altar of true consecration, ready to consume everyone who truly offers himself as a living sacrifice to God.

For a long time after her conversion, Mrs. Palmer had a great desire to be sanctified, but she felt as though the blessing was too great for her to ever think of attaining it. A close study of God's Word convinced her that He had commanded and expected all Christians to be holy, sanctified *"vessel[s] for honor, sanctified and useful for the Master"* (2 Tim. 2:21). Many passages of Scripture convinced her of her need of holiness, including, *"This is the will of God, your sanctification"* (1 Thess. 4:3), *"For God did not call us to uncleanness, but in holiness"* (v. 7), *"Be holy, for I am holy"* (1 Pet. 1:16), *"Pursue peace with all people, and holiness, without which no one will see the Lord"* (Heb. 12:14), and so on. Then she began to expect God to convict her deeply for the experience.

At last her eyes were opened to see that knowledge is conviction and that the only conviction necessary was to be convinced of her need. She then began earnestly to seek the experience. At first she felt that great agony and struggle of soul must be necessary to obtain the experience. But finally she was convinced that it was to be obtained by faith, as it was not necessary to struggle and agonize to obtain an experience that God commands and expects all Christians to have. She then trusted God for the experience and could say with the writer of the hymn,

> When I gave all trying over,
> Simply trusting, I was blessed.

In her widely circulated book, *The Way of Holiness*, she related her own experience, speaking in the third person, as follows:

> Over and over again, prior to the time mentioned, she had endeavored to give herself away in covenant to God. But she had never, until this hour, deliberately resolved on counting the cost, with the solemn intention to consider herself *"dead indeed to sin, but alive to God in Christ Jesus our Lord"* (Rom. 6:11); to account herself permanently the Lord's, and in truth no more at her own disposal, but irrevocably the Lord's property, for time and eternity. Now, in the name of the Lord Jehovah, after having deliberately counted the cost, she resolved to enter into the bonds of an everlasting covenant, with the fixed intention of counting *"all things loss for the excellence of the knowledge of Christ Jesus"* (Phil. 3:8), so that she might *"know Him and the power of His resurrection...[by] being conformed to His death"* (v. 10) and raised to an entire *"newness of life"* (Rom. 6:4). On doing this, a hallowed sense of consecration took possession of her soul.

✑

P. P. Bliss

One of the most consecrated Christians, as well as one of the greatest of gospel singers and hymnwriters, was Philip Paul Bliss. He was taken away early in life, but before his departure wrote some of our best hymns, among them being, "Let the Lower Lights Be Burning," "Hold the Fort," "Windows Open toward Jerusalem," "Free from the Law," "Only an Armour-Bearer," "Pull for the Shore, Sailors," "The Light of the World Is Jesus," "Whosoever Will," "Almost Persuaded," "I Am So Glad That Jesus Loves Me," "Hallelujah, 'Tis Done," "The Half Was Never Told," and many others.

P. P. Bliss was born in Pennsylvania in 1838, and was a poor country boy who was very fond of music. He was religiously inclined from his earliest youth and made a public confession of Christ at a Baptist revival in 1850. After his marriage, a short service in the Civil War, and a number of years spent in holding secular concerts, he became acquainted with D. L. Moody. Several years after this, he was led to consecrate his entire life and services to God for the purpose of spreading the Gospel in song.

In the memoirs of Bliss, by Major D. W. Whittle, we learn the story of how he was led to make the full consecration of his services. During the winters of 1873–74, Bliss received many letters from Moody, who was then in Scotland, urging him to give up his business, drop everything, and sing the Gospel. Similar letters came to Major Whittle, urging him to go out with Bliss and hold meetings. Mr. and Mrs. Bliss were ready for this if they could see it as the Lord's will. But there was much prayer and hesitation on the part of Mr. Bliss before he reached a decision in the matter. He doubted his ability, and he doubted whether the inclination he felt to go was from the Lord. But Moody continued to write, and Mr. H. G. Spafford, a mutual friend, also joined in urging Major Whittle and Mr. Bliss to go into the evangelistic work.

Finally a door opened for them. Reverend C. M. Saunders, of Waukegan, Illinois, invited them to his church for three or four evenings as an experiment.

Major Cole accompanied them on this trip. The first meeting was not an encouraging one in the matter of attendance, and there were no notable results except a powerful impression on the minds of the evangelists that the Lord was with them. The next day it rained, and they expected a small attendance, but the congregation was twice as large as the first, and a number of souls were led to Christ.

"Our hearts were very full," said Major Whittle,

> and a great responsibility was upon us. The next afternoon, the three of us met in the study of the Congregational church, where our meetings were held, and spent some hours in prayer. Bliss made a formal surrender of everything to the Lord. He gave up his musical conventions, gave up his writing of secular music, gave up everything; and in a simple, childlike, trusting prayer, he placed himself, with any talent and any power God had given him, at the disposal of the Lord, for any use He could make of him in the spreading of His Gospel. It was a wonderful afternoon. As I think back upon the scene in that little study, and recall Bliss' prayer and the emotions that filled us all in the sense of God's presence, the room seems lit up in my memory with a halo of glory.